MANAGING
PEOPLE

MANAGING PEOPLE

A PRACTICAL GUIDE
FOR LINE MANAGERS

MICHAEL ARMSTRONG

The
Industrial
Society

KOGAN
PAGE

YOURS TO HAVE AND TO HOLD
BUT NOT TO COPY

First published in 1998

Reprinted in 2001

Kogan Page Limited
120 Pentonville Road
London N1 9JN

British Library Cataloguing in Publication Data

A CIP record for this book is available from the British Library

ISBN 0 7494 2612 8

Typeset by Kogan Page
Printed and bound in Great Britain by Biddles Ltd, *www.biddles.co.uk*

CONTENTS

Part 3 Resourcing

Part 4 Performance management

Part 5 Developing people

Part 6 Managing reward

Part 7 Employee relations

Part 8 Managing the employment relationship

INTRODUCTION

This book is addressed to:

- Those in charge of an organization or a member of the top management team who do not have the benefit of advice from personnel specialists. This is the case in many small to medium sized enterprises. The 1990 Workshop Industrial Relations Survey of 2,061 workplaces found that only 17 per cent had a professional personnel manager.

- Line managers in organizations who have, in effect, to be their own personnel managers because there are no personnel specialists in their organizations.

- The considerable number of line managers to whom more responsibility has been devolved for making decisions about people even though there is a personnel department. Following an extensive study of the respective roles of line managers and personnel professionals conducted by the Institute of Personnel and Development in 1994 the conclusion was reached that: 'Most organizations reported a trend over the last five years towards greater line responsibility for personnel management'.

- Those line managers to whom significant additional responsibilities for personnel management have not been devolved but who are inevitably involved in people issues on their own initiative as well as in conjunction with the personnel specialists. Such managers will carry out this aspect of their duties more effectively if they have a better understanding of the rationale underpinning personnel policies and practices, how they operate in organizations, the benefits they bring to businesses, managers and employees generally, the part they play in these processes and the skills they need to develop and use.

PLAN OF THE BOOK

The book is divided into eight parts as described below.

Part 1 Managing people – the framework

In this part, a general background is provided to the rest of the book by descriptions of the respective people management roles of line managers and personnel specialists and how they work together.

Part 2 Managing people – the basic skills

In this part, the basic skills used by line managers in dealing with people are described. These skills comprise what managers do to motivate the members of their teams, manage the psychological contract, gain commitment, improve morale, exercise leadership, build their teams, delegate, communicate and organize their departments or sections. These skills, and the background knowledge which helps to apply them, underpin the personnel practices described in the rest of the book.

Part 3 Resourcing

The word 'resourcing' describes what managers need to do to ensure that they get the people they want in terms of numbers, skills and capabilities. The actions managers take include forecasting requirements and preparing plans to meet them, job, skills, role and competence analysis, writing job descriptions and role definitions, designing jobs, and recruitment and selection.

Part 4 Performance management

This part covers the ways in which managers working with their teams can improve performance and develop the capabilities of individuals and teams.

Part 5 Developing people

This part focuses on the role of line managers in developing people – providing learning opportunities and encouraging self-development.

Part 6 Managing reward

This part is mainly concerned with managing the financial elements of the reward package. By concentrating on pay, however, the importance of the non-financial rewards which can be made available by managers is not underestimated. These include recognition, praise and the provision of opportunities to use and develop skills and capabilities.

Part 7 Employee relations

This part covers the line manager's role in working with unions and the negotiating skills they may have to use. It also deals with the processes of involvement, participation and handling grievances which are applied whether or not there is a trade union.

Part 8 Managing the employment relationship

In this part the term 'employment relationship' is used generally to cover any aspects of people management which are generally concerned with the legal obligations of employers and their duty to provide healthy and safe working conditions. This part also deals with the individual aspects of the employment relationship, namely, handling downsizing, discipline, absenteeism and poor timekeeping. The part ends positively with a description of the process of counselling.

RECURRING PEOPLE MANAGEMENT THEMES

There are a number of recurring themes in this book. These are not prescriptions – there are no absolutes when it comes to dealing with people. But they do provide guidelines which can and should be taken into consideration whenever you are involved in the complex process of managing people, as individuals and in groups. The main themes are as follows.

■ Make clear what you expect people to achieve.

■ Give people feedback, recognizing achievements and spelling out where they have not met expectations.

■ Take action to encourage and develop high performers and to ensure that under-performers improve.

- Help people to work out for themselves where they need to improve and what they need to learn.

- Give people the opportunity to enhance their skills and abilities, encouraging them to develop themselves.

- Trust people and treat them as adults.

- Involve people so that they can contribute their ideas.

- Let people know about the things that matter to them at work.

- Listen attentively and intelligently to what people tell you.

- Reward people according to their contribution.

FURTHER READING

Institute of Personnel and Development (1995) *Personnel and the Line*, London.

Part 1

Managing people –
the framework

1

THE LINE MANAGER'S RESPONSIBILITY FOR PEOPLE

The responsibility of the line managers for people is best understood within the context of what managers have to do.

WHAT MANAGERS DO

Management is often defined as 'getting things done through people'. This is something of a cliché, but no less true for all that. By definition, managers cannot do everything themselves (although some try and fail).They have to rely on other people.

Managers are sometimes said to spend their time planning, organising, motivating and controlling. But this is an over-simplification implying that managers neatly parcel up their days into thirty minutes planning, one hour organizing etc. In practice, the work of managers is quite fragmented. It depends more on the demands of the situation and on the people concerned than on any theoretical division of the task into clearly differentiated elements. It is better to regard management as being about:

- getting things done
- maintaining momentum and making things happen
- finding out what is going on
- reacting to new situations and problems
- responding to demands and requests.

All these involve managers dealing with people (interpersonal relations): internally with their bosses, their colleagues and their staff; externally with their customers, suppliers, professional advisers and national or local government officials.

A leading writer on management, Henry Mintzberg has suggested that managers have:

- interpersonal roles – acting as leaders, providing guidance and motivation and maintaining a web of relationships with many individuals and groups

- informational roles – continually seeking and receiving information as a basis for action, passing on factual information, and transmitting guidance to subordinates in making decisions

- resource allocation roles – making choices about scheduling their own time, allocating tasks to people and authorizing actions

- 'disturbance handling' roles – dealing with involuntary situations and change beyond their control.

WHAT MANAGERS HAVE TO DO ABOUT PEOPLE

When it comes to dealing with people, managers:

- organize and allocate work

- get the right people to the work

- ensure that these people know what to do, are capable of doing it and then deliver the results expected of them

- develop skills and capabilities (competence)

- reward people, using both financial and non-financial methods

- involve people and communicate with them

- handle people issues and problems as they arise.

In some small and even medium-sized enterprises, managers do all these things without professional advice from personnel specialists. The National Workshop Industrial Relations 1990 survey established that only 17 per cent of the establishments it covered had a specialist personnel manager. But larger organizations with over 100 employees are much more likely to have full or part-time personnel practitioners and their role is described in the next chapter.

The role of managers and team leaders is changing in many organizations. They are no longer there simply to give orders. Instead they are responsible for leading their teams in the full sense of that word, by providing guidance and support as well as giving instructions and controlling results. An example of how this works is given below.

Team leaders at Dutton Engineering

At Dutton Engineering, supervisors have been replaced by team leaders, whose role is to act as 'coaches'. As Tina Mason, the company's Business Manager, says: 'The job of a team leader should be that of a facilitator, not someone who is going to play Superman, standing there telling everyone what to do.' Team leaders have had to be good communicators who can get the best out of employees and encourage a 'bring your brains to work' philosophy among workers who had previously been trained to leave them at home. Team leaders were given training to help them get the best out of their team members.

FURTHER READING

Armstrong, M (1990) *Management Processes and Functions*, Institute of Personnel and Development, London.
Mintzberg, H (1997) *The Nature of Managerial Work*, Harper & Row, New York.

2

THE ROLE OF THE PERSONNEL FUNCTION

THE BASIC ROLE

The role of the personnel function is to provide guidance and support on all matters relating to an organization's employees. The aim is to help management to deal effectively with everything concerning the employment, development, reward and well-being of people and the relationships that exist between management and the workforce.

INFLUENCE ON THE WORKING ENVIRONMENT

A further key role for the personnel function is to play a part in the creation of an environment which enables people to make the best use of their capabilities and to realise their potential to the benefit of both the organization and themselves. Increasingly personnel people are concerned with 'employability' – the scope individuals have to take on different roles within the organization or to find rewarding work elsewhere in the event of the end of a contract or redundancy as a result of 'downsizing'.

UPHOLDING CORE VALUES

Personnel professionals may also take on the role of helping to uphold the core values of the organization. Values refer to what is regarded as important. They are expressed as beliefs in what is best or good for the organization and what sort of behaviour is desirable. Values define the ways in which the business should relate to or deal with its key stakeholders. These include employees as well as the management and the owners. They also extend to customers, suppliers and the public generally. Values refer to such matters as care and consideration for people, equity in the sense of treating people fairly in comparison with other people, teamwork, social responsibility, customer care and quality.

AREAS OF RESPONSIBILITY

Personnel specialists may be concerned with any aspect of the management of people except the direct planning, direction and control of their activities. These aspects can include:

- organization structuring and development
- human resource planning – forecasting future requirements
- recruitment and selection
- performance management processes
- employee development
- employee reward
- employee relations
- health and safety
- dealing with people problems
- ensuring compliance with employment legislation.

The extent to which they are involved in any of these activities will vary enormously. There is no standard blueprint for what personnel people do. It depends on the type of organization and the views of management about their role. Powerful (or power hungry) personnel specialists can extend their influence by persuading management to give them more authority, having demonstrated that they are capable of making a bigger contribution. But it all depends on what management believes to be necessary. And in these days of global competition, rationalization, downsizing, cost reduction and re-engineering, many businesses are questioning the traditional role of the personnel function.

THE VARIOUS ROLES OF PERSONNEL PRACTITIONERS

The diversity of personnel practice means that personnel specialists can play any of the following roles:

- *business partners* – sharing responsibility with their line management colleagues for the success of the enterprise

- *strategists* – formulating personnel strategies which define the intentions of the organization on what needs to be done about its people and which support the achievement of its business plans

- *policy formulators* – drawing up personnel policies which provide guidelines to managers on people management practices

- *internal consultants* – advising their clients (line managers) on personnel practices and helping to implement new personnel processes

- *service providers* – providing efficient and cost-effective services to line managers in such areas as recruitment, training, pay and dealing with employee relations issues and problems with individuals

- *helpers and advisers* – assisting line managers to carry out their personnel responsibility and as necessary coaching them in the skills they need

- *monitors* – ensuring that corporate personnel policies and procedures are implemented consistently although not necessarily rigidly.

In some organizations, personnel professionals carry out all these roles. In others their role is limited to being service providers. However, whatever their role, it will always involve relationships with line managers and these are considered in the next chapter.

FURTHER READING

Armstrong, M (1996) *Handbook of Personnel Management Practice*, 6th Edition, Kogan Page, London.

3

PERSONNEL AND THE LINE

DEVOLUTION TO LINE MANAGERS AND WHY IT IS TAKING PLACE

The tendency to devolve more responsibility to line managers for personnel management has partially arisen because of the downsizing and delayering of the personnel function mentioned in the last chapter. Further contributory factors have been the decentralization and devolution of business decisions to strategic business units and the reduction of headquarters staff to one or two people who are only involved in strategic matters. Businesses like BP which ten years ago had over 100 personnel people in the centre may now have only a handful who are concerned with corporate personnel strategy and the personnel affairs concerning the most senior managers as a corporate resource.

There has, however, been another factor which has contributed to the devolution of personnel management decisions to line managers. This is the movement to empower line managers so that they take full responsibility for their major resource, the people they lead and manage.

THE INFLUENCE OF HUMAN RESOURCE MANAGEMENT

The thrust to make line managers more accountable for people decisions as well as decisions about their other key resources is associated with the human resource management (HRM) philosophy which first emerged in the 1980s. The emphasis of HRM is on:

- adopting a strategic approach – one in which HR strategies are integrated with business strategies and implemented by those responsible for meeting business targets, ie line managers

- treating people as assets (human capital) to be invested in to further the interests of the organization and to be utilized effectively by line managers

- obtaining added value from people by performance management and human resource development processes, both of which are regarded as key aspects of the responsibility of line managers for people

- gaining the commitment of people to the objectives and values of the organization (and largely relying on the efforts of the line managers to do this).

Human resource management is thus essentially a business-oriented philosophy concerning the management of people by line managers in order to achieve competitive advantage. Managements that subscribe to this philosophy (and explicitly or implicitly, many do) are more likely to devolve people management responsibilities to line managers.

AREAS FOR DEVOLUTION

Of course, what is devolved and how it is devolved will vary considerably, but here are some examples of how it has been done.

Organization

Line managers determine how they should structure and staff their departments as long as they can justify what it costs and keep within their budgets.

Recruitment and selection

Line managers take full responsibility for recruitment and selection although personnel specialists, if they exist, may provide such services as advertising, filtering applications, testing and taking up references.

Performance management

The processes of agreeing objectives, reviewing performance and drawing up personal development plans are entirely carried out by line managers. Assessment forms are retained by them and are not held by the personnel department.

Employee development

Line managers are responsible for training and developing their own staff on a 'self-managed learning basis'. The personnel or training function provides formal courses in areas where there are common training needs and/or a need to develop knowledge and skills in areas of general interest, for example, interviewing or conducting performance reviews.

Pay

Line managers make their own decisions on pay levels and increases in line with company pay structures and policies and within their payroll budgets. Personnel specialists may provide information on market rates, guidance, and advice. They may also monitor pay levels to ensure that line managers are consistent, fair and equitable in making pay decisions. Particular care may be taken to monitor the provision of equal pay for work of equal value.

Employee relations

Line managers deal with shop stewards and staff representatives on day-to-day issues. Major processes such as pay negotiations may be handled by senior line managers, while personnel specialists function in an entirely advisory role. Line managers are wholly responsible for joint consultation and communications in their departments.

Health and safety

Line managers are fully responsible for the achievement of required levels of health and safety in their departments. Personnel specialists and health and safety officers, for example, provide advice and help in conducting risk assessment surveys, investigate accidents and recommend actions to deal with health and safety hazards.

Employment

Line managers are accountable for dealing fairly with their staff and for meeting legal requirements in such areas as equal opportunity, sexual, racial and disability discrimination, and sexual harassment. Personnel specialists advise on the law and on dealing with particular issues. They also monitor the application of employment policies (e.g. ethnic monitoring).

Line managers are fully responsible for controlling absenteeism and timekeeping.

These examples set out above are only illustrations of how devolution may take place. There will be many variations in the degree of devolution in different parts of the same organization.

PROBLEMS OF DEVOLUTION

The IPD research into personnel and the line identified the following problems which may arise over devolution:

■ There is an underlying concern that line managers are not sufficiently competent to carry out their new roles. This may be for a number of reasons, including lack of training, pressures of work, because managers have been promoted for their technical rather than their managerial skills, or because they are used to referring certain issues to the personnel department.

■ Some personnel specialists also have difficulty in adopting their new roles because they do not have the right skills (such as an understanding of the business) or because they see devolution as a threat to their own job security.

■ Other problems over devolution include uncertainty on the part of line managers about the role of the personnel function, lack of commitment by line managers to performing their new roles, and achieving the right balance between providing line managers with as much freedom as possible and the need to retain core controls and direction.

The conclusions reached by the researchers were that:

■ If line managers are to take an effective greater responsibility for personnel management activities then, from the outset, the roles and responsibilities of personnel and line managers must be clearly defined and understood.

■   Support is needed from the personnel department in terms of providing a procedural framework, advice and guidance on all personnel matters, and in terms of training line managers so they have the appropriate skills and knowledge to carry out their new duties.

This excellent advice can only be acted upon within the organization but the intention of the rest of this book is to provide insight into the 'appropriate skills and knowledge' required by line managers so that the delicate process of devolution can be implemented more smoothly.

FURTHER READING

Institute of Personnel and Development (1995) *Personnel and the Line*, London.

Part 2

Managing people – the basic skills

4

MOTIVATING

Motivating other people is about getting them to move in the direction you want them to go in order to achieve the task. Motivating yourself is about setting the direction independently and then taking a course of action which will ensure that you get there. Motivation can be described as goal-directed behaviour. People are motivated when they expect that a course of action is likely to lead to the attainment of a goal and a valued reward ie one which satisfies their needs.

Well-motivated people are those with clearly defined goals who take action which they expect will achieve those goals. Such people may be self-motivated, and as long as this means they are going in the right direction to achieve what they are there to achieve, then this is the best form of motivation. Most of us, however, need to be motivated to a greater or lesser degree. The organization as a whole can provide the context within which high levels of motivation can be achieved by providing incentives and rewards and opportunities for learning and growth. But managers still have a major part to play in using their motivating skills to get people to give of their best, and to make good use of the motivational processes provided by the organization. To do this it is first necessary to understand the process of motivation – how it works and the different types of motivation that exist.

THE PROCESS OF MOTIVATION

How motivation works

Motivation starts when someone consciously or unconsciously recognises an unsatisfied need. This need establishes a goal and action is taken which it is expected will achieve that goal. If the goal is achieved the need will be satisfied and the same action is likely to be repeated the next time a similar need emerges (this is sometimes called the process of 'reinforcement'). If the goal is not achieved the action is less likely to be repeated. This sequence is modelled in Figure 4.1.

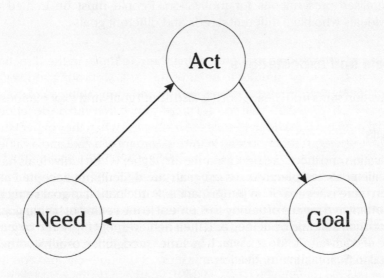

Figure 4.1   Motivation model

Needs

People are motivated by unsatisfied needs. A number of classifications of typical needs have been produced and these can be summarized as follows:

■ Existence needs – the need to survive and satisfy physiological requirements (food, drink, shelter etc.)

■ Social – the need for friendly relations with others.

■ Achievement – the need to feel a sense of achievement in what you have done.

■ Recognition – the need to be recognized for what you have achieved.

■ Growth – the need to develop one's capacities and potential and become what you believe you are capable of becoming.

■ Power – the need to control or influence others.

Everyone has existence and social needs. But the strength of the other needs will vary considerably between people and will vary for a person at different times. The need for power is certainly not universal. It is because of this diversity of needs that it is impossible to produce generalised prescriptions for motivation. People must be treated as individuals who have different needs and different goals.

Goals and expectations

Motivation starts from needs but it is also about goals and expectations.

Goals

Motivation and therefore performance are higher when individuals have specific goals or objectives, when goals are difficult but accepted and when there is feedback on performance. Participation in goal setting is important as a means of getting agreement to the setting of higher goals. Stretch goals should be agreed and their achievement furthered by guidance and advice. Feedback which includes recognition of achievement is vital in maintaining motivation.

Expectations

The strength of motivation depends on the extent to which people believe that their efforts will produce a worthwhile reward; that is, one that satisfies their needs. The strength of expectations may be based on past experiences (reinforcement). Promises are not enough. But individuals may often be faced with new situations such as a change in their jobs or a new payment system. Past experience may be an inadequate guide to the implications of the change and motivation may be reduced.

The two varieties of motivation

People can be motivated positively by what the organization does for them (pay, promotion, training opportunities etc) or what their managers do (award pay increases, give praise, recommend promotion). This is called extrinsic motivation because it describes what is done to or for people to motivate them.

People can also be motivated by factors which are inherent and not imposed from outside. These self-generated factors include responsibility (feeling that the work is important and having control over their own resources), a sense of achievement, freedom to act, scope to use and develop skills and abilities, interesting and challenging work and opportunities for advancement. This is called intrinsic motivation because it arises from the work itself and is not imposed from outside.

Extrinsic motivation can make an immediate and powerful impact but it will not necessarily last long. Intrinsic motivation which is concerned with the 'quality of working life' can have a deeper and longer lasting effect.

Extrinsic motivation can be described as the carrot. It is also possible to use the stick – punishment or criticism – to get people to correct the error of their ways. But the latter sort of negative motivation can cause resentment and do more harm than good. If used at all it has to be used judiciously.

APPROACHES TO MOTIVATION

The process of motivation as described above suggests the following points to remember about how it works:

- The significance of needs – people will be better motivated if both their psychological and their economic needs are satisfied.

- The influence of goals – individuals are motivated by having specific, attainable and agreed goals.

- The importance of expectations – the degree to which people are motivated depends on the strength of their expectations that work will bring them to the rewards they want.

- The relevance of the distinction between extrinsic and intrinsic motivation – extrinsic rewards will be important in attracting and retaining employees and, for limited periods, increasing effort. Intrinsic rewards related to responsibility, achievement, recognition and the work itself will have a longer-term and deeper impact on motivation.

ACHIEVING HIGH LEVELS OF MOTIVATION

The following actions will help you to motivate people more effectively:

1   Set and agree demanding goals.
2   Provide feedback on performance.
3   Create expectations that certain behaviours and outputs will produce worthwhile rewards.
4   Design jobs round the capabilities of people which will enable them to use their abilities and feel a sense of accomplishment, and will empower them to exercise control over, and take responsibility for, their work.
5   Provide appropriate financial incentives and rewards for achievement.
6   Provide appropriate non-financial rewards such as recognition and praise for work well done.
7   Ensure that people appreciate the link between performance and reward, thus enhancing expectations.
8   Select and develop team leaders or supervisors who will exercise leadership and motivating skills.
9   Give people guidance and encouragement and provide them with learning opportunities which will develop the knowledge, skills and capabilities they need to improve their performance.
10   Enable people to develop their potential and careers.

FURTHER READING

Robertson I T, Smith M and Cooper C (1992), *Motivation*, Institute of Personnel and Development, London.

5

MANAGING THE PSYCHOLOGICAL CONTRACT

Motivation is affected not only by what is done to or for people or what they do for themselves, it is also related to the beliefs people have about how they and others are expected to behave. This is the so-called psychological contract.

THE NATURE AND IMPORTANCE OF THE PSYCHOLOGICAL CONTRACT

A psychological contract consists of understandings about the behaviour employers expect from their employees on the one hand and the behaviour employees expect from their employer on the other. The essence of the psychological contract is that it consists of unwritten expectations. It is based on assumptions which may be held by one party but not the other. Psychological contracts are implied and inferred rather than stated and agreed.

The psychological contract is important because it creates attitudes and emotions which form and govern behaviour. Problems can arise with the employment relationship if there are misunderstandings, which are only too likely to occur.

EMPLOYEE EXPECTATIONS

Employees may expect the following from their employers:

- to be treated fairly as human beings
- to be provided with work which uses their abilities
- to be rewarded equitably in accordance with their contribution
- to be able to display competence
- to have opportunities for further growth
- to have security in employment
- to know what is expected of them
- to be given feedback (preferably positive) on how they are doing.

EMPLOYER EXPECTATIONS

Employers may expect the following from their employees:

- to be fully committed to the organization and its values
- to work hard
- to be loyal – 'to put themselves out'
- to be compliant
- to be competent
- to enhance the image of the organization with its customers, clients and suppliers.

CLARIFYING THE PSYCHOLOGICAL CONTRACT

Marked differences between the mutual expectations of employees and employers can damage the employment relationship. They can create confusion, conflict, dissatisfaction and poor morale.

As a line manager you can make an important contribution to clarifying the psychological contract by taking the following steps:

- during recruitment interviews – spelling out as clearly as possible what the job entails, not painting too glowing a picture and not glossing over the demands it will make on the job holder (this is sometimes called a 'realistic job preview')
- in induction programmes – telling new starters about the organization's values and what they are expected to do to uphold them

■ through performance management – getting agreement on the objectives and standards of performance an employee is expected to attain – the aim is to get employees to 'own', ie to be committed to those objectives and standards

■ through mutual contact – making the best use of semi-formal and informal contacts with team members to discuss and clarify mutual expectations

■ by adopting a general approach of transparency – ensuring that on matters which affect them employees know what is happening, why it is happening and how it will affect them

■ by involving team members in discussions about work plans and problems

■ by managing payment systems so as to achieve equity, fairness and consistency in all aspects of financial reward

■ by providing feedback to employees on how well they are doing

■ by encouraging team members to create personal development plans and helping them to develop their skills, improve their potential and increase their employability.

FURTHER READING

Guest, D (1996) *The State of the Psychological Contract in Employment*, Institute of Personnel and Development, London.
Hiltrop, S M (1995) 'The Changing Psychological Contract', *European Management Journal*, September, pp 286–292.

6

COMMITMENT AND MORALE

GAINING COMMITMENT

Commitment is about attachment and loyalty. It has three components:

■ identification with the organization – its purpose and values

■ a desire to remain with the organization

■ a willingness to work hard on behalf of the organization.

The significance of commitment

An American writer, Robert Walton first highlighted the importance of commitment. His theme was that improved performance would result if the organization moved away from the traditional control-orientated approach to managing people. He argued that the approach should be replaced by a commitment strategy. He suggested that people respond best and most creatively when they are given broader responsibilities, encouraged to contribute and helped to achieve satisfaction in their work. Effective response over the long-term is unlikely to happen when people are too tightly controlled by management, placed in narrowly defined jobs and treated like an unwelcome necessity. He expressed belief that in the new commitment-based organization:

> Jobs are designed to be broader than before, to combine planning and implementation, and to include efforts to upgrade operations, not just to maintain them. With management hierarchies relatively flat and differences in status minimized, control and lateral co-ordination depend on

shared goals. And expertise rather than formal position determines influence.

Tom Peters added weight to this belief in a commitment strategy. He wrote (in conjunction with Nancy Austin):

> Trust people and treat them like adults, enthuse them by lively and imaginative leadership, develop and demonstrate an obsession for quality, make them feel they own the business, and your workforce will respond with total commitment.

Enhancing commitment

The steps you can take to enhance commitment include the following:

■ get people involved in discussing the purpose and values of the organisation, listen to their constructive contributions and pass them on to higher management for incorporation in the organization's statement of purpose and values

■ talk to team members informally as well as formally about what is going on in the department and plans for the future that will affect them

■ involve team members in defining mutual expectations so that they 'own' and are committed to their objectives

■ take whatever steps you can to improve the quality of working life in your department or team – the environment in which they work, the ways in which their jobs are designed, the style with which they are managed and the scope to participate – a 'culture of consent' rather than a 'command and control' situation

■ help people to develop their skills and competences to improve their 'employability' within and, indeed, outside the firm

■ make no promises about 'a job for life', but emphasize, if this is true, that the company will do everything it can to increase employment opportunities and therefore security and will avoid compulsory redundancy if that is humanly possible.

■ Finally, bear in mind that in delivering any message about, for example, security, remember that the frame of reference for those who receive the message will not necessarily coincide with your own. Your views may be received with open or hidden expressions of doubt and cynicism, even hostility. You have to work hard to create trust and this will be achieved more by your deeds than your words.

As the Institute of Personnel and Development has emphasized: 'In too many organizations inconsistency between what is said and what is done undermines trust, generates employee cynicism and provides evidence of contradictions in management thinking.'

The IPD suggests that building trust is the only way in which commitment can be generated, and this will not be achieved if employees are simply treated as factors of production and in ways which are inconsistent with their status as the key business asset. And people will not feel committed to the organization unless they feel that they are valued by the organization.

Valuing people

People will not feel that they are valued just because there is a passing reference in the Annual Report by the Chairman that 'people are our most important asset' (according to Dilbert, one of the ten great lies of management). Valuing people is a matter of creating and maintaining a positive 'organization climate' (the atmosphere in the organization as indicated by how people feel about it and its management). This will include feelings about:

- responsibility – being trusted to carry out important work
- feedback – giving recognition for work well-done
- reward – ensuring that people are rewarded fairly according to their contribution, using both financial and non-financial rewards
- identity – being recognized as a valued member of a cohesive working team
- support – the helpfulness of managers and co-workers
- listening – managers, team leaders and co-workers ask for opinions, listen to what people have to say, take note and either act on what they have heard or at least give a reasoned explanation why action along the lines suggested is not possible or is only partly possible.
- Managers and team leaders are in a position to make the difference in all these areas. But remember that if you want people to be more committed because they feel more valued, it is deeds not words that count. Inconsistency between what is said and done is the best way to undermine trust and generate employee cynicism, lack of interest or even open hostility.

INCREASING MORALE

The word morale has a slightly old-fashioned ring about it, associated with the military and those head teachers who talk, or used to talk, about 'esprit de corps'. But it is a term which is frequently used, and it is a helpful one because it describes generally the feelings and attitudes of groups of people about their organization and their work. Morale is sometimes defined as being about group cohesion – the feelings shared amongst a group about the situation it is in – what it is there to do and the extent to which they believe generally that it is worthwhile and should be supported by their joint effort.

If morale is high, commitment, enthusiasm and teamwork is more likely to be high. If it is low people are likely to be uncooperative, argumentative in a negative way, and prone to conflict – with each other as well as management.

Assessing morale

Organizations can assess morale by the use of attitude or opinion surveys which ask questions about such things as:

- how well the organization is managed
- the quality of the organization as an employer
- the fairness with which people are treated by the organization and their bosses
- the extent to which people like working for the organization
- the amount of responsibility people are given
- satisfaction with the current job
- the extent to which the job makes the best use of skills and abilities
- the support provided by bosses and colleagues
- the extent to which achievements are recognised.

Such surveys can focus on particular departments or groups of employees but they are best prepared and administered by experts, often from outside the company. Held regularly, they can measure changes in attitudes and morale over the years and indicate where steps need to be taken to improve.

Of course, if you keep your finger on the pulse by talking and listening to people and by observing what is going on, you can produce a good picture of the state of morale in your department or team.

High morale will be indicated by enthusiasm, interest in and dedication to the task, effective teamwork and a willingness to discuss and resolve problems openly and without undue emotion.

Poor morale will be evidenced by conflict, an excessive number of grievances, absenteeism, lateness, uncooperative behaviour, inter-personal disputes, errors, and failures to provide good service to customers.

Improving morale

The best way to improve morale is to identify the reasons for the problem by talking and listening to people and their focus on corrective action. This action should be considered, planned and implemented with the active involvement of the team. Your task – not an easy one – is to convince them that they will benefit personally from participating in this process.

The following are examples of the action that can be taken in different circumstances:

■ lack of co-operation – get people to re-examine jointly what they and their colleagues are there to do, and establish how they can improve things by establishing mutually agreed aims and methods of working together

■ conflict – get team members together to define the problem and agree on the objectives to be attained in reaching a solution; then get the group to develop alternative solutions and debate their merits; finally, the group agrees on the preferred course of action and how it should be implemented.

■ lack of commitment – ensure that the team is involved in setting objectives, decision-making, monitoring performance and taking collective action.

Note that there are no universal prescriptions for improving morale. You can generally adopt a 'hearts and minds' approach to winning over people, but ultimately what you do and how you do it will depend on the situation you are in.

FURTHER READING

Institute of Personnel and Development (1994) *People Make the Difference*, London.

Peters, T and Austin, N (1995) *A Passion for Excellence*, Collins, Glasgow.
Walton R (1995) 'From control to commitment in the workplace', *Harvard Business Review*, March–April issue, pp 76–84.

7

LEADERSHIP

Leadership is the process of inspiring individuals to give of their best to achieve a desired result. It is about getting people to move in the right direction, gaining their commitment, and motivating them to achieve their goals.

THE ROLES OF THE LEADER

Leaders have two essential roles. They have to:

1 Achieve the task – that is why their group exists. Leaders ensure that the group's purpose is fulfilled. If it is not, the result is frustration, disharmony, criticism and, eventually perhaps, disintegration of the group.
2 Maintain effective relationships – between themselves and the members of the group, and between the people within the group. These relationships are effective if they contribute to achieving the task. They can be divided into those concerned with the team and its morale and sense of common purpose, and those concerned with individuals and how they are motivated.

John Adair, the expert on leadership, suggested some time ago that these demands are best expressed as three areas of need which leaders are there to satisfy. These are: (1) task needs – to get the job done, (2) group needs – to build and maintain team spirit, and (3) individual needs – to harmonise the needs of the individual with the needs of the task and the group.

Other more recent research, including that conducted by the Industrial Society as described towards the end of this chapter, has expanded and refined this model, but basically it still rings true as a basic description of what leadership is about.

LEADERSHIP STYLES

Leaders adopt different styles which can be classified as:

■ *Charismatic/non-charismatic*. Charismatic leaders rely on their personality, their inspirational qualities and their 'aura'. They are often visionary leaders who are achievement orientated, calculated risk takers and good communicators. Non-charismatic leaders rely mainly on their know-how (authority goes to the person who knows), their quiet confidence and their cool, analytical approach to dealing with problems.

■ *Autocratic/democratic*. Autocratic leaders impose their decisions, using their position to force people to do as they are told. Democratic leaders encourage people to participate and involve themselves in decision-taking.

■ *Enabler/controller*. Enablers inspire people with their vision of the future and empower them to accomplish team goals. Controllers manipulate people to obtain their compliance.

■ *Transactional/transformational*. Transactional leaders trade money, jobs and security for compliance. Transformational leaders motivate people to strive for higher level goals.

THE IMPACT OF THE SITUATION

The situation in which leaders and their teams function will influence the approaches that leaders adopt. There is no such thing as an ideal leadership style. It all depends. The factors affecting the degree to which a style is appropriate will be the type of organization, the nature of the task, the characteristics of the group and, importantly, the personality of the leader. A task-orientated approach (autocratic, controlling, transactional) may be best in emergency or crisis situations or when the leader has power, formal backing and a relatively well-structured task. In these circumstances the group is more ready to be directed and told what to do. In less well-structured or ambiguous situations, where results depend on the group working well together with a common sense of purpose, leaders who are more concerned with maintaining good relationships (democratic, enablers, transformational) are more likely to obtain good results.

However, commentators such as Charles Handy, are concerned that intelligent organizations have to be run by persuasion and consent. In *The Age of Unreason* he suggests that the heroic leader of the past 'knew all, could do all and could solve every problem'. Now, the post-heroic leader has come to the fore who 'asks how every problem can be solved in a way that develops other people's capacity to handle it'.

LEADERSHIP QUALITIES

The qualities required of leaders may vary somewhat in different situations, but research and analysis of effective leaders have identified a number of generic characteristics which good leaders are likely to have. John Adair lists the following qualities:

■ enthusiasm – to get things done which they can communicate to other people

■ confidence – belief in themselves which again people can sense (but this must not be over-confidence, which leads to arrogance)

■ toughness – resilient, tenacious and demanding high standards, seeking respect but not necessarily popularity

■ integrity – being true to oneself – personal wholeness, soundness and honesty which inspires trust

■ warmth – in personal relationships, caring for people and being considerate

■ humility – willingness to listen and take the blame; not being arrogant and overbearing.

WHAT ORGANIZATIONS REQUIRE OF LEADERS

Research conducted by the Industrial Survey and published in 1997 showed what organizations required of leaders and how these requirements fit into today's structures and cultures. What organizations want is:

- leaders who will make the right space for people to perform well without having to be watched over – not bosses

- flat structures where people can be trusted to work with minimal supervision

- a wide range of people who are able to 'take a lead', step into a leadership role when necessary and consistently behave in a responsible way

- a culture where people can be responsive to customer demands and agile in the face of changing technology.

BEHAVIOURS PEOPLE VALUE IN LEADERS

The respondents to the Industrial Society survey were asked to rank the importance of 35 factors in leader behaviour. The top twenty factors are shown in Table 7.1.

Rank	Factor
1	Shows enthusiasm
2	Supports other people
3	Recognizes individual effort
4	Listens to individuals' ideas and problems
5	Provides direction
6	Demonstrates personal integrity
7	Practises what he/she preaches
8	Encourages teamwork
9	Actively encourages feedback
10	Develops other people
11	Promotes other people's self esteem
12	Seeks to understand before making judgements
13	Treats mistakes as learning opportunities
14	Gives people doing the work the power to make decisions
15	Encourages new ways of doing things
16	Promotes understanding of the key issues
17	Looks at possible future challenges
18	Agrees targets
19	Takes decisions
20	Minimizes anxiety.

Table 7.1   Leadership behaviour factors in rank order

As the Industrial Society comments:

These behaviours are easy to recognize: managers can be seen setting targets, conducting team meetings, building teams, taking decisions, appraising and coaching their staff. But it emerged quite clearly that there is a vital link between how effectively managers achieve these things and whether they are trusted, and that it is their beliefs which determine whether they are trusted. For a manager to be regarded as a leader, to gain the genuine commitment of their staff, they must earn their trust.

LEADERSHIP CHECKLIST

The task

1 What needs to be done and why?
2 How does this task fit into the wider purposes of the organization?
3 What results have to be achieved and when?
4 Are the resources (people, money facilities) available to the task?
5 If not what needs to be done about them?
   What are the critical success factors affecting the satisfactory accomplishment of the task?
6 What problems have to be overcome?
7 How can it be established that the task has been well done? (ie what performance measures are available?)

The team

1 Is the team capable of achieving the task?
2 Has the team a sense of common purpose?
3 Do the members of the team work well together?
4 Are the members of the team flexible, ie capable of undertaking different tasks (multi-skilled)?
5 To what extent is it possible and desirable to empower the team to plan and control its work?

The individuals in the team

1 What are the strengths and weaknesses of each member of the team?
2 What sort of approaches are most likely to motivate individual team members?

3 How are they likely to respond individually to the different types of leadership styles that may be adopted?

FURTHER READING

Adair, J (1973) *The Action-Centred Leader*, McGraw-Hill, London.
Handy, C (1989) *The Age of Unreason*, Business Books, London.
Industrial Society (1997) 'Leadership – steering a new course', *Briefing Plus*, October issue, pp 4–5.
Turner, D (1998) Liberating Leadership – a manager's guide, The Industrial Society, London.

8

TEAM BUILDING

The importance of teamwork has increased significantly in organizations which have been 'delayered' and/or have undergone a business process re-engineering exercise. In the latter case, the organization is built around horizontal processes which are linked together and depend on good teamwork to function effectively. For example, in Bass Taverns, the responsibility for commissioning new pubs was divided between a number of different functions which operated independently.

An analysis of what was involved in setting up a pub led to a re-definition of the processes required and a decision to create multi-functional project teams to be responsible for the commissioning process from start to finish. As a result, the length of time taken was cut by half.

At the Nissan plant in Workington, Tyne and Wear, the general principles of teamwork are defined as being to:

- promote mutual trust and co-operation between the company, its employees and the union
- recognize that all employees, at whatever level, have a valued part to play in the running of the company
- seek actively the contributions of all employees in furthering these goals.

TEAMWORKING IN PRACTICE

The following is an example of teamworking in practice.

Dutton Engineering – teamworking

Following a reorganization of manufacturing operations at Dutton Engineering the next step was to introduce teamworking. The new arrangement was to organize employees into teams of up to ten workers. Instead of a job passing through everyone's hands to completion, it was seen through from start to finish by a single group of workers. This enabled members of the team to get much closer to the customer, helping them to improve the product. A key aspect of this method of working was that employees had to be multiskilled and this meant that a comprehensive training programme had to be planned and implemented.

Over time, the teams have become self-managing. Each team is effectively a self-contained small business. Members have been trained in basic cost accounting so they can set and monitor their own budgets. The quotes are given to customers by the team, and the team is responsible for getting the job done within that budget. Each team gets a monthly report on completed orders, detailing the cost of materials, labour and other overheads and whether it made money or not. If the job has run over budget, then it is up to the team to devise ways of improving the process so that the job is profitable next time round. Should customers be responsible for cost over-runs, perhaps because they changed the specifications, it again falls to the team to go back and ask for more money.

However, the organization has a 'no blame' culture. This means that employees are not punished if a project runs over budget. As Tina Mason, the company's business manager, points out: 'Control has been swapped for accountability. If you are asking people to make decisions, then it's very important that you support them when things go wrong, otherwise they'll never make one again... when things go pear-shaped, and occasionally they do, we try to treat it as a learning experience. We ask "What went wrong?" rather than "Whose fault is it?" We aren't looking for scapegoats. The key thing is to do better next time round so we don't repeat the mistake.'

APPROACHES TO TEAM BUILDING

All managers are essentially team leaders. To succeed as a manager you have to know what needs to be done to build effective teams. The key things you have to do to:

- establish urgency and direction

■ select members based on their skills and potential who are good at working with others

■ promote flexibility by developing multi-skilling, ie the capacity of individuals in the team to carry out more than one of the tasks which the team has to do

■ involve the team in setting objectives and targets

■ empower the team to make its own collective decisions about work programmes and how to deal with problems

■ encourage the team to monitor its own performance and to take initiative collectively to take corrective action

■ hold special 'off-the-job' meetings so that the team can get together and explore issues without the pressures of their day-to-day work

■ get the team to analyse its own performance using the checklist set out below.

Cellular working at GKN Westland Helicopters

GKN Westland Helicopters has made significant changes in working practices because of the increasingly high-tech helicopters they are making. These include the introduction of cellular-based teamworking. Previously, there had been relatively little planning or strategic management of the manufacturing process. Problems were often solved on an ad hoc basis by fitters. This was no longer possible. It was also clear that it would be difficult and costly to move the aircraft through a traditional production process. This determined a cellular approach in which parts are taken to the helicopter for its different stages.

Cellular working

The assembly and flight areas for the new helicopter (the EH101) were completely refurbished with the cellular idea in mind and the production staff were involved in designing the facility and its layout. A project team, which consisted of production staff, was established to look at all aspects of cellular working.

A cellular team is led by a cell leader and has about 12 production team members. The cell leader is at first-line management level. There is production engineering, logistical and administrative support within the cell. (The design function is outside the cell but is within the same building.) There is one leader per shift for each cell and production employees work double-day shifts.

Within helicopter assembly, production staff have either of two base skills – electrical or mechanical. The company is striving to get production team members to be able to do all the functions covered by either one of the base skills. Skills are spread across the cell with several employees able to complete every task.

There is also a move towards the dual-skilling of certain highly skilled employees. Ultimately, for example, the majority of electrical production staff would be partially skilled in mechanical areas so that they are able to carry out 50 per cent of mechanical tasks to the appropriate training standard. Accordingly the in-house apprenticeship has been revised to accommodate partial dual-skilling across mechanical and electrical trades.

Training

A 30,000-hour training programme has taken place for the 450 employees concerned. This took place in the 18 months prior to the setting up of the new facility. Cell members received a five-day training programme, which took place in company time. The first two days were used to explain the theory behind the teamworking concept and cellular working. A further three days were spent on Dartmoor for a series of teambuilding and problem solving exercises. An individual cell and its immediate support group took part in the training. This allowed employees within the extended cell to understand the different functions and how they all inter-linked.

Cell leaders were trained so that they possessed the skills to be able to manage employees and production. These included:

■ understanding the business process

■ an ability to solve problems logically, using the team and the extended team

■ developing the team by building relationships and by coaching and training.

CHECKLIST FOR ANALYSING TEAM PERFORMANCE

1 How well do we work together?
2 Does everyone contribute?
3 How well is the team led?
4 How good are we at analysing problems and taking collective action to deal with them?

5   How well do we use the skills of team members?
6   How flexible are we in carrying out our work?
7   Are there a sufficient number of team members who are multi-skilled, ie capable of carrying out different tasks?
8   If there is any conflict, to what extent is it openly expressed and is it about issues rather than personalities?

FURTHER READING

Katzenbach, J and Smith, D (1993) *The Magic of Teams*, Harvard Business School Press, Boston, Mass.

9

DELEGATING

You can't do everything yourself, so you have to delegate. This sounds easy. You just tell people what to do, then they do it. But there is more to it than that.

Delegation is difficult. You have to make decisions on what to delegate and then on how much control you want to exercise over what your subordinates do. You always have to remember that you carry the can. You can delegate work but you cannot delegate your responsibility for ensuring that the work is carried out properly. If you let go too much, will things get done? If you breathe down the necks of your subordinates will they ever learn the jobs and relieve you of the time-consuming business of checking up on them?

Delegation requires trust but you cannot leave it to chance. You have to delegate properly and develop your team so that they are capable of working on their own and delivering results without you getting involved.

WHEN TO DELEGATE

You should delegate when:

- you have more work than you can effectively do yourself

- you cannot allocate sufficient time to your priority tasks, including planning, staff development and monitoring performance

- you know that the task can be adequately performed by the subordinate

■ you want to develop your subordinate – the best way of learning is by doing; unless you give people the opportunity to do more they will not develop.

ADVANTAGES OF DELEGATION

If you delegate well:

■ you are relieved of routine tasks

■ it frees you for more important work

■ it allows decisions to be taken at the level where the circumstances are known or where people are in direct contact with the customer or supplier

■ it develops the capacity of people to take decisions and grow in their roles, thus increasing their employability.

WHAT TO DELEGATE

You delegate tasks that you don't need to do yourself. You also delegate to those who have the specialist knowledge and skills and/or the time to do work. You cannot do it all yourself.

HOW MUCH TO DELEGATE

How much you delegate to a person or group of people clearly depends on the nature of the task and the ability of those concerned to carry it out. But people won't grow unless they are extended. It is therefore a good idea to delegate rather more than people are capable of doing. It is a matter of judgement as to whether they will be capable of doing a bit extra, with your guidance and help. And much depends on your willingness to help them to learn their new tasks without interfering in the detail of how they carry them out.

GIVING OUT THE WORK

When you delegate you should ensure that the team or individuals understand:

■ why the work needs to be done

■ what they are expected to do

■ the targets or standards they have to achieve

■ the date by which they are expected to do it (unless it is a continuing task)

■ the authority they have to make decisions

■ the problems they must refer back to you

■ the progress reports they must prepare and submit

■ the dates of any 'milestone' meetings if this is a project

■ how you propose to guide and monitor them

■ the resources they will have to help them with the work.

The basis of delegation should be an agreement on what should be done – you delegate by the results you expect. You may sometimes have to specify to inexperienced people how the results should be achieved, but progressively you leave them to work it out for themselves. But it is often a good idea to ask people to tell you how they propose to deal with a problem. Then you have the opportunity to provide guidance at the outset. Guidance at a later stage may be seen as interference.

COACHING

Delegation not only helps you to get your work done, it also provides the basis for coaching people as described in Chapter 28.

MONITORING PERFORMANCE

You may have to monitor the performance of a new member of your team very carefully at first. But the sooner you can relax and watch progress informally the better.

It is important to define expectations – what you expect from your team members and what they expect from you. These should be agreed in advance in the form of targets or standards of performance.

The more you encourage your people to make suggestions to you about what they believe they can achieve the better – they will be much more committed to targets they have set themselves. Of course, you must ensure that individuals' targets and standards will ensure that the team's objectives will be achieved, and this means getting people to agree on more demanding targets where these are necessary.

As well as agreeing targets you should discuss performance measures – how you and the team will know whether the task has been done well. Project teams will have to work to target dates and methods of reviewing progress (reports and 'milestone' meetings) will need to be agreed. You cannot allow your team to become careless about meeting deadlines.

Without being oppressive you need to ensure that targets and standards are being achieved. This means that you must monitor outputs and levels of service delivery through reports and periodical meetings. You must be prepared to ensure that corrective action is taken if things are not going according to plan. But try to restrain yourself from constantly reviewing performance in great detail. It is, after all, the results that count. It is a matter of judgement to decide how much control information you require and how often. But don't overdo it.

There is a delicate balance to be achieved between hedging people around with petty restrictions and allowing them too much licence to do what they like. You must use your knowledge of your team members and the work situation to decide where the balance should be struck.

Remember always that you are the only person who is ultimately responsible. But if your people do not know what to do when they run into a problem you cannot always be there to help them. What they do may depend on a situation which only they can assess. Your responsibility is to ensure that, as far as possible, they acquire the skills, knowledge and experience which enables them to make good decisions without your help.

FURTHER READING

Armstrong, M (1994) *How to be an Even Better Manager* 4th edition, (Chapter 19), Kogan Page, London.

10

COMMUNICATING

Managers spend most of their time talking to other people and at least some of their time listening to them (the more of the latter the better). They are essentially communicators. To be able to communicate well you need to know something about the barriers to communication and how to overcome them. You also need to know something about listening skills.

BARRIERS TO COMMUNICATION

The main barriers to communication are:

■ *Hearing what we want to hear* – instead of hearing what people have told us, we hear what our minds tell us they have said. We have preconceptions about what people are going to say, and if what they say does not fit these preconceptions we adjust it until it does. What is said and what is heard may therefore be significantly different. The message will have failed to get through.

■ *Ignoring conflicting information* – we ignore or reject communications which conflict with our own beliefs.

■ *Perceptions about the communicator* – it is difficult to separate what we hear from our feelings about the person who says it.

■ *Influence of the group* – the group with which we identify influences our attitudes and feelings. People are more likely to listen to their fellow group members rather than outsiders such as managers.

■ *Words mean different things to different people* – it is easy to communicate words, it is much harder to convey meaning.

■ *Non-verbal communication* – we attend not only to what people say but to how they say it. We may feel that body language conveys more meaning than words. But there is a lot of scope for misinterpretation.

■ *Emotions* – our emotions colour our reception of the message. If we are angry or insecure we might reject what would otherwise be accepted as a sensible comment.

■ *Noise* – 'noise' in the literal sense of loud sounds or in the figurative sense of distracting or confused information can distract or obscure meaning.

■ *Size* – the greater the size or complexity of the organization the greater the problem of communication.

OVERCOMING THE BARRIERS

■ *Adjust to the world of the receiver* – try to predict the impact of what you are going to write or say on the receiver. Tailor the message to fit the receiver's interests, values and vocabulary. Be aware that people reject what they don't want to hear, can be prejudiced and may be under the influence of others.

■ *Use feedback* – get a reply from the receiver which tells you how much has been understood.

■ *Use face-to-face communication* – wherever possible talk to people rather than write to them. You can then adjust your message according to reactions and respond immediately to questions, doubts and fears.

■ *Use different channels* – some communications have to be in writing to get the message across. But supplement written communications with the spoken word.

■ *Use reinforcement* – present your message in different ways to get it across. Re-emphasize the key points.

■ *Use direct, simple language* – avoid jargon, long words and complex sentences.

■ *Reduce noise* – don't pass your message through a number of levels of management or supervision (if they still exist). Deliver it yourself.

LISTENING SKILLS

There are many good writers and speakers but few good listeners. Most of us filter the spoken words addressed to us, so only some of them are absorbed – usually those we want to hear. But a good listener will receive more information and get on better with other people.

Effective listeners:

- Concentrate on the speaker, following not only the words but also body language.

- Respond to points made by the speaker.

- Comment on the points, without interrupting the flow, in order to test understanding and demonstrate that the listener and the speaker are on the same wavelength.

- Make notes on the key points.

- Continuously evaluate the messages to check that they are understood.

- Are alert at all times to what the speaker is saying.

- Are prepared to let the speaker go on with the minimum of interruption.

11

ORGANIZING

Essentially, organizing is deciding who does what (individuals and teams) and how people and teams in an organization relate to one another. An organization's structure defines levels of authority and communication channels. This may be expressed through an organization chart with job descriptions for each of the posts included in the chart.

THE TRADITIONAL APPROACH TO ORGANIZING

Charles Handy makes the point that:

> One sign of the new sorts of organization is a perceptible change in the language we use to talk about them. Organizations used to be perceived as gigantic pieces of engineering, with largely interchangeable human parts. We talked of their structures and their systems, of inputs and outputs, of control devices, and of managing them, as if the whole was one large factory. Today the language is not of engineering but of politics, with talk of cultures and networks, of teams and coalitions, of influence or power rather than control, of leadership not management.

Traditionally, organizations were structured in accordance with a number of accepted 'principles'. These included such precepts as not having too many people reporting to a single person (span of control), one person must have one boss, job duties should be defined precisely, the organization should not be 'distorted' to fit the capacities of the people in it, lines of communication must be clearly defined to run from top to the bottom etc.

Managers tended to be given the structure of their department and told to live with it. They were not allowed to change it in any way. People were slotted into jobs and not given any real freedom to adapt what they were doing to changing situations.

Departments or functions were set up as 'chimneys'. Attention was focussed on vertical relationships and authority-based management – the 'command and control' structure. Little attention was given to how operations or processes which involved more than one function or department could work more smoothly and effectively together.

The problem with the traditional approach was that it led to bureaucracy, rigidity and failures in communication between different parts of the organization. The structure was designed to fit some abstract principles, not to represent the realities of the situation. It assumed that nothing would change. Traditional structures simply do not fit the ways in which many organizations now have to function.

THE NEW APPROACHES TO ORGANIZING

The new organization is flexible in the sense that it is capable of quickly adapting to new demands and can operate fluidly. It may take the form of what Charles Handy calls the 'shamrock' organization, with core workers carrying out the fundamental and continuing activities of the organization, while contract or temporary staff are employed as peripheral workers. Some of the work traditionally carried out within the organization may be 'outsourced' ie sub-contracted to outside suppliers or service providers. For example, an engineering firm may get its foundry work done elsewhere and a personnel department may get recruitment agencies to obtain staff.

The process-based organization

Much more attention is given to the horizontal processes that cut across organizational boundaries. John Welch, the dynamic leader of General Electric in the United States has stated that his aim is to create a 'boundaryless organization'.

The new organization is not based on hierarchies of static roles. Instead it is regarded as a portfolio of dynamic processes which overlay the vertical authority-based traditional structure. Bass Brewers abandoned the distinct traditional function of brewing, selling and distribution and now treats the organization as essentially consisting of one 'logistics' function which integrates the functionally separate tasks into unified horizontal work processes. This is what business process re-engineering exercises are intended to do.

Admittedly, they have often promised more than they have achieved and have recently had a bad press, mainly because they took insufficient account of the people implications of the considerable organizational changes they introduced. But the basic concept of looking at linked processes rather than separate activities is still valid.

Delayering

Another significant trend in the new organization is delayering – cutting out levels of management and supervision which are no longer required to produce a flatter structure.

This has sometimes gone too far, as Henry Mintzberg has written 'delayering means that the people who don't know what's going on in the organization get rid of those who do.' But the leaner organization is here to stay. Extended hierarchies are no longer appropriate where flexibility and ease of communication are necessary. And the increased use of information technology and electronic communications means that the function of some managers as simply links in a chain are no longer necessary. As Peter Drucker wrote:

> Whole layers of management neither make decisions nor lead. Instead, their main, if not their only, function is to serve as relays – human boosters for the faint, unfocussed signals that pass for communication in the traditional pre-information organization.

Role flexibility

Another feature of the new organization is 'role flexibility'. This is the concept that individuals and teams have to be much more prepared to adapt to new requirements, take on different responsibilities and learn new skills.

In many organizations, rigid job descriptions spelling out exactly what people have to do are a thing of the past. They are replaced by role definitions which focus on the roles people have to play in a position by using their skills and competencies to achieve results. Role definitions concentrate on what has to be achieved in broad terms rather than spelling out in detail the tasks that have to be carried out. The aim is to ensure that people who are expected to work flexibly cannot say: 'No, it's not in my job description'.

Cross-functional teams

One of the more important implications of the features of the new organization described above is the increased use of cross-functional teams. These will manage projects extending over a number of functions which are linked together as a unified horizontal process.

Customer focus

The increased emphasis on customer service has meant that the organization has to be more focussed on the needs of customers. Teams are therefore set up which are responsible for dealing with all aspects of the services that customers require. A company such as Pearl Assurance has set up teams which are responsible for a number of different processes (underwriting, claims etc) for defined groups of customers which were previously carried out by a number of different departments.

The changing role of the process worker

A report published in 1997 by the Institute of Employment Studies, *Productive Skills for Process Operatives* (L Giles, J Kodz and C Evans, IES Report 336), revealed that management structures designed in response to technological advances and competitive pressures are transforming the role of process workers. The study was based on detailed interviews with 20 employers in the chemicals, food and drink industries, mostly at the forefront of change in their respective sectors.

Increasing automation and the application of new technologies to the production process mean that low-skilled manual jobs continue to disappear, and that process workers are becoming progressively less involved in manual operating tasks. Instead, they are being given more responsibility for the processes they work on, while being expected to become more customer and business oriented and, in many cases, to carry out simple engineering and maintenance tasks.

The study identifies a number of areas where management strategies are creating a new context for process workers to carry out their changing roles:

■ Delayering was a common theme among survey respondents, with many having taken some supervisory and 'charge hand' roles out of the staffing structure while devolving their responsibilities down the line, thus creating space for the process worker function to develop.

■ Many of the surveyed employers emphasized teamworking in general, and cellular working in particular, entailing a move towards process operatives working on whole jobs, rather than different tasks or components within jobs, inside teams that have responsibility for whole processes.

■ Self-managed teams – which assume responsibility for staff management as well as production issues – were also 'beginning to become evident', according to the study's authors, although they tended to be at a fairly early stage of development.

■ Respondents also referred to new training initiatives, such as competency frameworks, and skills and training matrices, aimed at ensuring a structured means of developing people.

■ In some areas, pay enhancements and performance-related pay were being used as incentives to enhance individual productivity and development.

■ Moves towards multi-skilling and flexible working were not universal, but tended to take the form of 'variations upon a theme across processing sites', with a corresponding erosion of traditional job demarcations between process operatives and craft occupations.

Expanding the final point, the report suggests a three-part typology for the range of approaches to increasing flexibility outlined by respondents:

■ *Multiple skilling* – where all process operators are trained in all areas of a new skill to a similar level. A problem with this approach can be that many operators do not get the opportunity to practise their newly acquired skills and so do not retain them.

■ *Flexible skilling* – process workers operate the plant or piece of machinery as their core function, but are also trained in an extended area. This has the advantage that it can be focused on tasks that the individual will be regularly carrying out. It also allows different individuals to learn and use different skills depending on their wishes and abilities.

■ *Multi-functional teams* – in which the necessary skills are spread within the team, without all process operators having to be trained in all skills. This allows for individuals with particular aptitudes to be trained in certain specialisms.

IMPLICATIONS FOR LINE MANAGERS

In the new organization, line managers have more freedom to decide how they are going to allocate work to the teams and individuals for which they are responsible. If you are in this position, there are no rigid principles for you to act upon. But there are certain guidelines which you should take into account. These are:

- *Best fit* – purpose: whatever else you do, you must ensure that the way in which your unit, department or section is organized fits the purpose for which it exists. This means being clear about what the purpose is and what activities are likely to be required to achieve it. You have to take account of the extent to which these activities are prescribed and the extent to which they may change. The need for flexibility in response to new demands and for teamwork should also be considered.

- *Best fit* – people: you must also take into account the people you have in your team and the sort of people you are likely to recruit in the future. This does not mean distorting the organization to fit individual idiosyncrasies. But it does mean building roles round the strengths of people to ensure that they can maximize their contribution.

- *Job design*: establish or modify meaningful jobs in accordance with the principles of good job design as described in chapter 12.

- *Skill and competence requirements*: while you may have to start by making the best use of the people you have, or can get, you should also analyse very carefully what skills and competences you will need to have in the future in order to meet new demands and improve the performance of your team. This means, first, defining what your team as a whole must be good at doing – its core competences. You can then look at what individual members have to be good at doing – the role competences. If there are any gaps between what your existing team members can do and what they should be able to do you can then take steps to fill them. Skills and competence analysis and developing people are dealt with in chapter 19 and part 5 respectively.

- *Defining expectations:* you must get the agreement of your team or teams and individual team members about what they are expected to achieve and the basis upon which their performance will be measured.

■ *Team building*: the effectiveness of your organization will depend largely on how well team members work together. Team building programmes as described in chapter 6 are therefore necessary.

■ *Organizational change* – changing organizational arrangements can be a painful process for those affected by them who face uncertainty about their future and may be concerned about their ability to cope with new demands. The reasons for the changes and the impact they will make on employees need to be explained carefully. It is even better if people are involved in the process of redesigning work methods. People do not necessarily resist change, but they do resist being changed. And steps must be taken to ensure that the training necessary to learn new skills is provided.

THE APPROACH TO REORGANIZATION

At GKN Westland Helicopters, the introduction of cellular working as described on page 40 was carried out with the full involvement of production staff. Dutton Engineering also involved their employees in the change programme described below

Dutton Engineering – organizational change

Dutton Engineering is a small company which acts as a sub-contractor, specializing in the precision fabrication of stainless steel, mild steel and aluminium.

In 1984, long before 'Japanisation' became all the rage, the managing director, Ken Lewis, went to the Far East to see how manufacturers did business there. What struck him was not so much the teamworking but the culture of mutual trust between management and workforce, something that was extended to the relationship between the company and its suppliers.

Production was previously organized on a 'one man, one job' basis. But as Tina Mason, the company's business manager has said: 'In a manufacturing operation one person is very dependent on another. It did not make sense to put people in little boxes in this way. It also made life difficult for us as managers, because when you have one person, one job, there has to be high degree of forward planning – for instance, we couldn't let all the welders go on holiday together'.

The company therefore went back to first principles to achieve the goal of a flexible workforce. It examined the manufacturing process to find out what core skills it needed. Thirteen key skills were identified as a result of this process. The workforce was then analysed to match the required expertise to individual employees. The goal was to equip everyone with a minimum of three core skills. Some, like welding, were difficult to learn and the company had to invest in quite a lot of external training. Others, like packing, were easier. The company soon found that, far from there being resistance to the concept of flexibility, employees were eager to learn new skills.

Another aspect of operations – inspection – was also tackled. Previously, the responsibility for quality lay at the end of the line with the inspection department. But as Ken Lewis, the company's founder and managing director, says: 'You cannot inspect quality into a product, you've got to build it in'.

ORGANIZING CHECKLIST

☐ Are you clear about the purpose and objectives of your department or team?

☐ How do you know when the overall purpose has been achieved?

■ What are the key areas in which results have to be obtained if your department/team's objectives are to be achieved?

☐ How do you know when you have achieved the required results in each of these key result areas?

■ What are the critical success factors that determine the effectiveness of your department or team?

☐ Are you satisfied that the work required in each of the activities within the key result areas is logically allocated to teams or individuals?

☐ Is each team or individual job a natural work unit which makes a significant and measurable contribution to achieving the results expected from your department?

☐ Do teams and individuals clearly understand what they are accountable for, to whom they are accountable, the objectives and standards they are expected to achieve and how their performance will be measured?

☐ Does the way in which work is allocated to teams and individuals facilitate co-ordination and communication?

■ Are teams and individuals capable of working flexibly in response to new demands and changing situations?

☐ How would you describe the quality of teamwork in your department? If it is just acceptable or poor, what can you do to improve it?

■ How would you describe morale in your department (what people feel about their work, their colleagues, their bosses and the organization?) If it needs to be improved, how will you set about doing it?

■ How would you describe the levels of motivation and commitment in your department? How would you achieve any necessary improvements?

■ How skilled and competent are the members of your department or team? How would you raise the skill base or increase levels of competence?

FURTHER READING

Drucker, P (1988) 'The coming of the new organization', *Harvard Business Review*, January–February, pp 45–53.

Handy, C (1981) *Understanding Organizations*, Penguin Books, Harmondsworth.

Handy, C (1996) *The Age of Unreason*, Business Books, London.

Part 3

Resourcing

12

PLANNING PEOPLE REQUIREMENTS

As a line manager you have to decide or recommend how many people and what skills you need now and at least in the short-term future. This is the process of human resource planning, and it is up to you. If there is a personnel function it may provide you with data on such things as the availability of people from the labour market, the output of trainee schemes and employee turnover rates. It may even in some large organizations use computer models to make projections. But only you know what you are doing now and will be doing in the future and it is those activity levels that form the basis of human resource plans.

AIM OF HUMAN RESOURCE PLANNING

Human resource planning aims to match human resources to business needs, expressed as activity levels.

Plans are often long-term (one year ahead or more) but may look at shorter-term needs. Planning for people is concerned with:

- getting and keeping the number and quality of staff you need
- identifying skill requirements and how to satisfy them (see also Chapter 23)
- dealing with surpluses and deficits of employees
- developing flexible work arrangements (see Chapter 15)
- improving the utilization of employees (see Chapter 16)

DECIDING HOW MANY PEOPLE YOU NEED

Decisions on how many people you need are based on demand and supply forecasts.

Demand forecasting

Demand forecasting is the process of estimating the future number of people required and the skills and competences they will need. The basis for the forecast will be present and projected activity levels in such terms as outputs or the number of items to be processed. Forecast activity levels are usually derived from the business plan and the related functional or departmental plan and budget. In a manufacturing company such as Cummins Engines the sales budget is translated into a manufacturing plan, giving the number of types of product to be made in each period. From this information the number of hours to be worked by each category of employee to meet the budget for each period is computed.

In an insurance company such as Pearl forecasts are made of how many new policies will have to be prepared, how many claims will have to be dealt with and how many customer enquiries will have to be answered. These will be based on the business plan with some of the figures extrapolated from past experience.

A project engineering company such as Cegelec Project Ltd will examine its current projects and how they are likely to develop. It will also do its best to forecast acquisition of new business by reference to current and prospective bids. Firm forecasts can be made by the analysis of current projects but the longer-term future may be more difficult to forecast. In these circumstances human resource planning is more art than science and can only indicate broad trends and the likelihood of action when the future is more assured.

Demand forecasting will also be affected by any corporate plans which may result in increases or decreases in the demand for employees. These might include, for example, setting up a new regional organization, introducing a new product or service, rationalizing production or distribution, and plans 'to drive cost out of the business'. Expected changes in productivity arising from new working methods or the introduction of new technology may also affect demand.

As the above demonstrates, human resource demand planning can be a complex process. But the basic data will always consist of forecast activity levels and there are four methods of doing this as described below.

Managerial judgement

This is the most typical method. It simply requires you to sit down, think about future work loads, and decide how many people you need. Experienced managers can do this quite well but it often involves a lot of guesswork. It usually only works in the short-term and this may not present too much of a problem if increases in levels of work can easily be dealt with by recruitment, overtime, sub-contracting or outsourcing. Unforeseen decreases in activity levels may create more problems. It may not be so easy or desirable to make people redundant, lay them off or reduce their working hours. It may even be difficult to get out of a sub-contract quickly. That is why you have constantly to attempt to forecast requirements as far ahead as you can see by monitoring trends, finding out how business plans are progressing, checking on sales forecasts and results and so on. You cannot rely entirely on your own resources to plan ahead. You must get data from other people.

Ratio-trend analysis

Ratio-trend analysis is carried out by studying past ratios between, for example, the number of direct (production) workers and indirect (support) workers in a manufacturing unit. Forecast activity levels can then give you a good idea of how many direct workers you will need (so many people to make so many widgets) and the ratio of indirects to directs will tell you how many support workers you are likely to need.

Work study techniques

Work study techniques can be used when it is possible to apply work measurement to calculate how long operations should take and the number of planned hours, and therefore people, required.

In a manufacturing company the starting point is the production budget set out as the volume of saleable products for the plant as a whole and the output volumes for each department. If standard hours for units of output have been determined by work measurement, the budgets of productive (planned hours for the year) are then compiled by multiplying standard hours per unit of output by the planned output in units. This is decided by the number of actual working hours for an individual worker, having allowed for absenteeism and forecast idle or down time to show the number of operators required. The following is a simplified example of this process:

■   planned output for year = 2000 units

■ standard hours per unit = 5 hours

☐ planned hours for year = 100,000 hours

☐ net productive hours per person year = 2,000 hours

☐ number of direct workers required (planned hours divided by productive hours per person) = 50

Work study techniques for direct workers can be combined with ratio-trend analysis to calculate the number of indirect workers needed.

Forecasting skill requirements

Forecasts of skill requirements start from an analysis of the current range of skills required. They then analyse the impact of forecast product-market developments, the acquisition of new or different types of business, projected changes in work methods and the effect of the introduction of new technology. The latter would include information technology, computerized production methods such as manufacturing requirements planning (MRP) or computer integrated manufacturing (CIM), or some form of automation or robotics.

Skill forecasts are largely a matter of judgement based on experience and a thorough analysis of likely trends in the type of work to be carried out and working methods.

Supply forecasting

Supply forecasting estimates this number of people likely to be available from within and outside the organization (ie what are sometimes called the internal and external labour markets). The supply analysis covers:

☐ existing people available – how many have you got and what skills do they possess?

■ potential losses to existing resources through employee wastage – what are the present and forecast employee turnover figures?

☐ effect of absenteeism – what is the present rate and what will it be in the future?

☐ sources of supply from within the organization – who have we got now with the right skills? Who is going to be available in the future, and when?

☐ sources of supply from outside the organization – what are the chances of being able to recruit the sort of people we need?

■ Defining sources of future supply and reaching satisfactory conclusions on availability may be difficult. It depends on a number of factors out of your control, for example, the outputs from universities in particular disciplines. Cegelecs Project Ltd, an electrical contracting company found that the universities are producing plenty of computer specialists, but an insufficient number of good old-fashioned electrical engineers who can get stuck into developing a metro system for Istanbul.

ACTION PLANNING

Together, demand and supply forecasts indicate the extent to which there are likely to be surpluses or deficits of people.

Surpluses

If surpluses are, or are likely to be, the problem, action can be taken to stop recruitment, encourage early retirement or voluntary redundancy and provide help to people who may have to be made redundant. A downsizing plan should set out:

■ the size to which the workforce has to be reduced

■ the number of people who may have to go and when this needs to take place

■ arrangements for informing and consulting with employees and their trade unions

■ any financial or other inducements to encourage voluntary redundancies

■ a forecast of the likely numbers who will volunteer to leave

■ a forecast of the balance of employees, if any, who may have to be made redundant (the plan should, of course, aim to avoid this through natural wastage and voluntary redundancy)

■ arrangements for retraining employees and finding them work elsewhere in the organization

■ the steps to be taken to help redundant employees find new jobs by counselling, contacting other employers, arranging special services from the Employment Agency or offering the services of outplacement consultants

■ arrangements for keeping trade unions informed and for telling individual employees about the redundancies, and how they will be affected and what will be done to help them.

■ Plans to retain key workers, who might otherwise leave – these sometimes include financial incentives to stay.

Deficits

If there are likely to be future shortages, you should take steps to initiate recruitment, training and retraining programmes. Attention can also be given to reducing a deficit problem by taking action which will ensure that more of the people you want to keep are retained.

RETAINING PEOPLE

It is clearly very desirable to do whatever you can to keep your best people if they are needed in the future. The retention plan should be based on an analysis of why people leave. It is a good idea to conduct exit interviews to establish why they are going, but the information can be unreliable. If your company conducts regular surveys to establish people's attitudes to the organization and their work, this may provide better information. When preparing a retention plan you should consider the following actions you could take:

■ Ensure that rates of pay are competitive and that payment levels and systems are equitable and fair.

■ Take steps to ensure, as far as possible, that the work people do provides for job satisfaction by using their skills and by being given the opportunity to take responsibility and develop.

■ Ensure that people know what is expected of them and recognise their achievements in meeting or exceeding expectations.

■ Provide training to enable people to deliver the results required and to develop their careers.

■ Ensure that recruitment and selection procedures do produce people that are likely to succeed and stay with the company.

FURTHER READING

Brabham, J (1994) *Manpower Planning*, Institute of Personnel and Development, London

13

JOB ANALYSIS

It is the responsibility of line managers to analyse the jobs of the members of their teams. Personnel specialists may help but should not do it for them. Job analysis is a key management technique because it provides the information required for designing or developing organizations, recruitment, performance management, training and development and pay.

This chapter deals solely with job analysis and the associated process of skills analysis. Techniques of writing job descriptions are covered in Chapter 16. But an important distinction can be made between jobs and roles and the associated analysis techniques, and this distinction is defined in Chapter 14 before dealing with role analysis techniques. An aspect of people management that has received a lot of attention in recent years is competence analysis which is often linked to role analysis. This is a complex area which is dealt with exclusively in Chapter 15. Techniques of writing role definitions which may incorporate competence profiles are described in Chapter 16.

JOB ANALYSIS – BASIC INFORMATION

Job analysis produces the following basic information about a job:

- overall purpose – why the job exists and what the job holder is expected to contribute

- organization – where the job fits into the organization, covering reporting arrangements (to whom job holders report and who reports to them)

■ job content – the tasks to be performed or duties to be carried out

■ dimensions – quantitative indicators of the size of the job, covering such aspects as the size of the plant, equipment, property and facilities for which the job holder is responsible.

COLLECTING THE DATA

If you are thinking of creating a new job or making major changes to an existing one you will mainly be doing this yourself in accordance with the job design techniques described in Chapter 14. But it will be worth checking out your ideas with other members of your team who, after all, will be working with whoever carries out the new or changed job. It will undoubtedly impinge on their roles and if they are consulted they may be able to give you useful tips as well as having the opportunity to raise questions, doubts or fears. You would almost certainly consult your boss to get approval for your proposal. You might also sound out people in other departments who are going to work with the new job holder.

JOB ANALYSIS CHECKLIST

To obtain the data you need you should obtain answers to the following questions:

■ why does the job exist?

■ overall, what is the job holder expected to achieve?

■ how does the job fit in with other jobs in the team?

■ to whom does the job holder report?

■ who reports to the job holder?

■ what are the key tasks the job holder carries out?

■ what results are expected for each of these tasks? (quantify if possible)

■ what knowledge and skills are required to do the job?

■ who are the main people with whom the job holder relates (colleagues, customers, suppliers etc)?

■ what resources does the job holder control? (financial budget, equipment, plant, property etc)

- how much authority does the job holder have to make decisions?
- how can the performance of the job holder be measured?
- does the job present any special difficulties or problems to the job holder?
- what are the conditions under which the job holder works?

This checklist covers the content of the job and refers to knowledge and skills. But more detailed skills and competence analysis as described below may be needed to define the demands made on the job holder in terms of the type and variety of skills they must possess to do the job and the level of competence required.

SKILLS ANALYSIS

Skills analysis establishes the skills required in manual and clerical jobs. It determines not only what job holders do but also the skills and abilities they need to do it. Skills analysis is used to prepare person specifications for recruitment purposes and learning specifications for training purposes. The skills to be analysed will include:

- physical skills requiring various degrees of manual dexterity
- the skills required to operate or use particular equipment, facilities or machines
- procedural skills required to carry out sequences of activity
- diagnostic, analytical and problem solving skills
- the skills required to interpret or use written manuals and other sources of information such as diagrams and charts.

An analytical approach to establishing skill requirements is carried out in the following steps:

1 Identify and describe each task
2 Breakdown each task into its elements
3 Define the sequence in which the tasks and their elements are carried out.
4 Define what the job holder has to know and be able to do to perform each task and the whole sequence of tasks satisfactorily.

This means establishing:

- the knowledge and skills required to operate pieces of equipment, machines or plant
- the type and level of manual dexterity required
- what the job holder needs to know about company operational procedures
- any analytical or diagnostic skills required
- any communicating skills required
- the degree to which the job holder is expected to work flexibly, using different skills at different times, or taking on differing roles requiring different skills within a team (multiskilling requirements)

Analyse the typical faults which may occur when performing tasks, especially the more costly faults. This provides the basis for a faults specification which provides job holders, especially trainees, with information on what sort of faults occur, how they can be recognized, what causes them, what effect they have, what action should be taken when a fault occurs and how a fault can be prevented from recurring.

Skills analysis is particularly important as a means of preparing and operating training programmes and courses as described in chapter 25.

FURTHER READING

Armstrong, M (1996) *Handbook of Personnel Management Practice,* 6th edition, (Chapter 12), Kogan Page, London.

14

ROLE ANALYSIS

JOBS AND ROLES

A distinction should be made between jobs and roles. These terms are sometimes used interchangeably but they describe different things.

A job is a group of tasks which have to be done by someone to achieve an overall purpose. A role is the part played by people in carrying out their jobs, achieving results and using their skills to reach a satisfactory level of performance. Role analyses and definitions are not simply concerned with the content of jobs. They will focus on outcomes and the behaviours required to achieve these outcomes. These behaviours may include such aspects of roles as working flexibly, working with others, leading a team, communicating with others and relating to customers.

THE DIFFERENCES BETWEEN ROLE AND JOB ANALYSIS

In some ways role analysis is an extension of job analysis. It starts from the same point – a definition of the overall purpose of the role. And it proceeds by breaking this overall purpose down into its main elements. But then the similarity ends. The main points of difference are described below.

Organizational context

A role analysis does not simply define reporting relationships so that the job can be placed in the appropriate box in an organization chart. Role analysis is more concerned with how the role fits into the organization by establishing relationships not only with superiors and subordinates, but also with colleagues, people in other functions and departments, customers, suppliers and outside agencies or bodies.

A role analysis may therefore incorporate a piece of narrative which describes the organizational context within which the role holder operates and the nature and scope of what the role holder does. This analysis will cover such important aspects of the role as flexibility requirements, interpersonal relationships, the particular pressures under which role holders have to operate, and the extent to which the role is built round the strengths and capacities of people, rather than the other way round.

Focus on results

Role analysis aims to determine the key result areas of the role – what the role holder is expected to achieve in terms of outputs and standards of performance. Unlike job analysis, which concentrates on identifying the tasks job holders carry out, role analysis focuses on the purposes of those tasks – the outcomes of what the role holder does.

Role analysis is concerned with the contribution that role holders make to attaining the goals of their team, department and the organization as a whole. In fact, this aspect of role analysis could be called contribution analysis because, ultimately, that is what roles are all about.

The various elements of a role are sometimes called principal account abilities, meaning those aspects of the role for which the role holder is held to account by a higher authority.

Focus on competence/competency requirements

Role analysis usually incorporates competence or competency analysis. This form of analysis including a definition of what these terms mean is covered in Chapter 15.

CONDUCTING A ROLE ANALYSIS

Role analysis may be conducted in a similar way to the methods used for job analysis. This will include interviewing existing role holders and their colleagues. You can, however, usefully extend this approach by getting groups of role holders together and conducting what is in effect a workshop which goes into the characteristics of the role in some depth and ensures that different perspectives are taken into account (and there will be different perspectives). It is often useful to have a facilitator who can help workshop members to carry out the analysis. The facilitator could be a personnel specialist or a colleague who has facilitating skills.

Role analysis checklist

The analysis of the purpose and context of the role should provide answers to the following questions:

What contribution does this role make to achieving the goals of the team/department?

What are the key areas in which the role holder is expected to achieve results?

What are the critical success factors which affect the level of contribution made by the role holder?

■ What measures can be used to assess the extent to which the results have been attained?

To what extent and in what ways does carrying out the role require role holders to operate flexibly?

■ What are the particular pressures and demands with which the role holder has to cope?

■ To what extent are these pressures and demands subject to change?

To what extent is the role ambiguous in the sense that it is difficult to define exactly the part role holders play, because for example, of constantly changing demands and circumstances?

■ To what extent does the role require its holder to interact with other people?

To what extent is the role holder dependent on other people (specify) to make an effective contribution?

What are the most typical problems role holders have to solve – themselves, or in conjunction with other people?

Does the role holder have to cope with conflicting priorities (specify)?

About how long would it normally take for a mistake or error by the role holder in a major key result area to be identified?

To what extent does this role require strategic thinking on the part of the role holder?

■   How much leadership does the role involve?

■   To what extent does the role holder have to be a good team worker?

■   In what ways and in which areas is the role holder required to innovate?

■   How much freedom to act has the role holder?

In addition, information will need to be obtained about competence requirements as described in the next main section of this chapter.

Use of the analysis

Role analysis goes into much greater depth than job analysis. It is necessary when an in-depth study of role requirements has to be made as a basis for performance management, performance or competence-related pay, or for employee and career development processes. A full programme of role analysis is too time-consuming for most line managers and help is generally required from personnel specialists or outside consultants.

But it is useful to be aware of the principles of role analysis with its emphasis on the person in the job rather than on the content of the job. And it is always possible to add some of the techniques of role analysis to more conventional job analysis to obtain a fuller understanding of the context in which the job is carried out and the outputs required from job holders. Role analysis techniques can enhance job analysis in order to provide the additional information required for recruitment and training purposes.

Role analysis is most appropriate for managerial, team leader, professional and technical roles where the person can influence the role and where flexibility – the need constantly to adapt to changes in the context of the role and in the demands made on role holders – is an important factor.

Because role definitions and profiles, as discussed in Chapter 16, frequently incorporate competence or competency schedules, this important aspect of people management is covered specifically in the next chapter.

15

COMPETENCE AND COMPETENCY ANALYSIS

The concept of competence or competency and the language associated with it is much used now in larger or more complex organizations. It is a concept which has largely been the preserve of academics, management consultants and personal specialists. The language is not one which is familiar to many line managers who are often bemused by the jargon with which the concept is almost overwhelmed. In fact Professor John Storey of the Open University regards it as the most over-used concept in the whole field of human resource management.

However, if you are in an organization which has gone overboard for competence or competency you need to know something about it because undoubtedly you will be involved in its application. Even if the whole area is riddled with jargon the application of the fundamental notions of competence has value in the fields of performance management and development. It can also clarify and inform personal specifications used in recruitment.

Before describing the process of competence analysis it is necessary to define what competence and competency are (the reason for the two terms will be explained below).

COMPETENCE AND COMPETENCY DEFINED

The gurus in this field feel very strongly that it is necessary to distinguish between competence (hence competences) and competency (hence competencies). Disaster, they claim, will overtake anyone who confuses the two terms. Whether this is true or not, the received view of the distinction between them needs to be understood.

Competence defined

Competences describe what people need to be able to do to do a job well. They are about stripping jobs down into their component parts and linking together the two basic elements of performance – what has to be done and to what standard. In National Vocational Qualification (NVQ) language, an element of competence is a description of something which people carrying out particular types of work should be capable of doing. The NVQ system assesses people as being competent or not yet competent. The accent is on what people should be able to do rather than on how they should behave in doing it.

Competences are concerned with effect rather than effort; with output rather than input. Some people adopt what may be called the 'output' model of competence which is based on the proposition that the concept of competence is only meaningful when it can be demonstrated that competences have been applied effectively. It is therefore a matter not of having competences but of using them to good effect.

Competences can be defined at three levels:

1   Core competences – these are the competences which apply to the organization as a whole. They refer to what the organization has to be good at doing if it is to succeed. This could include such factors as customer orientation, producing high quality goods or delivering high quality services, innovation, adding value through the effective use of resources and managing costs (driving unnecessary cost out of the business). Core competences can be linked to its 'balanced score card' meaning if measuring organizational success as developed by Kaplan and Norton. This requires managers to take a balanced look at the business from four key perspectives.
    (i)   How do customers see us? (customer perspective)
    (ii) What must we excel at? (internal perspective)
    (iii) Can we continue to improve and create value? (innovation and learning perspectives)
    (iv) How do we look to shareholders? (financial perspective).
2   Generic competences – these are the competences shared by a group of similar jobs – financial accountants, systems analysts, team leaders etc. They cover the aspect of the work which they have in common and define the shared abilities they have to apply to deliver the results they are expected to achieve.
3   Role specific competences – these are the competences which are unique to a particular role and they define anything special which

they have to be able to do in addition to any generic competences they may share with other people carrying out broadly similar roles.

Competence is analysed by a process called functional analysis which is described later in this section.

Competency defined

Competency is sometimes defined as referring to the dimensions of behaviour which lie behind competent performance. These are often called behavioural competencies because they are intended to describe how people will behave when they carry out their role well.

When defined as competencies these behaviours can be classified in areas such as the following used by Manchester Airport for senior managers:

■ Understanding what needs to be done – critical reasoning, strategic capability, business know-how.

■ Getting the job done – achievement drive, a proactive approach, confidence, control flexibility, concern for effectiveness, persuasion, influence.

■ Taking people with you – motivation, interpersonal skills, concern for output, persuasion, influence.

Many organizations have now developed their own lists of 'generic competencies' which describe the behaviour they believe to be important. These are sometimes called competency frameworks when they cover all the key jobs in an organization. They may refer to all the jobs in a 'job family' – a job family being a related set of jobs with similar skills or competencies but applied at different levels, often in a hierarchy, such as retail assistants, departmental managers and store managers in a retailing company. The use of 'generic' for competencies is another example of the confusion that permeates the whole concept of competence. It can be used either to denote the competencies shared by those carrying out similar roles or to the competencies which apply throughout the organization. Confusion is worse confounded when consultants and personnel managers refer to generic competencies as core competencies.

Because competencies refer to behaviour they can be regarded as 'soft'. The assumption is made that if you behave as required by the competency definitions of good behaviour then you will deliver good results. This assumption is based on an analysis of the behaviours of people who do perform well. If so, it is said, other people who behave in the same way will also perform well.

The analysis of competencies will sometimes produce a list of differentiating competencies which list positive and negative indicators of the level of competence. These are derived from analysis of how good and poor performers behave in this area of competency. For example, the differentiating competencies for a typical competency, judgement, might be defined as follows:

Definitions

Reaching appropriate conclusions and making sensible decisions on the basis of analysis and experience.

Positive indicators

- alternative courses of action are carefully explored before reaching a decision.
- decisions are founded on logical inferences and are based on factual information.
- quickly identifies what needs to be achieved in a given situation.
- reaches sound decisions which indicate clearly the most appropriate course of action and the goals to be achieved.
- decisions or recommendations can be and are implemented effectively.

Negative indicators

- fails to take account of some of the key factors in situations.
- fails to think through the implications of the decision.
- frequently comes to an incorrect conclusion, because of flawed assumptions, inadequate analysis, or inability to make good use of experience.

COMPETENCE ANALYSIS

The concept of competence is more meaningful in practical terms than that of competency because it is about what people have to do to achieve results. It is not about how they do it, which may or may not result in the required performance and tends to produce lists of generalised personality characteristics such as persuasiveness, assertiveness and achievement motivation. In fact, a number of well known organizations such as ICL and the Midland Bank have rebelled against using the term 'competence' and adopt the term 'capability' instead to denote the things that people are able to do effectively. These are measurable in terms of results in more objective ways than any attempt to measure personality characteristics or traits can be.

Competence or capability analysis is therefore more likely to be useful to line managers. It is something you can do yourself because there is no mystique about it. You simply say 'there is a job, these are the tasks which comprise the job and these are the outcomes I expect in terms of workplace performance'. In NVQ language these outcomes are called functions and this technique is known as functional analysis. This provides a framework for measuring performance on the assumption that 'what you measure is what you get'. The competences are defined in terms of what job holders should be capable of doing. They can then be used as the basis for obtaining evidence of what they can do (for recruitment purposes) and what they have done (for performance management). The gaps between what people should be able to do and what they can actually do indicate areas for personal development – learning and training activities.

Methods of analysis

To analyse competences it is necessary to obtain answers to the following questions:

- what are the elements of this job – what does the job holder have to do (expressed as main tasks or key result areas)?
- for each element, what is an acceptable standard of performance?
- what levels and types of knowledge and skills are required to ensure that the job holder is fully capable in each element of the job?
- how will role holders and their managers know that the required levels of competence have been achieved?

You can obtain answers to these questions yourself, but it is useful to get other views. The best approach is to get a group of people together in similar jobs and ask them three questions:

1   What do you think are the most important things someone in your sort of job (or one similar to yours) has to be capable of doing?
2   What do people do when they are carrying out each part of their role well?
3   How can you tell that they are doing well?

The answers to these questions from the group should be written up in their own language on flip charts. Brainstorming rules should apply – any contribution is welcome and no one will be allowed to rubbish it.

The brainstormed list of answers is then discussed by the group and distilled into a number of statements to the effect that:

> People will be carrying out this part of their job well when they ....

The blank is filled up by statements of what they do, what they have to know to do it, and how they do it. This is in line with the Glaxo Wellcome definition of competence which states that competence is 'what you do, what you know and how you do it to perform effectively in a role'. The 'how' part of this process in the Glaxo Wellcome definition refers to behaviour, but it is always behaviour which is anchored to what people do to get results in a specific element or area of a job. It is not about generalized statements of behavioural characteristics or traits.

The most important feature of this approach is that your team members are involved in writing the competence definitions in their own language. This means that they are much more likely to be acceptable and used as a basis for agreeing performance targets and standards. This establishes evidence of the performance achieved, applying performance measures to that evidence and reviewing performance by reference to targets and measures. When it comes to agreeing personal development plans (see Chapter 23), participation in the competence definition process and familiarity with the language used to define competences will help people to identify learning needs and subscribe to a programme for meeting them.

Competence analysis at the Derby General National Health Hospital Trust

Competence analysis along these lines was carried out by this Trust. Nurses were invited to attend workshops in which they were asked to describe in their own words situations in which nursing staff could be carrying out their work well or badly. The contributions made at workshops were then edited to produce an agreed list of competencies using the original words.

Competence analysis at Portsmouth Housing Trust

A comprehensive competence analysis programme was completed in 1997 by line management at the Portsmouth Housing Trust (PHT). The personnel department was not involved. The first step was to define the core competencies of PHT, which provides care in the form of accommodation and help for people with learning difficulties, young people, ex-offenders and others in need of assistance.

A working group consisting of managers, team leaders, and support (care) workers and trade union representatives was set up to define the PHT core competencies using the techniques discussed above. The essential question was 'what has PHT got to be good at doing if it is to achieve its purpose?' The agreed core competence headings were:

■ provide a quality service

■ manage the business and the provision of services effectively

■ ensure that accountabilities are defined, accepted and fulfilled

■ acquire, develop and use professional expertise to deliver services

■ develop and apply interpersonal skills to achieve aims and standards and to comply with PHT's core values.

The core competences provided the framework for generic role and role-specific competence definitions. The aim was to integrate the generic and specific competences with the organizational core competencies. This was to emphasise that they were defined areas of competence at all levels which had to be linked and were linked and that if this did not happen, then the organization was much less likely to thrive or even survive.

Generic competences were developed for the key roles in PHT using the same core competence headings as the framework. Workshops were held with groups of team leaders and support workers to produce competence schedules expressed in their words.

The next step was to define role specific competencies. This was done by team managers with small groups of people with special responsibilities or with individuals.

Finally, the generic and role specific schedules were combined to produce role profiles. These could be generic for some roles (eg team leaders) but could be a specially tailored mix of generic and specific competencies in certain cases.

The role profiles were used as the basis for performance management processes (called 'competence management' in PHT).

Using National Vocational Qualification (NVQ) competence schedules

A number of schedules have been provided by the various NVQ lead bodies defining competence requirements at each of the NVQ levels.

These can be used to provide a competence framework as long as they fit the roles carried out within the organization. However, this is not always the case, although some organizations have referred to the NVQ schedules for comparable workers and adapted them to suit their requirements.

COMPETENCY ANALYSIS

Competency analysis is concerned with the behavioural dimensions of roles as distinct from competence analysis, which considers what people have to do to perform well.

Approaches to competency analysis

Some organizations have adapted standardized competency lists developed by occupational psychologists or management consultants. Those produced by reputable people or firms will have been thoroughly researched by reference to actual people who are carrying out their roles well or not so well. The basic questions are: 'how do people in this role behave when they carry it out effectively?' and 'how do people behave in this role when they are carrying it out ineffectively?'. The evidence from the answers to these questions is used to derive competency headings and produce definitions of differentiating competencies – positive and negative examples of behaviour.

Management consultants who advise on competency frameworks often produce 'competence dictionaries' which contain examples of differentiating competencies under various headings. They can be applied in an organization as they stand or, preferably, modified to meet the special requirements of the business.

The advantage of adopting this approach is that ready-made competence lists such as those produced for managers by the Management Charter Institute (MCI) save a lot of work and will have been properly researched. But they may not fit the particular circumstances of the business. Generalized definitions, however well based, are not necessarily universally applicable. Rather than painstakingly adapting ready-made lists, some organizations prefer to develop their own tailor-made competence schedules. They do this by conducting workshops, as discussed earlier in relation to competence analysis, but the questions will focus on identifying good and bad behavioural characteristics rather than concentrating on the output factors – those referring to workplace performance.

The preparation of a tailor-made competency schedule is usually carried out by personnel specialists and/or management consultants. Line managers may be consulted but eventually the competency frameworks are issued to them to use in accordance with procedures laid down for such processes as performance management.

Although the first draft of a tailor-made competency schedule may be developed in-house, it is frequently the practice to reference home-made schedules to a consultant's dictionary of competence or the standards issued by Management Charter Institute.

16

WRITING JOB DESCRIPTIONS AND ROLE DEFINITIONS

JOB DESCRIPTIONS

Job descriptions contain details of reporting relationships (to whom the job holder reports and who reports to the job holder), a statement of the overall purpose of the job, and a list of the main tasks, activities or duties (whichever term is used) that the job holder has to carry out.

Desirable characteristics of job descriptions

Job descriptions should be clear and succinct. They should not go into too much detail. They should certainly not attempt to spell out exactly how a job holder carries out a task. It is, for example, sufficient to say of one of the tasks of a marketing analysis 'Maintain database of information on sales, retail prices and discounts' without describing precisely how the database is maintained. Wherever possible job descriptions should be continued within the dimensions of the proverbial 'one side of one sheet of paper'.

A job description should fulfil its purpose, whether it is to place a job in the organization structure, inform job holders of their duties, provide data for recruitment, training and job evaluation purposes or set out the framework for setting objectives and reviewing performance. The format and content of a job description may vary somewhat depending on the purpose or purposes it serves. These variations usually take the form of additional data, for example:

■ *organization* – critical dimensions (budget, people managed, responsibility for plant, machinery, equipment, property etc.); a description of the relationships between the job and other jobs in the organization, details of the customers served

■ *recruitment* – a person specification setting out the experience, qualifications, knowledge, skills and personal qualities the job holder requires

■ *training* – a training or learning specification describing the skills that need to be learned and the methods of training that will be used

■ *job evaluation* – an analysis of the job in terms of the factors contained in a job evaluation scheme (see Chapter 32)

■ *performance management* – statements of objectives to be attained, which are updated regularly and, possibly, a list of competences. If these are included, the job description begins to take on some of the characteristics of a role definition.

Statement of overall purpose

The statement of the overall purpose of a job sets out in general terms what the job exists for – how it contributes to achieving the objectives of the team, department or organization.

The definition of purpose should place the job in its setting within the organization and provide a basis for making an overall assessment of the job holder's contribution.

The statement should convey in one sentence a broad picture of the job which will distinguish it from other jobs. When preparing the job description you might find it easier to defer writing down the definition of overall purpose until the main tasks or activities have been analyzed and described.

The following are some examples of overall purpose statements:

■ Production director – 'Plan and control all production management activities to ensure that output, quality and customer service targets and standards are achieved within agreed expenditure budgets'.

■ Human resource manager – 'Advise on human resource strategies, policies and practices to ensure that the company has the high quality, well-motivated and committed workforce it needs'.

■ Retail marketing analyst – 'Provide monthly and annual forecasts of retail sales on the basis of given assumptions to assist in generating and updating retail sales plans'.

■   Word processor operator – 'Use word processor to produce letters, memoranda, reports and tables from tapes and hand written drafts'.

Main tasks

The list of main tasks (often called activities, responsibilities or duties) covers the key aspects of the job which together contribute to achieving its overall purpose. To avoid unnecessary complexity, the number of task areas should normally be limited to seven or eight. If care is taken in analysing the things that job holders do which really count, there are very few jobs with more than that number of key tasks.

The aim, as mentioned earlier, is to describe what the job holder is there to achieve under a concise list of main headings, not to go into details of the ramifications of each of those key areas by spelling out everything the person does. If an attempt is made to do this it will inevitably fail. The job description will be so long that no one will ever look at it again. It will tie people down too much and restrict their flexibility. If it does not cover every eventuality, which it cannot, it opens the door to the remark 'It's not in my job description'. The task statements should only give broad indications of the key result areas of the job. How these results are achieved is a matter for continuous review depending on new demands and changing circumstances. Over-detailed job descriptions are out-of-date as soon as they are written. Job descriptions should aim to do no more, or less, than broadly indicate the key areas of responsibility and then define them in one sentence, as described below.

Defining a task

Start with a verb in the active voice, which provides a positive indication of what has to be done and eliminates unnecessary wording. Examples of such verbs are:

achieves	informs
advises	maintains
carries	outmakes
co-ordinates	operates
conducts	plans
controls	prepares
deals with	produces
Decides on	provides
develops	supervises
dispatches	takes part in
ensures that	tests

Describe the object of the verb (what is done) as succinctly as possible, for example:

- Ensures that management accounts are produced.
- Prepares marketing plans.
- Posts cash to the nominal and sales ledgers.
- Schedules production.
- Tests new systems.

State briefly the purpose of the activity (why it is done) in terms of objectives or standards, for example:

- Ensures that management accounts are produced *which provide the required level of information to management and individual managers on financial performance against budget and any variances.*
- Prepares marketing plans *which support the achievement of the marketing strategies of the business, are realistic and provide clear guidance on the actions to be taken by the development, marketing, sales and production departments.*
- Posts cash to the nominal and sales ledgers *in order to provide up-to-date and accurate financial information.*
- Schedules production in order to meet laid-down output and delivery targets.
- Tests new systems to ensure that they meet agreed systems specifications.

The following is an example of a basic job description.

Regional Sales Manager

Overall purpose

- Plans, directs and controls regional sales effort to achieve and, as far as possible, exceed sales volume and contribution targets.

Organization

- Reports to: Sales Director
- Report to job holder: five area sales managers

Main tasks

■ Opens new accounts in the region to achieve sales development targets

■ Develops existing accounts to increase sales to meet targets

■ Controls the direction of sales effort to ensure that contribution is maximized

■ Achieves agreed levels of customer service with regard to delivery, handling queries and complaints and after-sales service

■ Takes part in new product launches, including pilot testing to contribute to successful product/market developments

■ Maintains close contact with customers in order generally to promote sales and specifically to obtain marketing intelligence on trends in customer wants and needs

■ Tracks competitive activity in order to provide information which will help to develop marketing strategies

■ Staffs the region with high quality area managers and sales representatives who are trained, developed and motivated to achieve demanding sales targets and high levels of customer service.

ROLE DEFINITIONS

Role definitions or profiles start, like job descriptions, with a statement of overall purpose and organizational details. However, the list of main tasks is replaced by a list of key result areas. The latter place more emphasis on what has to be achieved in the shape of objectives, targets and standards than a typical task definition in a job description.

Key result area definitions

Key result area definitions, like task definitions, start with an active verb and are limited to a single sentence to make them as succinct and telling as possible. As the term implies, however, they focus on outcomes. Thus the key result area definitions for a Production Director might be set out as follows:

■ Meets demand forecasts consistently by achieving the manufacturing programmes incorporated in the Master Production Schedule.

■ Reduces the level of defects to achieve agreed targets.

■ Increases units produced per employee by an agreed percentage over the next budgeting period.

■ Reduces cost per unit of output by an agreed percentage over the next budgeting period.

■ Reduces downtime by an agreed percentage over the next budgeting period.

■ Ensures that delivery schedules are met.

■ Settles disputes and grievances at shop floor level before industrial action is taken.

■ Reduces absenteeism by an agreed percentage over the next budgeting period.

For a personal assistant/secretary the key result areas could be:

■ Uses the word processor and its associated programmes to produce high quality documents.

■ Provides an accurate, speedy and helpful service.

■ Carries out filing accurately and keeps the backlog down to no more than one working week.

■ Deals with colleagues, members of other departments and outside contacts efficiently and politely.

■ Deals with telephone callers efficiently and helpfully.

■ Carries out additional tasks effectively, as delegated by the manager.

■ Manages the manager's appointments diary efficiently.

These examples illustrate key result areas for which specific objectives and targets can be agreed and updated as necessary. Some of the definitions provide a standard of performance, in other cases the definitions indicate where standards of performance may have to be agreed to ensure that expectations are clearly defined and understood. Approaches to agreeing objectives and standards of performance are discussed in Chapter 22.

Context

Role definitions may include a description of the organizational context in which the role is carried out. This is not an essential part of the

definition but it can help increase understanding and improve performance by indicating some of the broader characteristics of the role
which may not be covered elsewhere. Context statements can add
'flavour' to the role definition. These could include flexibility requirements, the need to operate from time-to-time as a member of a
cross-functional project team, any particular pressure to which role
holders will be subjected, an indication of priority areas and further
information on how the role holder will function as a member of a team.

Context descriptions are particularly useful as a means of providing
information to people about a role 'in the round' when they are being
recruited, when considering promotion or when planning a career.
They can also help to clarify the psychological contract by defining
special features of the role and how people are expected to carry it out.

There is no formula for writing context statements and their useful-
ness will be more dependent on the extent to which they increase
understanding of the conditions under which the role is performed so
that role holders are in a position to improve their contribution. The only
requirement is that context statements should be brief and to the point.
The following is an example of a context statement:

Regional Sales Manager

A Regional Sales Manager is expected to work closely with the other
Regional Sales Managers. The priority is to maximize sales for the whole
company not to maximise sales in one region at the expense of the
higher levels and sales that could be achieved if there is co-operation
between Regional Sales Managers in matters such as handling major
accounts. Regional Sales Managers work under pressure. Sales targets
are exacting and the need to develop new business is of prime importance. The company is particularly anxious to develop and improve
long-term relationships with its customers and this is a prime
responsibility of Regional Sales Managers.

Competence or capability profile

If generic or role specific competences have been profiled, you can add
these to the role definition to provide a full picture of what the role
holder has to be able to do. This is particularly helpful when you are
recruiting, reviewing performance or preparing personal development
plans.

If you or your organization are not into competence profiling it may
still be helpful to work out capability requirements, ie what the role
holder should be able to do. These can be developed yourself but it is

better to involve existing role holders in your team in defining capability requirements.

Capability profiles can be generic as in the following example of a team leader's profile:

- Builds effective team relationships, ensuring that team members are committed to the common purpose.

- Encourages self-direction amongst team members but provides leadership and guidance as required.

- Shares information with team members.

- Trusts team members to get on with things – not continually checking.

- Treats team members fairly and consistently.

- Supports and guides team members to make the best use of their capabilities.

- Provides opportunities for team members to acquire additional experience and skills.

- Encourages self-development.

- Actively offers constructive feedback to team members and positively seeks, and is open to, constructive feedback from them.

FURTHER READING

Armstrong, M and Murlis, H (1994) *Reward Management* (Chapter 8), Kogan Page, London.

17

DESIGNING JOBS

You will find that the role of your department or team will evolve as circumstances change and it is necessary to adapt to new demands. This means that the nature and scope of the jobs carried out by your existing team members will also change or new jobs may have to be created. You will then be involved in job design for individual jobs or in defining the functions of a team.

This chapter starts with a discussion of what job design means to line managers – what it is and what it aims to do. The following aspects of job design are then examined:

- deciding on the content of the job
- deciding on how the job fits into the department or team
- designing jobs to provide for intrinsic motivation
- fitting jobs to people rather than people to jobs.

In some ways the techniques of job and role design are similar and whenever the term 'jobs' is used on its own it also refers to 'roles'.

THE MEANING OF JOB DESIGN

Job design is the specification of the contents, methods and relationships of jobs in order to satisfy business requirements as well as the personal needs of the job holder. It is also concerned with the work carried out by teams. Job design has four aims:

1   To satisfy the demands of the organization for operational effi-
    ciency, productivity and quality of service.
2   To meet the needs of the organization for flexibility and the capacity
    to operate through horizontal work processes rather than as a series
    of separate hierarchies.
3   To meet the needs of the individual for interest, challenge and
    accomplishment.
4   To ensure that team responsibilities are defined in ways which
    improve the quality of teamwork and team effectiveness.

These needs are interrelated, and an associated aim of job design is to
integrate the needs of individuals with the needs of the organization.

JOB CONTENT

The basis of job design – task structure

Job design requires the assembly of a number of tasks into a job or a
group of jobs. An individual may carry out one main task which consists
of a number of interrelated elements or functions. Or task functions may
be allocated to a team working closely together in a manufacturing
'cell', a customer service unit, or strung along an assembly line.

In more complex jobs, individuals may carry out a variety of intercon-
nected tasks, each with a number of functions. Similarly a team may
carry out a number of different but related tasks. Complexity in a job may
be a reflection of the number and variety of tasks, the different skills to
be used, or the range and scope of the decisions to be made.

The internal structure of a task contain three elements:

1   *Planning* – deciding on the course of action, its timing and the
    resources required.
2   *Executing* – carrying out the plan.
3   *Controlling* – monitoring performance and progress and taking
    corrective action when required.

A completely integrated job includes all these elements for each of the
tasks involved. The worker, or group of workers having been given or
agreed objectives in terms of output, quality and cost targets, decides on
how the work is to be done, assembles the resources, eg material or
information, performs the work, and monitors output, quality and costs.
Responsibility in a job is measured by the amount of authority a person
or group of people have to do all these things.

Factors to take into account in job design

The factors you should take into account in designing jobs are as follows:

- Create or modify jobs so that they consist of logically related tasks and form natural work units on their own.

- The job should make an appropriate and measurable contribution to the achievement of the objectives of the department or team when performed well.

- The job should be worth doing – it should occupy the full attention of workers for whatever period of time they have to carry out.

- The demands made by the job on workers in terms of effort, concentration and time allowed should be achievable by any able person working at a normal pace. This could be defined at the British Standard Institute of level 100 for an average worker – this is often equated to someone walking at four miles an hour.

- However, these demands must be modified to suit the capacities of workers with disabilities.

- Except in the case of workers with disabilities, the demands should not therefore be set at a level below which an individual working normally and without being subjected to undue pressure could achieve.

- However, where feasible, there should be scope for above average workers to exceed the norm and be rewarded accordingly.

- The demands made by the job, the conditions under which it is carried out and the machinery and tools used should not result in health hazards or the risk of accidents.

- So far as possible, the jobs should be integrated in the sense described above, ie they should include planning and controlling elements as well as executing tasks. This process of increasing responsibility or 'empowerment' provides intrinsic motivation as discussed in a later main section of this chapter.

- Consideration should be given to the need for flexibility – for job holders to be able to carry out different tasks and for them to have the skills to do it as individuals or as members of a team (multiskilling).

■ It also needs to be remembered that job demands will inevitably change and the content of the job should be capable of being amended as required. It should not be regarded as fixed for all time.

■ Finally, and importantly, job design has to take account of the capabilities and preferences of the people who carry out the work. The design of jobs may have to be modified to fit the people available, although plans can and should be made to develop their capabilities so they can take on greater or wider responsibilities, thus enlarging or 'enriching' the job. This is a motivating factor for them and constitutes the basis for processes of continuous development and improvement.

FITTING THE JOB INTO THE TEAM

Jobs should not be treated as isolated units of work. Consideration has always to be given to how the job carried out by workers fits with that carried out by co-workers. Obviously, when creating or modifying teams this is an essential requirement. Particular attention will have to be given to how individual members of the team work together and the needs for flexibility and multiskilling. Job design is as much about deciding how teams should function as about allocating tasks to individuals.

PROVIDING INTRINSIC MOTIVATION

The significance of intrinsic motivation

Intrinsic motivation was defined in chapter 4 as the self-generated factors which influence people to behave in particular ways or to move in certain directions. Intrinsic motivation can be increased by the work itself which provides rewards that are directly under the control of the worker. This is related to the fundamental concept that people are motivated when they are provided with the means to achieve their goals. Money is an essential method of satisfying these needs, which is why it is important as a powerful motivator. But the impact of financial rewards on motivation does not necessarily persist. Intrinsic motivation tends to have a deeper and longer-term effect because it is not imposed from outside.

Providing intrinsic motivation

The following characteristics are required in jobs if they are to provide intrinsic motivation:

- *Integration* – the job should be integrated in terms of planning, execution and control.

- *Autonomy* – as high a degree of autonomy as possible should be given to the worker or the team in terms of setting goals, exercizing discretion, responsibility and self-control.

- *Task significance* – the worker or team must believe that the task they carry out is significant, is worth doing. Ideally, they should work on a complete product or provide a full service, or at least a significant part of the product or service which can be seen as a whole.

- *Use and development of abilities* – workers should believe that the job will enable them to use and develop their abilities. The work should fit what they are and are capable of becoming.

- *Variety* – the more variety in the tasks carried out the better.

- *Feedback* – workers should be able to get feedback on their performance and development needs. This should be provided by their managers or team leaders, but ideally it should be self-generated. In other words, people should be in a position in which they can monitor and evaluate their own performance against targets and standards which they have been involved in setting.

Job enrichment

Although not so much is heard of it nowadays, the job enrichment movement of the 1960s, which was largely inspired by the research and writings of Frederick Herzberg, has had a considerable influence on job design.

The aim of job enrichment is to maximize the interest and challenge of work by providing employees with jobs having the following characteristics:

- they are complete pieces of work in the sense that workers can identify a series of tasks or activities that end in a recognisable and definable product or service

- they provide employees with as much variety, decision-making responsibility and control as possible in carrying out the work

■ they provide direct and quick feedback through the work itself on how well the employees are doing their jobs.

Quality of working life

The phrase 'quality of working life' came to the fore in the 1970s. It was based on the belief that the level of performance depends on the job satisfaction that could be provided by job enrichment. In the hard-nosed 1980s the quality of working life and job enrichment concepts were dismissed as a 'soft' approach to management.

However, the quality of working life (QWL) has made something of a comeback in the present post-entrepreneurial era. This was exemplified by the statement produced by ACAS (the Advisory, Conciliation and Arbitration Service) which suggested that the following contributions to improved performance can be made through a QWL strategy:

■ people will be better motivated if their work experience satisfies their social and psychological needs as well as their economic needs

■ people work more effectively if they are managed in a participative way

■ the factors which satisfy people at work such as responsibility, achievement and recognition are essentially different from the factors which cause dissatisfaction (pay, the behaviour of management, working conditions) – this is essentially what is called the two-factor model of motivation developed by Herzberg

■ individual motivation and therefore greater effectiveness can be enhanced by attention to the design of jobs and work organization

■ there is a need to see an organization as a balance between its technical systems (the ways goods and services are produced) and its social systems (the ways in which people are organized, managed, trained and consulted).

FITTING JOBS TO PEOPLE

The traditional approach to designing organizations was to treat them like machines. In such mechanistic environments job design was based on the principle of 'Taylorism'. Work processes were standardized and every task was prescribed. The main requirements were control, order, formality and predictability. Workers did what they were told. People existed to fill boxes in organization charts.

Some people believe that the human resource management (HRM) philosophy is tainted with the belief that people are no more than resources or factors of production to be treated as human capital. As such, they are invested in when the business believes it can get a good return on that investment and, when pressured to demonstrate a healthy bottom line, are divested like any other asset.

It is possible to argue that HRM focuses on the interest of the employer and only pays lip service to the interests of the employees. But even if that is the case, it is in the interest of the business to use its people in ways that will maximize their contribution to the bottom line. And except in traditional highly bureaucratic organizations, the mechanistic model of prescribed jobs into which people have to fit, whether or not their talents are effectively used, no longer works. In the new organization flexibility and the capacity to adapt rapidly to different situations and challenges are all-important. Jobs can no longer be allowed to act as straitjackets in these circumstances.

The aim should be to build the organization and therefore design jobs in the organization around the strengths of people and their capabilities. The starting point may be an idealized version of what a job should contain. But if someone comes along with different skills and aptitudes who can make a better contribution by being given the opportunity to use them, then the 'ideal' job design must be abandoned.

The argument that fitting jobs to people rather than people to jobs will enhance their ability to perform better and more flexibly is a powerful one. It may well be that when jobs are built around people's capabilities it will be easier to develop their roles in new directions by simply getting them to use the same skills in different situations. They will not have to learn the new job from scratch.

The capacity to adapt quickly will be further enhanced if a policy of continuous development is adopted which enables people to grow their talents in their present roles thus preparing them for new roles. And in a flexible, process-based organization, people will be able to grow their roles – and should be encouraged to do so – as well as grow in their roles.

FURTHER READING

Robertson, I T and Smith, M (1985) *Motivation and Job Design*, Institute of Personnel and Development, London.

18

RECRUITING

THE RECRUITMENT PROCESS

As a line manager one of your key tasks is to ensure that you have the right people to do the work. You have to replace those who leave, are promoted or are transferred with people who are just as good, if not better. You have to find people who meet your specifications for new roles.

The four stages of recruitment are:

1   *Defining requirements* – specifying what sort of person you want to do a particular job or carry out a role.
2   *Deciding or confirming conditions of employment* – pay, benefits, hours etc.
3   *Attracting candidates* – sifting and processing applications, assessing candidates by interviews and tests, offering employment, taking up references and preparing contracts of employment.

These three stages are considered in turn in this chapter except that interviewing, as a key part of the process deserves its own chapter (Chapter 19).

DEFINING REQUIREMENTS

You need to be clear about what you are looking for before you set out to find it. This means specifying your requirements in terms of the qualifications, training, skills, capabilities, experience and personal qualities needed to carry out the job or role effectively.

The starting point will be a job description or role definition which can be prepared along the lines described in Chapter 16. Your next step is to prepare a person specification.

Person specifications

Person or employee specifications describe the sort of person you are looking for. They provide the basis for advertising the post (internally or externally) and the criteria you will use for sifting or short-listing candidates and for assessing their suitability through interviews and tests. The information you need to record in a person specification is described below.

Capabilities

You should define what the jobholder needs to know and be capable of doing in terms of knowledge, skill and competence requirements. These should be specified as precisely as possible by reference to the job description or role definition supported by any skills analysis schedules or competence profiles that are available (see Chapter 13).

You need to identify actual examples of the knowledge required and the skills and competences that have to be applied in the job or role. These can be used as reference points when assessing candidates and as the basis for specific questions to candidates to find out whether what they know and can do will meet the requirements of the job. For this purpose you should get answers to the following questions:

What does the person need to know?

■ technical knowledge – manufacturing, engineering, computing, process control, biochemistry, pharmaceuticals etc.

■ professional knowledge – finance, legal, banking, insurance, surveying, personnel etc.

■ procedural knowledge – how to deal with national and local government bodies, agencies, QUANGOS, export documentation and planning applications etc. and where to obtain information

■ business awareness – business and economic factors affecting the firm.

What does the person need to be able to do?

■ be skilled in operating or managing particular machines, equipment, processes or procedures, or driving vehicles – specify which ones and the level of skill required

■ carry out work requiring manual dexterity – the amount of work and the level of dexterity required

■ carry out work which requires physical fitness or strength

■ apply technical, professional or procedural knowledge and skills to deliver results – specify the activities or tasks in which the knowledge is applied, how the knowledge is applied, what results are expected, what problems and challenges is the jobholder likely to meet in applying the knowledge and skills

■ interact with other people, eg colleagues, supervisors, customers, clients, suppliers, members of the public, officials – specify what people the jobholder interacts with, the subjects covered and the extent to which dealings involve persuasion, handling queries and problems (give examples), or simply supplying or processing information

■ lead a team of people – specify the size and type of team, the type of leadership skills required, the sort of leadership problems the jobholder may meet

■ communicate in writing – specify type of communication (letters, memoranda, reports, sales literature) and to whom it is addressed

■ communicate orally – specify the subjects, frequency of communication and to whom it is addressed

■ work as a member of a team – specify the type of team, the sort of work the team carries out, the jobholder's position in the team and the contribution the jobholder is expected to make to team effort

■ innovate or be creative – specify, with examples, where innovation and creativity is required and indicate the extent to which the jobholder will be working as a member of a research team or independently

■ sell or persuade people to take a course of action – specify what the jobholder sells and to whom, and the occasions when persuasion is required

■ make things happen, seeing things through and meeting deadlines – specify the jobs, the time scales and the problems the jobholder may have to overcome to get results

- manage projects – specify the type of projects, their objectives, time scales and the resources available

- think strategically – specify the role of the jobholder in formulating strategy

- plan and organise work – specify the type of plans made (business, operational, sales etc.) and what is involved in organizing work to achieve the plan

- prepare, manage and control financial budgets – specify the size and scope of the budgets

- manage physical resources – specify type and size, eg plant, machinery, property

- work alone – specify situations when this might happen

- take initiative – specify the type of situations in which initiatives have to be taken and the extent to which the job holder will be expected to take action without reference to higher authority

- exercise judgement – specify the type of decisions to be made, the situations when they arise and the degree of uncertainty that has to be taken into account.

How will the person have acquired the knowledge, skills and expertise to do the work?

- by acquiring an academic or professional qualification – specify the type of qualification, subject(s), level or class achieved

- by acquiring a diploma or certificate – specify type and subject(s)

- by completing a formal training course – specify type, duration and the skills acquired during the training

- by experience – specify the type of experience, the type of organization or business in which the experience was acquired, what should have been learnt through this experience and the length of the experience which would lead to acquiring the necessary degree of knowledge, skill or expertise.

What sort of person is best suited for this work?

☐ motivation – how well motivated should this person be (especially in some cases, the level of achievement motivation)?

☐ self-sufficiency – to what extent will the jobholder have to be self-sufficient, relying on his or her own resources?

☐ self-starter – to what extent will the jobholder have to get things moving himself or herself?

☐ self-confidence – how much confidence will the person require to do the work?

☐ impact – what capacity for making an impact on events and people does this person need to possess?

☐ resilience – how resilient must the jobholder be to stress and pressure?

☐ flexibility – how flexible does the person need to be in carrying out new or different tasks and in accepting changes in his or her role?

☐ outgoing – how outgoing (extroverted) has this person to be in relating to other people such as colleagues, customers and suppliers?

■ assertiveness – to what extent will the person have to be assertive, standing his or her ground in discussions, arguments and when under attack?

■ political sensitivity – how sensitive will this person have to be in dealing with the internal politics of the organization?

☐ toughness – how tough will this person have to be in dealing with crises and making unpopular decisions?

■ tolerance – how should this person be able to tolerate difficult colleagues, customers or suppliers or ambiguous situations?

☐ numeracy – how good has this person got to be with figures?

☐ articulateness – how articulate does this person need to be?

What conditions of work will the jobholder have to accept?

☐ flexible working hours?

☐ compulsory overtime?

☐ call-outs?

☐ travel in the UK or abroad (including time away from home)?

- postings to new locations in the UK or abroad to meet business requirements?

- working flexibly within the organization (unit, plant, department or team) taking on different types of work and exercising different skills?

- driving long distances or, within reason, long hours?

- working in unpleasant conditions?

- being subject to considerable pressure to get things done?

- working against tight deadlines?

- having to meet high standards of output, quality and customer care?

- being prepared to learn new skills, undertaking training courses and implementing personal development plans as required?

The specification should not indicate in any way that there will be any prejudice or discrimination against candidates on the grounds of sex, race, disability, age or religion. The legal requirements on discrimination are summarised in chapter 35.

When specifying your requirements under the above headings you should attempt to strike a balance between overstating and understating them. You do not want to set too high standards because they may restrict your opportunity to recruit people. And if you do recruit them, they may be too well-qualified for the job with the result that they are dissatisfied and leave. Clearly, you do not want to set low standards just to get your numbers right.

It is a good idea to indicate in the specification what you think are the minimum essential requirements as well as the ideal requirements. This sets the threshold for recruitment but enables you to select those whose qualifications for the job are above the minimum (but not too far above).

The person specification can be set out as illustrated in Figure 18.1 overleaf and used as the basis for assessing candidates.

PERSON SPECIFICATION		
Job title:	**Department**	
Education, qualifications and special training		
Essential	Desirable	
Experience		
Essential	Desirable	
Knowledge and skills		
Essential	Desirable	
Competencies		
Essential	Desirable	

Figure 18.1   Person Specification form

CONDITIONS OF EMPLOYMENT

You will need to determine in advance or obtain guidance from the personnel department the conditions of employment for the position. These will form the basis for a contract of employment. The conditions should cover:

■ *Type of contract* – fixed, short-term (if the latter, the period of the contract and the circumstances in which it might be renewed)

■ *Remuneration* – pay grade, basic pay, pay scale, arrangements for performance, skill-based, or competence-related pay, profit sharing or bonus schemes, and allowances (shift, overtime, call out, special working conditions, travel and subsistence)

- *Hours of work* – including shift, overtime and flexible or annual hours arrangements

- *Holidays and leave* – holiday entitlement, statutory holidays, maternity and paternity leave, other forms of leave (eg for jury service)

- *Period of notice* – length of notice required from the employer and the employee

- *Retirement* – normal retirement age

- *Employee benefits* – pension, sick pay, maternity pay, redundancy pay, life, permanent health and medical insurance, loans, house purchase assistance, relocation help, discounts, company cars and petrol (specify arrangements for private use)

- *Special requirements* – the requirements to travel, to work away from home, to move to different locations and to work flexibly.

ATTRACTING CANDIDATES

The main sources of candidates are from inside the company (other things being equal in terms of suitability for the job, these should be given priority unless, there is an equal opportunities policy which requires internal and external candidates to be considered on an equal footing) and from outside. In the latter case the sources are:

- internal or external advertising, dealt with in detail in the next main section of this chapter

- promotion or transfer from within the organization

- recruitment consultants, agencies and executive search consultants (head hunters)

- employment centres

- straight from universities, further education colleges and schools

- getting in touch with former employees to ask them back

- casual applicants by letter or calling in person.

You may readily be able to fill the post by internal promotion or transfer without advertising. But many organizations believe that this does not conform with their equal opportunities policies and therefore insist on all posts being advertised internally, often before an external advertisement or an approach to an agency has been made.

You may easily be able to fill vacancies for manual, service, secretarial and clerical employees through employment centres and agencies. Some agencies specialize, for example, in accounting, legal, computing or catering staff. Vacancies can sometimes be filled by casual applicants but you can seldom rely on this source.

At more senior or professional levels you may well want to engage a recruitment consultant or even a head hunter. They will help to prepare a specification, and will advertise the post, search their database or approach likely candidates. Next they will interview likely candidates and let you have a shortlist with comments. They also take up references. Recruitment consultants can charge a fee based on a percentage of the basic salary for the job which can be 20 per cent or more. Head hunters can charge up to 50 per cent or so of the first year's salary. Recruitment agencies and consultants can save you time and trouble and the good ones will have expertise in drafting person specifications and advertisements, selecting media and assessing candidates.

In spite of these advantages you may prefer to do it yourself, thus keeping complete control and saving money. If there is a personnel department it will, of course, provide all the services a recruitment consultant can, at less cost and with, it is to be hoped, a better feel for your requirements.

If you decide to go it alone (if allowed to) or have to do it yourself, the next section of this chapter covers advertising procedures.

ADVERTISING

The objective of an advertisement should be to:

- attract attention

- create and maintain interest

- stimulate appropriate action, ie applications from an adequate number of qualified candidates.

You can prepare and place advertisements yourself or get help from an advertising agency which, if selected carefully, should have expertise in writing good copy, designing attractive advertisements and selecting the appropriate media. If you are doing it yourself the main actions you have to take are to write the copy, decide on the layout and select the media.

Writing the copy

The advertisement should start with a compelling headline which is usually the job title in bold type. If you can quote the rate of pay (always desirable) you can give the exact rate, a range, or state that it will be around (circa) £X000.

The advertisement should state the name of the organization and, as succinctly as possible:

■   details of the job – the essential features of what the job is should be summarized in a way which will attract the right sort of application

■   qualifications and experience required – don't overstate what you are looking for

■   personal qualities – this is optional, platitudes such as the candidate has to have qualities of drive, initiative etc., are often meaningless

■   how the candidate should apply – a letter, card/or CV or resume, or a request for an application form to a named person.

Advertising copy should avoid any discrimination as laid down by the Sex, Race and Disabilities Discrimination Acts. It is unlawful in an advertisement to discriminate by referring specifically to either sex, except for a few jobs which can only be done by one sex. Advertisements must therefore avoid a sexist job title such as 'salesman' and use a neutral title such as 'sales representative'. If no neutral title is available, the job title should be amplified to cover both sexes; for example 'steward or stewardess'. It is best to avoid any reference to the sex of the candidate by using only neutral, or 'unisex' titles and referring only to the 'candidate' or 'applicant'. Otherwise you must specify 'men or women' or 'he or she'.

Designing the advertisement

The design of the advertisement will depend on which of the following varieties is used:

■   *classified/run-on*, in which copy is run-on in standard type and there is no space around the advertisement and no paragraph spacing or indentation – this variety is cheap but only suitable for lower grade clerical or manual workers

■   *classified/semi-display*, in which standard type is still used but there is more 'white space', headings can be emphasized and paragraphs indented – this variety is still fairly cheap but it can be more effective than run-on advertisements for more senior administrative staff and skilled manual workers

■ *full display*, in which the advertisement can be bordered, any typeface and illustrations can be used and you can have as much 'white space' as you like – this category can be expensive but will make the most impact for managerial, professional or technical staff.

'White space' means the space left round the text. A reasonable amount of such space can focus attention on the text.

It can be helpful to look at other advertisements in the media of your choice to obtain ideas on how to draft and lay out your advertisement.

Choice of media

Newspapers and journals are the most obvious choice. Local papers are best for office and manual workers, the 'quality' national broadsheets for more senior staff and journals for specialized or professional staff. In the latter case, you may advertise in both national papers and an appropriate journal. If you advertise frequently it is a good idea to analyse the response you get in terms of both quantity and quality to provide guidance on the most productive media for future use.

SIFTING AND PROCESSING APPLICATIONS

The steps required to sift applications are as follows:

■ Record the applications as they arrive for control purposes.

■ Send a standard acknowledgement to each applicant; if you want to get more details and obtain a standard basis for comparing applicants, send them an application form to complete.

■ Compare the applications (letters, CVs and completed application forms if the latter has been sent out) with the criteria set out in the person specification and sort them initially into three categories: possible, marginal and unsuitable.

■ Draw up a short list from the 'possibles' for interview; for a single position it is not normally necessary to invite more than seven or eight people if a sufficient number of 'possibles' is available.

■ If some possible or marginal candidates still remain, select half a dozen or so of them as a reserve list in case no one on the short-list is suitable. Send them a 'holding' letter indicating that they are still under consideration and will be informed in due course as to whether or not they will be invited for interview.

■ Send a reject letter to the unsuccessful applicants; the text of the letter could be along these lines:

> We have given very careful consideration to your application for the above position. However, I regret to inform you that we have decided not to invite you for an interview. I should like to thank you for the interest you have shown.

■ Invite the short-listed candidates to interview, using a standard letter. At this stage you should ask them to complete an application form if they have not already done so. This helps to ensure that all applicants are being considered against the same headings and may fill in gaps in the information provided by the original application. It may be worth sending candidates brief details of the company and the job at this stage.

■ When the selection process has been completed and the successful candidate has accepted your offer, write to the rejected short-list candidates and any applicants you have kept on hold. This could be expressed as follows to unsuccessful short-list candidates:

> Since your recent interview I have given very careful consideration to the qualifications of all the short-listed candidates for this post. I regret to inform you that another candidate has more appropriate qualifications for this particular position and I therefore cannot offer it to you. However, I was impressed with your application and your performance at the interview. I am therefore sure that you will find no difficulty in finding a post which suits your talents. Thank you for the interest you have shown and the time and trouble you took to attend the interview.

SELECTING CANDIDATES

The usual method of selecting candidates is, of course, an interview, as considered in Chapter 19. But interviews are not entirely reliable and you might want to obtain additional information to assist in your decision by using a test.

The basic form of test which you can in theory administer yourself is one which tests the ability of the candidate to perform a typical task – using a machine, making something, or producing a letter or schedule on a word processor. But such tests should be used with caution. A test is no good unless it is valid – it measures what it is intended to measure – and reliable – it always measures the same thing. A good test will have been evaluated by comparing test results with actual performance to establish how valid and reliable the test is. It is wise to get advice from an expert before placing too much reliance on a home made test.

The other tests which can be used are:

- *Intelligence tests* which may express the results as an intelligence quotient (IQ).

- *Aptitude and attainment tests* which cover such aspects of work as clerical aptitude, numerical aptitude, mechanical aptitude and dexterity.

- *Personality tests* which attempt to assess various aspects of personality such as emotional stability, sociability, thinking style, feelings and emotions.

- *Graphology* which purports to draw conclusions about the personality of candidates by a study of their handwriting.

Tests can provide useful, dispassionate and revealing information that might not be obtained through a standard interview. But they have to be properly validated (and graphology falls down on this point) and it is best to obtain them from a reputable test agency. The agency will validate the test against people within your organization and train people to administer it (proper administration is important).

OFFERING EMPLOYMENT

An offer of employment confirms the basic terms and conditions applying to the job – the job title, the department or team in which the jobholder will work, the person to whom the jobholder will be responsible, pay, benefits, working hours, holidays and any special working requirements (eg flexibility or mobility) will be specified. This is in effect a basic contract of employment, and it is important to get it right. It is a good idea to get a second opinion, preferably from a personnel specialist before making an offer. Apart from anything else, the terms must conform to the terms and conditions policies of the organization. An offer is normally made subject to satisfactory references and, sometimes, passing a medical examination.

REFERENCES

References can provide essential factual information to confirm what the candidate has told you, but should only be taken up after a provisional offer has been made. Candidates sometimes exaggerate (CVs can be works of art). Some candidates tell outright lies. It is worth checking with at least the present employer and the previous employer (if this was not too long ago) the following basic facts:

■   What job did this person do?

■   How long has he/she been doing it?

■   What was the person's rate of pay or salary?

If the person is no longer in the employment of the company from which a reference is being sought you can ask why he or she left and, a useful question, if answered honestly is, 'would you re-employ?' Such questions are more likely to be answered over the telephone.

Employers are generally cautious about giving references which, although privileged, could be the basis for legal action when an aggrieved candidate claims that the information was false or malicious. That is why it is best to use them only to obtain factual information. If you ask for an opinion it may be refused or expressed in such generalized terms as to be misleading. Character references are of only limited use.

If, incidentally, you are at the receiving end of a request for a reference, it is best to confine yourself to facts not opinions.

CHECKING ON QUALIFICATIONS

Candidates can claim qualifications (academic or professional) which they do not possess. If these are key criteria you should always check with the educational or professional institution that the candidate is telling the truth. Even if the qualification or membership is not essential a check would establish that a candidate has lied. And you will know what to do about that.

GOOD RECRUITMENT PRACTICE

A study commissioned by The Institute of Personnel and Development's Recruitment Forum found that good recruitment practice may be costly but that it can minimize the risk of failing to achieve the business strategy. This can be jeopardized if the people who are appointed are not capable of contributing effectively, if appointments are not timely, or if no appointment is made. Recruitment can also undermine organizational effectiveness if it is inconsistent with organizational policies. For example, if the organization is committed to equal opportunity, but recruitment practices are discriminatory or alienate applicants from minority groups.

Unnecessary expense can arise from remedial costs such as re-recruitment, unplanned extra training, management time spent sorting out problems and complaints by applicants about non-compliance with equal opportunity and other legislation. Cost can also be incurred through inefficiency in the recruitment process itself such as over-elaborate, time-consuming recruitment activities.

The most common failings established by the research were:

■ no obvious links with HR strategy, resourcing strategy and broader business and organizational goals

■ a lack of job analysis and, therefore, possible inappropriate use of job descriptions and personal criteria

■ important details missing from recruitment advertisements

■ use of references for shortlisting

■ inadequate use of structured interviews

■ insufficient use of occupational psychologists where psychometric testing is used, together with a lack of feedback and counselling

■ insufficient test piloting and validation

■ use of invalid prediction methods

■ lack of monitoring of results or, if monitoring has taken place, lack of remedial action.

The last problem was confirmed by an issue of the Industrial Society publication *Managing Best Practice in Recruitment and Selection*. This noted that while more than half of the organizations surveyed monitored recruitment, only between 4 and 5 per cent acted on the results.

RECRUITMENT IN PRACTICE

The following are two examples of how organizations undertake large scale recruitment programmes.

Unisys

Unisys is a global information management business operating in three major areas: information services, computer services and global customer services. Unisys has been growing rapidly in the last few years and, as for other IT companies, recruiting experienced technical staff has become harder. Given the size of the current recruitment target, the company is using a range of different resourcing media to reach candidates.

Internal on-line vacancy information

All vacancies are advertised internally as a matter of course. Unisys uses a Lotus Notes system on which it runs an application called *Information Online*. As well as general company information and news there is a separate HR section which currently lists all vacancies in the form of a word document. Each vacancy contains a description of the job, the job grade (which influences salary) location, the skills and experience required and details of the relevant manager to contact for further information.

The ability to identify vacancies by date of entry enables resourcing managers to track vacancies and monitor progress more efficiently. Finally, the resourcing team can keep 'closed files' of CVs submitted for vacancies which have been filled but where similar positions are likely to arise in other areas of the business. Previous applicants who would already have been screened as suitable can then be contacted again.

Refer a friend scheme

Unisys runs an incentive scheme to encourage existing employees to refer suitably qualified and experienced friends and/or former colleagues to apply for a position. If the friend is appointed, the employee who referred them receives a 'commission' of £1,000 for new employees on a starting salary up to £25,000, or £2,000 for those starting on salaries over £25,000. Employees refer CVs to the resourcing team but have no involvement thereafter. Referrals are not accepted from people who are working for one of Unisys' clients.

External recruitment

The company uses a variety of media to source external recruits. The largest source of applications currently is direct advertising in the national press and specialist magazines. Recruitment agencies are also a significant source of candidates. Other methods are used to access potential recruits, such as the Internet and specialist careers fairs.

The company also receives a significant number of applications on a speculative basis. Mostly from graduates, these are screened in the same way as applications from other sources. The company has used the Internet for recruitment purposes for some time.

Interviews

Due to the technical nature of the work, interviewing is conducted by line management, usually the immediate technical manager and a senior manager. (The central resourcing team interviews new graduates only.) The resourcing managers act in an advisory capacity to managers and talk to candidates about terms and conditions and other contractual matters. Managers can refer to a policy document prepared by the resourcing team which gives details of the sort of information that candidates require, eg the job role, the company and the relevant employee benefits. Most interviews are on a one-to-one basis although the precise format depends on the individual department.

Central resourcing is responsible for completing the recruitment process and agreeing the terms of the job offer. They also give feedback to candidates about their performance at interview where requested.

Tesco

Tesco employs more than 110,000 staff in about 514 supermarkets across the UK. It opens about 30 new stores, of varying sizes, each year. Around 60 per cent of its employees are members of the shop workers' union, USDAW.

New stores

When the decision to open a store in a new location is taken, the research department provides a new stores department with a demographic breakdown of the area, analysing, for example, the numbers of students and one-parent families as both of these may affect staffing and shift patterns. The research department also provides details of how recruitment campaigns in similar areas have worked in the past.

Once an opening date is set, recruitment proceeds according to a tight schedule.

Recruitment Centre

At week minus 30 (30 weeks before opening) a manager for the store is selected. He or she meets with the new stores team and they establish a recruitment centre within the catchment area for the store. A recruitment centre needs to have 6,000 to 8,000 square feet of office space, with interview rooms and areas for group training.

The team takes occupation of the recruitment centre at about week minus 14. The intervening weeks are spent recruiting the store's senior team from within the company. This is followed by the recruitment of section managers. A good proportion are recruited internally, in accordance with Tesco's succession plan. Section managers have experience ranging from six months to a couple of years within retailing.

Employment service

At about week minus 24 Tesco briefs the local Job Centre in detail about the recruitment needs for the new store. A member of the Employment Service staff is taken on to the team from about week minus 14, to control the administration of the recruitment exercise, and use local knowledge. This tends to be a developmental posting.

Recruitment

The major recruitment activity comes in the last 14 weeks. The bulk of the jobs available are for cashiers, and general assistants (in areas such as delicatessen, fruit and vegetables, meat, dairy, systems or customer service). At week minus 13, an advertisement is placed in the local newspaper inviting applicants to ring and book a slot at the Tesco Open Day, held at the recruitment centre.

Open days

Open days are held on Fridays, Saturdays and Sundays with about 50 people attending each one-hour session. They are provided with information about the job, about the benefits of working for Tesco and about the pay and training on offer. The store's manager gives specific information about the new store.

Other interested groups set up stalls at the open day: the local Job Centre attends to help potential applicants calculate how any earnings from Tesco would affect their benefits; women's groups discuss childcare; banks give advice on mortgages and similar issues. USDAW also attends to give out literature and explain the union's involvement in giving legal advice, help and discounts on services to members. This may be vital for the union in the South of England, where there is little history of trade unionism for many new recruits. The application forms for Tesco include a union membership form.

Attending the open day is how applicants can get application forms. This allows people to decide for themselves whether working for Tesco would be the right choice for them. The Tesco management team screen the forms, looking for a customer-service orientation.

Tesco takes the view that skills can be taught more easily and are best built upon a basis of service-oriented behaviour. The forms offer a space for the applicants to tell Tesco about themselves. This is their chance to sell themselves, and give Tesco a chance to find out more about them.

Section managers invite suitable candidates to an interview and about three or four candidates are seen for each job. Interviews last about 20 to 30 minutes. Candidates are asked to give examples of their customer service skills or appropriate transferable skills, for example bringing up a family. Interviewers are trained in the skills needed to persuade interviewees to raise examples of relevant behaviour.

FURTHER READING

Armstrong, M (1996) *A Handbook of Personnel Management Practice*, 6th Edition, (Chapter 24) Kogan Page, London.

19

SELECTION INTERVIEWING

In this chapter the following aspects of selection interviewing are covered:

- the overall purpose of selection interviews
- aims of a selection interview
- the nature of a selection interview
- who conducts the interview
- interviewing arrangements
- preparing for the interview
- the content of an interview
- sequencing the interview
- interviewing techniques
- questioning techniques
- completing the interview
- assessing the data
- do's and don'ts of selection interviewing.

THE OVERALL PURPOSE OF A SELECTION INTERVIEW

Selection interviews provide the information required to assess candidates against a person specification. If well-conducted, they enable you to make a reliable prediction about the potential capacity of candidates to do the job. On completing an interviewing programme you should be in a position to compare candidates and select the right person.

AIMS OF A SELECTION INTERVIEW

A selection interview should provide you with the answers to three fundamental questions:

1   Can the individual do the job? Is the person capable of doing the work to the standard required?
2   Will the individual do the job? Is the person well motivated?
3   How is the individual likely to fit into the team? Will I be able to work well with this person?

THE NATURE OF A SELECTION INTERVIEW

A selection interview should take the form of a conversation with a purpose. It is a conversation because candidates should be given the opportunity to talk freely about themselves and their careers. But the conversation has to be planned, directed and controlled to achieve your aims in the time available.

Your task as an interviewer is to draw candidates out to ensure that you get the information you want. Candidates should be encouraged to do most of the talking – one of the besetting sins of poor interviewers is that they talk too much. But you have to plan the structure of the interview to achieve its purpose and decide in advance the questions you need to ask – questions which will give you what you need to make an accurate assessment.

Overall, an effective approach to interviewing can be summed up as the three Cs:

■   *Content* – the information you want and the questions you ask to get it

■ *Contact* – your ability to make and maintain good contact with candidates; to establish the sort of rapport that will encourage them to talk freely, thus revealing their strengths and their weaknesses

■ *Control* – your ability to control the interview so that you get the information you want.

All this requires you to plan the interview thoroughly in terms of content, timing, structure and use of questions. But before doing all this you need to consider who is to conduct the interview and what arrangements need to be made for it.

WHO CONDUCTS THE INTERVIEW?

Although whoever is going to make the final selection decision (ie the manager) should always conduct the main interview, there is much to be said for a second opinion. This may help to avoid a biased or superficial decision. The second opinion can be the manager's boss or any other manager or team leader with whom the jobholder will work. If the jobholder is going to be a member of a closely knit team the other members of the team could be involved, if only to meet candidates and talk to them informally. This has the additional advantage that the candidates will meet their future colleagues. Panel interviews or selection boards often used for public sector appointments allow more people to have a say in the selection, but candidates may not do justice to themselves because they are seldom able to expand on their replies. Selection boards tend to favour the confident and articulate candidate, and these are not the only qualities they should be looking for.

■ Next step – candidates should be told what the next step will be following the interview. They may be asked at this stage if they have any objections to references being taken up.

■ Recording decisions – it is essential to spell out the reasons why someone was rejected, explaining that this was on the grounds of their qualifications for the job and had nothing to do with the sex, race or disability (except in the latter case when it is absolutely clear that the disability precludes the candidate from doing the job or even a specially modified version of it).

PREPARING FOR THE INTERVIEW

Initial preparations

Your first step in preparing for an interview should be to familiarize or re-familiarize yourself with the person specification. It is essential to list the key points to be covered and to identify the critical criteria you will use when making a choice, ie the minimum you could accept in terms of qualifications and experience. It is also advisable at this stage to pre-pare questions that you can put to all candidates to obtain the informa-tion you require. If you ask everyone some identical questions you will be able to compare the answers.

You should then read the candidates' CVs and applications. This will identify any special questions you should ask about their career or, to fill in the gaps, – 'what does this gap between jobs C and D signify'? (although you would not put the question as baldly as that; it would be better to say something like this: 'I see there was a gap of six months between when you left your job in C and started in D. Would you mind telling me what you were doing during this time?').

Timing

You should decide at this stage how long you want to spend on each interview. As a rule of thumb, 45 to 60 minutes are usually required for serious, professional or technical appointments. Middle ranking jobs need about 30 to 45 minutes. The more routine jobs can be covered in 20 to 30 minutes. But the time allowed depends on the job and you do not want to insult a candidate by conducting a superficial interview.

THE CONTENT OF AN INTERVIEW

The content of an interview can be analysed into three sections: the interview's beginning, middle and end.

Beginning

At the start of the interview you should put candidates at their ease. You want them to talk freely in response to your questions. They won't do this if you plunge in too abruptly. At least welcome them and thank them for coming to the interview, expressing genuine pleasure about the meeting. But don't waste too much time talking about their journey or the weather.

Some interviewers start by describing the company and the job. Wherever possible it is best to eliminate this part of the interview by sending candidates a brief job description and something about the organization.

If you are not careful you will spend far too much time at this stage, especially if the candidate later turns out to be clearly unsuitable. A brief reference to the job should suffice and this can be elaborated on at the end of the interview.

Middle

The middle part of the interview is where you find out what you need to know about candidates. It should take at least 80 per cent of the time, leaving, say, 5 per cent at the beginning and 15 per cent at the end.

This is when you ask questions designed to provide information on:

- the extent to which the knowledge, skills, capabilities and personal qualities of candidates meet the person specification

- the career history and ambitions of candidates and, sometimes, on certain aspects of their behaviour at work such as sickness and absenteeism.

End

At the end of the interview you should give candidates the opportunity to ask questions about the job and the company. The quality of these questions can often give you clues about the degree to which applicants are interested and their ability to ask pertinent questions.

You may want to expand a little on the job. If candidates are promising, some interviewers at this stage extol the attractive features of the job. This is fine as long as these are not exaggerated. To give a 'realistic preview' the possible downsides should be mentioned, for example the need to travel or unsociable working hours. If candidates are clearly unsuitable you can tactfully help them to de-select themselves by referring to aspects of the work which may not appeal to them, or for which they are not really qualified. It is best not to spell out these points too]quirement of the job, how do you feel about it?' You can follow up this general question by more specific questions: 'Do you feel you have the right sort of experience?' 'Are you happy about (this aspect of the job)?'

At this stage you should ask final questions about the availability of candidates, as long as they appear promising. You can ask when they would be able to start and about any holiday arrangements to which they are committed.

You should also ask their permission to obtain references from their present and previous employers. They might not want you to approach their present employer and in this case you should tell them that if they are made an offer of employment it would be conditional on a satisfactory reference from their employer. It is useful to ensure that you have the names of people you can approach.

Finally, you inform candidates of what happens next. If some time could elapse before they hear from you, they should be told that you will be writing as soon as possible but that there will be some delay (don't make a promise you will be unable to keep).

It is not normally good practice to inform candidates of your decision at the end of the interview. You should take time to reflect on their suitability and you don't want to give them the impression that you are making a snap judgement.

SEQUENCING THE INTERVIEW

When planning interviews you should give some thought to how you are going to sequence your questions, especially in the middle part. There are two basic approaches as described below.

Biographical approach

The biographical approach is probably the most popular because it is simple to use and appears to be logical. The interview can be sequenced chronologically, starting with the first job or even before that at school and, if appropriate, college or university. The succeeding jobs, if any, are then dealt with in turn ending with the present job on which most time is spent if the candidate has been in it for a reasonable time. If you are not careful, however, using the chronological method for someone who has had a number of jobs can mean spending too much time on the earlier jobs, leaving insufficient time for the most important recent experiences.

To overcome this problem, an alternative biographical approach is to start with the present job, which is discussed in some depth. The interviewer then works backwards, job by job, but only concentrating on particularly interesting or relevant experience in earlier jobs.

The problem with the biographical approach is that it is predictable. Experienced candidates are familiar with it and have their story ready, glossing over any weak points. It can also be unreliable. You can easily miss an important piece of information by concentrating on a succes-sion of jobs rather than focusing on key aspects of the candidates' expe-rience which illustrate their capabilities.

Criteria-based or targeted approach

This approach is based on an analysis of the person specification. You can then select the criteria on which you will judge the suitability of the candidate which will put you in a position to 'target' these key criteria during the interview. You can decide on the questions you need to ask to draw out from candidates' information about their knowledge, skills, capabilities and personal qualities which can be compared with the cri-teria to assess the extent to which candidates meet the specification. It is up to candidates to select from their experience incidents or examples illustrating what they know, what they can do, what they have done and how they have done it. These instances will probably be drawn mainly from recent experience but relevant earlier experiences can also be mentioned.

This is probably the best way of focusing your interview to ensure that you get all the information you require about candidates for comparison with the person specification.

INTERVIEWING TECHNIQUES

Questioning

The most important interviewing technique you need to acquire and practice is questioning. Asking pertinent questions which elicit informa-tive responses is a skill which people do not necessarily possess, but it is one they can develop. To improve your questioning techniques it is a good idea at the end of an interview to ask yourself: 'Did I ask the right questions?', 'Did I put them to the candidate well?', 'Did I get candidates to respond freely?'

There are a number of different types of questions as described below. By choosing the right ones you can get candidates to open up or you can pin them down to giving you specific information or to extend-ing or clarifying a reply. The other skills you should possess are establish-ing rapport, and listening, maintaining continuity, keeping contact and note-taking. These are considered later in this section of the chapter.

Questioning techniques

There are a number of different ways of putting questions ranging from open questions which ask for general replies and are good for getting the interview going in its early stage to probe, to closed questions which ask for specific replies and can be posed later. The main types of questions are described below.

Open questions

Open questions are the best ones to use to get candidates to talk – to draw them out. These are questions which cannot be answered by a yes or no and which encourage a full response. Single word answers are seldom illuminating. It is a good idea to begin the interview with one or two open questions thus helping candidates to settle in.

Open-ended questions or phrases inviting a response can be phrased as follows:

- I'd like you to tell me about the sort of work you are doing in your present job.
- What do you know about...?
- Could you give me some examples of...?
- In what ways do you think your experience fits you to do the job for which you have applied?
- How have you tackled...?
- What have been the most challenging aspects of your job?
- Please tell me about some of the interesting things you have been doing at work recently.

Open questions can give you a lot of useful information but you may not get exactly what you want, and answers can go into too much detail. For example, the question: 'What has been the main feature of your work in recent months?', may result in a one-word reply – 'marketing'. Or it may produce a lengthy explanation which takes up too much time. Replies to open questions can get bogged down in too much detail, or miss out some key points. They can come to a sudden halt or lose their way. You need to ensure that you get all the facts, keep the flow going and maintain control. Remember that you are in charge. Hence the value of probing, closed and the other types of questions which are discussed below.

Probing questions

Probing questions are used to get further details or to ensure that you are getting all the facts. You ask them when answers have been too generalized or when you suspect that there may be some more relevant information which candidates have not disclosed. A candidate may claim to have done something and it may be useful to find out more about exactly what contribution was made. Poor interviewers tend to let general and uninformative answers pass by without probing for further details, simply because they are sticking rigidly to a pre-determined list of open questions. Skilled interviewers are able to flex their approach to ensure they get the facts while still keeping control to ensure that the interview is completed on time.

A candidate could say to you something like: 'I was involved in a major business process re-engineering exercise that produced significant improvements in the flow of work through the factory.' This statement conveys nothing about what the candidate actually did. You have to ask probing questions such as:

- What was your precise role in this project?
- What exactly was the contribution you made to its success?
- What knowledge and skills were you able to apply to the project?
- Were you responsible for monitoring progress?
- Did you prepare the final recommendations in full or in part? If in part, which part?
- How was the success of the project measured?
- How successful was the project?

The following are some other examples of probing questions:

- You've informed me that you have had experience in... Could you tell me more about what you did?
- Could you describe in more detail the equipment you use?
- What training have you had to operate your machine/equipment/computer?
- What else is involved in this task?
- Why do you think that happened?
- What influenced you to make that decision?
- How did you deal with that situation?

- How much supervision/guidance were you given?
- Who else was involved?
- What contribution did you make to the end-result?

Closed questions

Closed questions aim to clarify a point of fact. The expected reply will be an explicit single word or brief sentence. In a sense, a closed question acts as a probe but produces a succinct factual statement without going into detail. When you ask a closed question you intend to find out:

- what the candidate has or has not done – 'What did you do then?'
- why something took place – 'Why did that happen?'
- when something took place – 'When did that happen?'
- how something happened – 'How did that situation arise?'
- where something happened – 'Where were you at the time?'
- who took part – 'Who else was involved?'

Capability questions

Capability questions aim to establish what candidates know, the skills they possess and use and what they are capable of doing. They can be open, probing or closed but they will always be focused as precisely as possible on the contents of the person specification referring to knowledge, skills and capabilities.

Capability questions should therefore be explicit – focused on what candidates must know and be able to do. Their purpose is to obtain evidence from candidates which show the extent to which they meet the specification in each of its key areas. Because time is always limited it is best to concentrate on the most important aspects of the work. And it is always best to prepare the questions in advance.

The sort of capability questions you can ask are:

- What do you know about...?
- How did you gain this knowledge?
- What are the key skills you are expected to use in your work?
- How would your present employer rate the level of skill you have reached in...?
- What do you use these skills to do?

■ How often do you use these skills?

■ What training have you received to develop these skills?

■ Could you please tell me exactly what sort and how much experience you have had in...?

■ Could you tell me more about what you have actually been doing in this aspect of your work?

■ Can you give me any examples of the sort of work you have done which would qualify you to do this job?

■ Could you tell me more about the machinery, equipment, processes or systems which you operate/for which you are responsible? (the information could refer to such aspects as output or throughput, tolerances, use of computers or software, technical problems)

■ What are the most typical problems you have to deal with?

■ Would you tell me about any instances when you have had to deal with an unexpected problem or a crisis?

Behavioural event questions

Behavioural event questions aim to get candidates to tell you how they would behave in situations which have been identified as critical to successful job performance. The assumption upon which such questions are based is that past behaviour in dealing with or reacting to events is the best predictor of future behaviour.

The following are some typical behavioural event questions:

■ Could you give an instance when you persuaded others to take an unusual course of action?

■ Could you describe an occasion when you completed a project or task in the face of great difficulties?

■ Could you describe any contribution you have made as a member of a team in achieving an unusually successful result?

■ Could you give an instance when you took the lead in a difficult/unusual situation in getting something worthwhile done?

■ Could you tell me of an incident in which you successfully dealt with an awkward customer/supplier/colleague?

■ Could you tell me of an instance when you had to deal with a member of your team who was not performing particularly well and what you did about it?

- Could you give me an example of an incident when you had to decide for yourself on an entirely new way of tackling the project/task?

Questions about motivation

The degree to which candidates are motivated is a personal quality to which it is usually necessary to give special attention if it is to be properly assessed. This is usually achieved by inference rather than direct questions. 'How well are you motivated?' is a leading question that will usually produce the response: 'Highly'.

You can make inferences about the level of motivation of candidates by asking questions about:

- Their career – replies to such questions as: 'Why did you decide to move on from there?' can give an indication of the extent to which they have been well-motivated in progressing their career.

- Achievements – not just 'What did you achieve?' but 'How did you achieve it?' and 'What difficulties did you overcome?'

- Triumphing over disadvantages – candidates who have done well in spite of an unpromising upbringing and relatively poor education will indicate that they are better motivated than those with all the advantages that upbringing and education can bestow, but who have not made good use of these advantages.

- Spare time interests – don't accept at its face value a reply to a question about spare time interests which, for example, reveals that a candidate collects stamps. Find out if the candidate is well-motivated enough to pursue the interest with determination and to achieve something in the process. Simply sticking stamps in an album is not evidence of motivation. Becoming a recognized expert on 19th century stamps issued in Mexico is.

Continuity questions

Continuity questions aim to keep the flow going in an interview and encourage candidates to enlarge on what they have told you, within limits. Here are some examples of continuity questions:

- 'What happened next?'
- 'What did you do then?'
- 'Can we talk about your next job?'
- 'Can we move on now to…?'

■ 'Could you tell me more about...?'

It has been said that to keep the conversation going during an interview the best thing an interviewer can do is to make encouraging grunts at appropriate moments. There is more to interviewing than that, but single words or phrases like 'good', 'fine', 'that's interesting', 'carry on' can help things along.

Hypothetical questions

Hypothetical questions put a situation to candidates and ask them how they would respond. They can be prepared in advance to test how candidates would approach a typical problem. Such questions may be phrased: 'What do you think you would do if...?' When such questions lie well within the candidate's expertise and experience the answers can be illuminating. But it could be unfair to ask candidates to say how they would deal with a problem without knowing more about the context in which the problem arose. It can also be argued that what candidates say they would do and what they actually do could be quite different. Hypothetical questions can produce hypothetical answers. The best data upon which judgements about candidates can be judged are what they have actually done or achieved. You need to find out if they have successfully dealt with the sort of issues and problems they may be faced with if they join your organization.

Play-back questions

Play-back questions test your understanding of what candidates have said by putting to them a statement of what it appears they have told you, and asking them if they agree or disagree with your version. For example, you could say: 'As I understand it, you resigned from your last position because you disagreed with your boss on a number of fundamental issues – have I got that right?' The answer might simply be yes to this closed question, in which case you might probe to find out more about what happened. Or the candidate may reply 'not exactly' in which case you ask for the full story.

Career questions

As mentioned earlier, questions about the career history of candidates can provide some insight into motivation as well as establishing how they have progressed in acquiring useful and relevant knowledge, skills and experience. You can ask such questions as:

■ What did you learn from that new job?

- What different skills had you to use when you were promoted?
- Why did you leave that job?
- What happened after you left that job?
- In what ways do you think this job will advance your career?

Focused work questions

These are questions designed to tell you more about particular aspects of the candidate's work history, such as:

- How many days absence from work did you have last year?
- How many times were you late last year?
- Have you been absent from work for any medical reason not shown on your application form?
- Have you a clean driving licence? (for those whose work will involve driving).

Questions about outside interests

You should not spend much time asking people with work experience about their outside interests or hobbies. It is seldom relevant, although, as mentioned earlier, it can give some insight into how well motivated candidates are if the depth and vigour with which the interest is pursued is explored.

Active interests and offices held at school, colleges or universities can, however, provide some insight into the attributes of candidates in the absence of any work history except, possibly, vacation jobs. If, for example, a student has been on a long back-pack trip some information can be obtained about the student's initiative, motivation and determination if the journey has been particularly adventurous.

Unhelpful questions

There are two types of questions that are unhelpful:

- *Multiple questions* such as 'What skills do you use most frequently in your job? Are they technical skills, leadership skills, teamworking skills or communicating skills?' will only confuse candidates. You will probably get a partial or misleading reply. Ask only one question at a time.

■ *Leading questions* which indicate the reply you expect are also unhelpful. If you ask a question such as: 'That's what you think, isn't it?' you will get the reply: 'Yes, I do'. If you ask a question such as: 'I take it that you don't really believe that...?' You will get the reply: 'No, I don't'. Neither of these replies will get you anywhere.

Questions to be avoided

Avoid any questions that could be construed as being biased on the grounds of sex, race or disability. Don't ask:

■ 'Who is going to look after the children?' This is no concern of yours, although it is reasonable to ask 'Do the hours of work pose any problems for you?'

■ Are you planning to have any more children?

■ Would it worry you being the only black face around here?

■ With your disability, do you think you can cope with the job?

Ten useful questions

The following are ten useful questions from which you can select any that are particularly relevant in an interview you are conducting:

1 What are the most important aspects of your present job?
2 What do you think have been your most notable achievements in your career to date?
3 What sort of problems have you successfully solved recently in your job?
4 What have you learned from your present job?
5 What has been your experience in...?
6 What do you know about...?
7 What is your approach to handling...?
8 What particularly interests you in this job and why?
9 Now you have heard more about the job, would you please tell me which aspects of your experience are most relevant?
10 Is there anything else about your career which hasn't come out yet in this interview but you think I ought to hear?

Establishing rapport

Establishing rapport means establishing a good relationship with candidates – getting on their wavelength, putting them at ease, encouraging them to respond and generally being friendly. This is not just a question of being 'nice' to candidates. If you achieve rapport you are more likely to get them to talk freely about both their strengths and weaknesses.

Good rapport is created by the way in which you greet candidates, how you start the interview and how you put your questions and respond to replies. Questions should not be posed aggressively or imply that you are criticizing some aspect of the candidate's career. Some people like the idea of 'stress' interviews but they are always counter-productive. Candidates clam up and gain a negative impression of you and the organization.

When responding to answers you should be appreciative, not critical: 'Thank you, that was very helpful; now can we go on to...?', not 'Well, that didn't show you in a good light, did it?'

Body language can also be important. If you maintain natural eye contact, avoid slumping in your seat, nod and make encouraging comments when appropriate, you will establish better rapport and get more out of the interview.

Listening

If an interview is a conversation with a purpose, as it should be, listening skills are important. You need not only to hear but also to understand what candidates are saying. When interviewing you must concentrate on what candidates are telling you. Summarizing at regular intervals forces you to listen because you have to pay attention to what they have been saying in order to get the gist of their replies. If you play back to candidates your understanding of what they have told you for them to confirm or amend it will ensure that you have fully comprehended the messages they are delivering.

Maintaining continuity

So far as possible link your questions to a candidate's last reply so that the interview progresses logically and a cumulative set of data is built up. You can put bridging questions to candidates such as: 'Thank you, that was an interesting summary of what you have been doing in that aspect of your work. Now, could you tell me something about your other key responsibilities?'

Keeping control

You want candidates to talk, but not too much. When preparing for the interview you should have drawn up an agenda and you must try to stick to it. Don't cut candidates short too brutally but say something like: 'Thank you, I've got a good picture of that, now what about…?'

Focus on specifics as much as you can. If candidates ramble on a bit ask a pointed question (a 'probe' question) which asks for an example illustrating the particular aspect of their work that you are considering.

Note taking

You won't remember everything that candidates tell you. It is useful to take notes of the key points they make, discreetly, but not surreptitiously. However, don't put candidates off by frowning or tut-tutting when you are making a negative note.

It may be helpful to ask candidates if they would mind you taking notes. They can't really object but will appreciate the fact that they have been asked.

COMPLETING THE INTERVIEW

At the end of the interview you need to:

- give the candidates the opportunity to ask questions
- check on obtaining references
- ask possible candidates when they would be able to start
- ask about fixed holiday plans
- tell them about the next steps, for example, when they will hear from you about the outcome of the interview.

ASSESSING THE DATA

If you have carried out a good interview you should have the data to assess the extent to which candidates meet each of the key points in the person specification. You can summarize your assessments by marking candidates against each of the points – 'exceeds specification', 'fully meets specification', 'just means the minimum specification', 'does not meet the minimum specification'.

You can assess motivation broadly as 'highly motivated, 'reasonably well motivated', 'not very well motivated'.

You should also draw some conclusions from the candidate's career history and the other information you have gained about their behaviour at work. Credit should be given for a career that has progressed steadily, even if there have been several job changes. But a lot of job hopping for no good reason and without making progress can lead you to suspect that a candidate is not particularly stable.

No blame should be attached to a single setback – it can happen to anyone. But if the pattern is repeated you can reasonably be suspicious. Redundancy is not a stigma – it is happening all the time.

Finally, there is the delicate question of whether you think you will be able to work with the candidate, and whether you think he or she will fit into the team. You have to be very careful about making judgements about how you will get on with someone. But if you are absolutely certain that the chemistry will not work, then you have to take account of that feeling, as long as you ensure that you have reasonable grounds for it on the basis of the behaviour of the candidate at the interview. But be aware of the common mistakes that interviewers can make. These include:

- jumping to conclusions on a single piece of favourable evidence – the 'halo effect'

- jumping to conclusions on a single piece of unfavourable evidence – the 'horns effect'

- not weighing up the balance between the favourable and unfavourable evidence logically and objectively

- coming to firm conclusions on inadequate evidence

- making snap or hurried judgements

- making prejudiced judgements on the grounds of sex, race, disability, religion, appearance, accent, class or any aspects of the candidate's life history, circumstances or career which do not fit your preconceptions of what you are looking for.

Coming to a conclusion

Compare your assessment of each of the candidates against one another. If any candidate fails in an area which is critical to success he or she should be rejected. You can't take a chance. Your choice should be made between the candidates who reach an acceptable standard against each of the criteria. You can then come to an overall judgement by reference to their assessments under each heading and their career history as to which one is most likely to succeed.

In the end, your decision between qualified candidates may well be judgmental. There may be one outstanding candidate but quite often there are two or three. In these circumstances you have to come to a balanced view on which one is more likely to fit the job and the organization and have potential for a long-term career, if this is possible. Don't, however, settle for second best in desperation. It is better to try again.

Remember to make and keep notes of the reasons for your choice and why candidates have been rejected. These together with the applications should be kept for at least six months just in case your decision is challenged as being discriminatory.

DO'S AND DON'TS OF SELECTION INTERVIEWING

To conclude, here is a summary of the do's and don'ts of selection interviewing:

Do

■ give yourself sufficient time

■ plan the interview

■ create the right atmosphere

■ establish an easy and informal relationship – start with open questions

■ encourage the candidate to talk

■ cover the ground as planned, ensuring that you complete a prepared agenda and maintain continuity

■ analyse the candidate's career to reveal strengths, weaknesses and patterns of interest

■ ask clear, unambiguous questions

■ get examples and instances of the successful application of knowledge, skills and the effective use of capabilities

■ make judgements on the basis of the factual information you have obtained about candidates' experience and attributes in relation to the person specification

■ keep control over the content and timing of the interview.

Don't

■ attempt too many interviews in a row

- start the interview unprepared
- plunge too quickly into demanding (probe) questions
- ask multiple or leading questions
- pay too much attention to isolated strengths or weaknesses
- allow candidates to gloss over important facts
- talk too much or allow candidates to ramble on
- allow your prejudices to get the better of your capacity to make objective judgements.

FURTHER READING

Edwards, L (1997) *Interviewing*, Industrial Society, London.
Hackett, P (1995) *The Selection Interview*, Institute of Personnel and Development, London.

Part 4

Performance management

20

MANAGING PERFORMANCE – THE OVERALL APPROACH

Managers exist to achieve results. To do so they have to manage the performance of their department or team and the individual members of the team. In carrying out this responsibility for managing performance the aim of managers is to contribute to the improvement of the overall performance of the organization by getting better results from their teams and individuals. This is what Jose Pottinger, Personnel Director of Cummins Engines Limited told the IPD researchers on performance management:

Performance management can deliver:

- clarity about expectations
- linkage between individual and organisational objectives
- a focus on improvement – establishing what data is required to achieve improvement and what is helpful in the shape of feedback.

Essentially, the process should encourage dialogue – a reflective conversation about performance and development. Performance management should not be seen as an end in itself – it is simply one of the dimensions that can be used in improving the performance of the organization. Performance management should address the needs of both the organization and individuals. They want feedback on how they are doing. The direction performance management should take is to move from a controlling/critical process to an enabling process. Managers have to answer the question: 'how can we help individuals to realize their potential?' They have to be involved in helping individuals to understand what skills they need and in helping them to develop these skills. Coaching is important.

As long as human resources drives performance management, line managers will feel that all they have to do is fill in the form. Performance management should be treated as a business process. Line managers may feel reluctant to give quality time to performance management. To do so they must have an inherent feeling that the investment of their time will pay off.

The process of managing performance is therefore a natural process of management. It is not a 'system' of performance appraisal or performance management imposed on managers and team leaders by top management aided and abetted by personnel. Performance management belongs to managers, not the personnel department. It is your responsibility, not their's.

Managing performance is not just a matter of filling in an elaborate form once a year and then conducting an appraisal meeting which produces a rating determining a pay increase. Managing performance is about raising performance not rating performance. It is a continuous process not an annual event. Forms and formal review processes have their uses. But forms are completed for the benefit of managers and individuals. They are not completed for the benefit of the personnel department, to be filed away and then forgotten. Formal reviews provide a means for both parties to reflect on the past and plan for the future (with much more emphasis on the latter). But they are not the be all and end all of a performance management system as has been the case traditionally, and still is in many organizations.

MANAGING EXPECTATIONS

Managing performance is concerned with the management of expectations. The organization defines its purpose and its objectives and strategic plans to meet the expectations of its shareholders, the City, regulators or trustees and the public at large. The organization may define its values as well as its purpose – how it wants its members to behave in achieving the organization's goals.

The expectations of the organization determine what functions, departments and teams are expected to do to contribute to the achievement of the organization's purpose. These define what individual line managers and team leaders are expected to achieve. Finally, organizational, departmental and team expectations define what individuals are expected to do in terms of achieving targets and standards of performance and upholding corporate values.

Similarly, the organization defines core competences – what it is expected to do well in order to ensure that its goals are achieved, having paid proper attention to the critical success factors which affect organizational performance. Expectations about the competences which individuals should possess are defined within the context of the organization's core competences.

INTEGRATION

What has been described above are processes of integration – the integration of corporate, team and individual objectives, the integration of core values, and the integration of competence requirements. The reason for this emphasis on integration when managing performance is that expectations are shared and understood, and, if it is put into effect properly, everyone will be moving in the same direction towards the achievement of corporate goals.

THE CASCADING PROCESS

The integration of objectives and competences as described above is frequently defined as a process of 'cascading' down from the top to the bottom of the organization. Thus at each level people know what they are expected to contribute to the achievement of higher level objectives.

The only problem of this concept of cascading is that it gives the impression of a waterfall pouring down through the organization and drowning those at the bottom. It is a top down process. People lower down have to accept the objectives and like them – or else. Cascading provides no room for people contributing to the agreement of their objectives. Waterfalls don't cascade upwards.

Of course, if organizations and departments exist to fulfil a purpose and if certain overall targets have to be achieved, everyone must work towards them. To this extent at least, there will always have to be a strong top-down element in objective setting. But there is no reason why there should not be a bottom-up process as well – individuals and teams being given the opportunity to contribute to the formulation of their objectives within the framework of overall corporate and departmental expectations. In fact, there is every reason why they should be given scope to contribute. This is the principle of 'ownership'. If people contribute to establishing their objectives they are much more likely to be committed to achieving them – to own them.

PERFORMANCE MANAGEMENT AS A CONTINUOUS PROCESS

Performance management takes place within the framework of agreed expectations and objectives in the context of the mutual understanding of competence or capability requirements. It should be regarded as a continuous process.

It is also a cyclical process as illustrated in Figure 20.1.

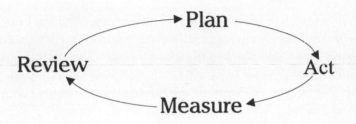

Figure 20.1   The managing performance cycle

The managing performance cycle comprises the following activities which are carried out jointly by the manager and the individual:

- Plan – the agreement of objectives, targets and needs for the development of competences or capabilities and the preparation of plans to achieve objectives, improve performance and develop capabilities.

- Act – the implementation of the plan in the normal course of work and through special improvement and development programmes.

- Measure – monitor performance (actions) by reference to performance measures – what has been achieved (outcomes) with what should have been achieved (plans). Also monitor the implementation of personal development plans by measuring, so far as this is possible, improvements in capability.

- Review – take stock at regular interviews, but not just once a year, of achievements in relation to the plan as established by measuring outcomes. Reflect on how capabilities have developed and how well they have been applied. Use any points agreed at reviews as the basis for forward plans, the next stage in the cycle.

And so on...

WHAT MANAGERS CAN DO ABOUT MANAGING PERFORMANCE

To manage performance effectively you need to:

- be clear about what you are expected to achieve in terms of objectives, targets and standards of performance

- be clear about what the teams and individuals reporting to you are expected to achieve

- ensure that your expectations concerning objectives, targets, standards of performance, capability requirements and areas for improvement or development are made clear and agreed with your teams

- identify performance measures which you and your team can use to monitor performance so that action can be taken to achieve improvements as required

- develop and apply your skills in agreeing objectives and capability requirements, reviewing performance (including the provision of feedback), helping people to formulate and implement personal development plans, dealing with the under-performers, coaching and counselling. These skills are dealt with in later chapters of the book.

PERFORMANCE APPRAISAL AND PERFORMANCE MANAGEMENT

Performance appraisal

Performance appraisal schemes are the traditional methods developed by organizations to assess and rate performance.

A typical performance appraisal scheme has the following features:

- it is owned by the personnel department which lays down the rules on how it is to be applied by line managers

- it concentrates on a one-to-one relationship between managers and their subordinates which may include setting objectives against which performance will be appraised

- the centre point of the scheme is a performance appraisal meeting during which managers appraise the performance of their subordinates and, usually, rate that performance overall or under a number of headings against a scale – this is sometimes described as merit rating which involves allocating points under headings such as judgement and initiative, a largely discredited procedure

- the outcome of the appraisal meeting is documented on an appraisal form, often an elaborate affair

- the appraisal form is held by the personnel department, quite often not to be referred to again unless it is pulled out and used as evidence in an unfair dismissal case.

Performance appraisal schemes with these characteristics frequently fail. Neither managers nor subordinates like them. They are seen, especially by managers, as an unnecessary intrusion engineered by personnel which gets in the way of their real work. The recipients of appraisals may resent the top down nature of the system and believe that it is intrinsically unfair because it depends entirely on the judgement, which could be biased, of managers. Performance appraisal meetings conducted by unwilling and unskilled managers are more likely to demotivate people than to motivate them. Above all, they are perceived as isolated from what really matters and irrelevant to the manager's task of managing performance.

Performance management

The concept of performance management first emerged in the 1980s. It was seen as a means of overcoming the weaknesses of traditional performance appraisal schemes described above.

Performance management processes incorporate performance appraisals or, as it is more frequently called, performance reviews, as an important feature. The term review is preferred by some people because it can be interpreted as a joint process while performance appraisal has a from high to low – a top down – connotation.

The characteristics of a fully developed performance management process are that it:

- is concerned with the total performance of the organization and how the efforts of teams and individuals contribute to that performance

- is seen as an integrating process – integrating corporate, functional, team and individual objectives and linked closely with other aspects of personnel management

- is regarded as a normal, everyday process of management, not an administrative chore imposed by the personnel department

- is based on the principle that managers, their teams as a whole and the individuals in those teams are partners in the process – it is not something administered by bosses to their subordinates

- is concerned as much with team performance as individual performance

- is a continuous process, not relying on a once-a-year formal review

- focuses on competence or capability requirements as well as the achievement of objectives (ie inputs and outputs)

- is concerned primarily with performance improvement and personal development, in some cases more importance is attached to the developmental aspects of performance management

- may or may not be linked to a performance-related pay scheme – more and more organizations are severing the connection on the grounds that it contaminates the developmental aspects of performance management

- may or may not include performance ratings, partly because they are believed to be unnecessary if there is no direct link to performance-related pay, but also because it is deemed impossible and invidious to sum up a person's whole performance by one figure or letter (in fact, many organizations have dropped ratings even when they have a performance pay scheme because it turns the attention of people away from their development needs to how much money they are going to get after the review)

- does not rely on elaborate forms or procedures – the records of agreements and reviews are retained by individuals and their managers and are often not held by the personnel department

- recognizes the need for the thorough training of both parties (ie managers and individuals, in the skills required to agree objectives, establish capability requirements, measure and review performance, provide and accept feedback and implement personal development plans

- overall, attaches much more importance to the 'processes' of jointly forming agreements, managing performance throughout the year and monitoring and reviewing achievements than to the content of what is sometimes called a 'performance management system' – by implication a set of mechanisms to get people to do certain things in certain ways.

PERFORMANCE MANAGEMENT AS A PROCESS

The process of performance management is essentially holistic. It takes an all-embracing view of the constituents of good performance and how it contributes to desired outcomes at individual, team, department and organizational, levels.

Performance management is about improving both results and the quality of working relationships. The effective use of performance management processes means that people are clear about what they are expected to achieve and their priorities, know what they should be doing now and in the future to improve their performance and capabilities, and what they can do individually and as team members to contribute to the attainment of team and corporate objectives. At SEEBOARD the introduction of new performance processes was driven by the realisation that management did not know enough about how staff perform; appraisal and reward tended to be based on 'gut feeling' rather than performance.

THE APPROACH TO MANAGING PERFORMANCE

It cannot be emphasized strongly enough that the management of performance is something you are doing all the time. It is not a separate system or procedure. But there are certain approaches to managing performance which, suitably adapted to your own circumstances and natural management style, can help you to do it better. These approaches can be summarized as follows:

■ remember that every time you agree with people that something needs to be done, review with them how they have done it and, where necessary, discuss how they can do it better next time, you are managing performance

■ treat managing performance as a continuing dialogue between you, your team and individual team members – it is a two-way process; you have to take account of their views

■ regard yourself and your team as partners working within a framework which sets out how you can best co-operate to achieve the required results

■   use the plan-act-measure-review model as the framework for managing performance but do not apply it too rigidly.

APPROACHES TO PERFORMANCE MANAGEMENT

The following are three examples of approaches to performance management.

A packaging company

The objective of the 'performance review' system in this company is to focus shop floor teams on business objectives. As the HR Manager said:

> It's to focus them, as a team, on how they can contribute towards the success of the business in terms of their objectives. How can we get rid of the things that are stopping them achieving their objectives and enhance the things that are helping them to achieve their objectives? How can we give them the training and development needed to do better in their own jobs? It is all linked around the needs of the business.

The reasons for introducing this blue-collar scheme were as follows:

■   The need to increase capacity in line with targets set by the parent company.

■   The need to reflect objectives set at levels higher up (eg for total site capacity) at the lowest level by cascading site objectives down to each shift (and shift managers), and each team (and team co-ordinators) within each shift.

There was no systematic way of agreeing targets with teams, reviewing performance, giving feedback or identifying training needs. As the HR Manager said:

> It seemed ludicrous not to be doing something for the bulk of our workforce for whom objectives, and improvement and training, were absolutely paramount.

The nature of the working environment – large teams working for one manager. In general people in each team face the same problems. There was a need for a team-based approach where people couldn't blame others in the team for failure to perform individually and which would encourage people to get together in teams and talk about problems.

Bass Brewers

Performance management at Bass Brewers represents best practice in the following ways:

- emphasis on developing people to increase the added value they can provide for the business
- focus on competencies – their definition, assessment and development
- a powerful personal development planning process
- link to a broad-banded pay structure.

A shipping company

The reasons for introducing performance management in this company were:

- there was no focused development – training was providing 'buffet style', where employees were given a list of courses and told to say what training they wished to do
- people were uncertain of what was expected of them – there was no formal method of feedback so people didn't know how they were doing. They knew only that people who didn't perform were asked to leave at the end of the year
- the career structure was traditional and hierarchical – people promoted to management positions tended to be those who had joined the firm as office juniors and worked their way up
- pay was unstructured – reward increases were granted on the basis of the chairman's decision or in response to a direct request. People wanted pay to be based more directly on performance
- the concept of annual appraisal was totally discredited – five previous attempts had been made to introduce it, but without adequate training or preparation, and it was perceived as being too subjective.

FURTHER READING

Armstrong M (1994) *Performance Management*, Kogan Page.
Walters, M (ed.) (1995) *The Performance Management Handbook*, Institute of Personnel and Development, London.

21

MANAGING EXPECTATIONS

A fundamental aspect of the process of managing performance is the management of expectations. This takes place by reaching agreement on the objectives to be achieved and the capabilities or competencies required to attain them. The performance management cycle starts from this point with a performance agreement which forms the basis for the performance and personal development plan.

OBJECTIVES

What are objectives?

An objective describes something which has to be accomplished, either as a point to be aimed at (a target), a plan or a project to be implemented or completed, a standard of performance to be achieved and maintained, personal development objectives to be achieved, or values to be maintained. These are described below.

Targets

Objectives can be expressed as quantified targets such as:

- increase output by 3 per cent over the next six months
- meet sales targets as set out in the three monthly sales budgets for the region

■ reduce cost per unit of output by 2 per cent over the next twelve months

■ open at least 10 potentially profitable new accounts over the next six months

■ reduce downtime by 3 per cent over the next six months

■ reduce the level of defects from 1.5 to 1.0 per cent over the next three months

■ reduce inventory levels to £12m within six months

■ increase the customer satisfaction index as established by the customer reaction survey by 2.0 per cent over the next twelve months

■ reduce employee turnover by 1.0 per cent over the next twelve months

■ reduce absenteeism by 1.0 per cent over the next twelve months.

Characteristics of a good objective

The characteristics of a good objective when expressed as a target is often summed up by the acronym SMART:

S = stretching/specific
M = measurable
A = agreed
R = relevant/realistic (appropriate and achievable)
T = time related

Plans and projects

An objective can be expressed as a plan to be implemented or a project to be completed satisfactorily. The agreement on what has to be achieved could be summarized in a line or two, possibly referring to the detailed plan or the project terms of reference and timetable to provide supporting information.

Objectives in the form of plans or projects can be described as follows:

■ plan and introduce a fully effective system of MRP2 within the next 12 months

■ develop a skill-based pay with supporting training programmes to be introduced within two years

■ conduct the pilot testing and product launching of new product X over the next three months

■ contribute as a member of the project team to the business process re-engineering exercise planned to take place over the next 12 months

■ set up and facilitate a project team to develop and launch by the end of next year a new approach to performance management.

The SMART criteria for a good objective applies also to projects and plans.

Standards of performance

Performance standards define the level of performance expected for a particular aspect of the work on a continuing basis. However, they will be modified from time to time as circumstances change, especially when it is thought that the standards should be tightened or the expected level of performance increased. A performance standard in effect completes the statements: 'This aspect of the work will have been well done when...' or 'Performance will be up to standard when...'

Here are some examples of how these statements could be completed:

■ '... the JIT system operates consistently at the rate determined by the final product-assembly schedule'.

■ '... systematic recruitment and selection procedures are maintained which provide a wholly acceptable service to line managers'.

■ '... queries on products and prices from customers are answered to their satisfaction within one working day'.

■ '... proposals for new product development are fully supported by data provided from properly conducted product research, market research and product testing'.

■ '... customer orders are acknowledged the same day and deliveries out of stock are made within the next three days in the UK'.

■ '... co-operative and productive relationships are maintained with fellow team members'.

■ '... a level of customer satisfaction is maintained in which complaints do not exceed 0.1 per cent (1:1,000 transactions)'.

- '… 90 per cent of customer complaints are dealt with inside 24 hours – the remaining to be acknowledged the same day and answered within three working days'.

- '… an accurate, speedy and helpful service is provided to users'.

Some of these examples are quantified and these figures may be changed, as required. But the underlying objects (level of service delivery to internal and external clients, swift turnaround, delivery to time, customer satisfaction) remain as standing or continuing objectives.

Some performance standards cannot be quantified. They have to be defined qualitatively. But this definition can spell out what the qualitative requirements mean in terms of expectations about a satisfactory standard of service delivery or behaviour. For example, a performance standard for a personnel manager may be to provide an acceptable and efficient recruitment service. The standard may state that the level of service meets this requirement is one that includes:

- a prompt response to requests for advice and help in recruitment

- the rapid delivery of acceptable person specifications, draft advertisements

- the use of psychometric tests which have been properly validated and provide useful insights for selection purposes

- the delivery by an agreed deadline of a short list of candidates who meet the specification, supported by helpful profiles.

Even in this example, some of the qualitative standards could be quantified. It could be agreed that the response to requests should be made within one working day, and person specifications delivered within three working days.

Personal objectives

Personal objectives set out what individuals agree to do to develop their capabilities and improve their performance. They may be expressed in a personal development plan as discussed in Chapter 28.

Values

Objectives may be agreed which describe how individuals and teams are expected to uphold the core values of the organization.

The typical values which can be incorporated in a set of objectives are:

■ customer service (internal as well as external)

■ teamwork

■ developing people (for managers and team leaders).

Definitions of the behaviour expected to support such values are agreed with teams and individuals as objectives. For example, a team's objectives for teamwork could be expressed as follows:

We recognize that our objectives for teamwork are to:

■ agree work plans and critical success factors

■ ensure that every team member is given the opportunity to contribute to the maximum of his or her potential

■ work together flexibly and co-operatively, accepting that we are inter-dependent and rely on the support and contribution of fellow team workers

■ jointly review our progress and performance and agree on any corrective actions that may be required.

Agreeing objectives

So far as possible, you should get your team as a whole and its individual members to take part in setting objectives and obtain their agreement to them. Of course, this has to be done within the context of the objectives to which you have agreed and the overall objectives of the organization to which you and your team contribute. You have to say, for example: 'This is the target set by top management for improving productivity over the next financial year. This, amongst other targets, is the target I have agreed to achieve for reducing downtime in this department. Now, how are we going to work together to achieve this target? What contribution do you think you can make?'

Or: 'Top management has set me the task of improving levels of customer service, especially our speed of response. Let's look at what we are achieving now and discuss what room there is for improvement and how we are going to do it together'.

Sometimes you may not be able to reach agreement. You will then have to say something to the effect that: 'I'm sorry, but we really do have to improve our turn round of enquiries. I think we must try to reduce the time taken to one working day. Now, how are we going to do this?' If you get the response that this is impossible you may have to state firmly that it can be done, if that is really the case. You can explain how and, possibly, quote benchmark examples of teams or organizations facing the same situation, and with similar systems and resources, who have done it. This is where your qualities of leadership come to the fore. Good leaders are capable of taking people with them and getting them to accept challenges which they did not feel they were capable of meeting. But good leaders also explain why and how, and tell people what support they are going to get.

The steps required to agree objectives

1 Identify and agree the key result areas for the team or individual.
2 As appropriate, indicate for key result areas the targets, plans, projects, standards of performance or values which have been defined at organizational and departmental levels and which must be taken into account in coming to an agreement on what the team or individual should be expected to achieve.
3 Ask the team as a whole, or individual members, what targets or tandards of performance they believe can be achieved for the key result areas.
4 Discuss the suggested targets and standards and agree on any modifications.
5 Agree on the performance measures that can be used or the sort of evidence that can be obtained to indicate the extent to which targets and standards have been attained.

AGREEING TO CAPABILITY REQUIREMENTS

Capability or competence requirements can be analysed for roles as described in chapter 15. But it is a good idea to go through these with individuals to discuss how they apply in their particular case. You can ask them to tell you what they think they need to know and be able to do to perform their job well. If this is agreed you can then discuss how you will both know that these capabilities are being used well.

PERFORMANCE MEASURES

Measurement is a key aspect of managing performance – 'if you can't measure it, you can't improve it'. You will waste your time if you agree objectives and standards unless you and the individuals concerned know how performance will be measured.

The four basic types of measurement are:

- *Money measures*, including income, expenditure and rates of return
- *Effort or impact measures* include the achievement of a target, completion of a task or project, the level of take-up of a service and the influence exerted over the behaviour of colleagues, clients or customers
- *Reaction measures* indicate how other colleagues, customers etc. judge the jobholder
- *Time measures* express performance against timetables or deadlines, the speed of response and the amount of backlog.

The following are guidelines for defining performance measures:

- measures should relate to results, not efforts
- the results must be within the jobholder's control
- measures should be objective and observable
- data must be readily available for measurement
- existing measures should be used or adapted wherever possible.

The following is an example of a list of performance measures for a factory manager:

1 Output – production targets
2 Product quality – statistical quality control returns indicating variances outside specified limits; number of justified complaints on quality received from customers.
3 Productivity – output per employee; added value per employee.
4 Cost control – cost per unit of production; maintaining variances in standard costs within prescribed limits; keeping within cost budgets; waste or scrap levels in relation to budget.
5 Stock control – ratio of inventory to current assets; achievement of agreed customer service levels; incidence of stockouts.
6 Utilization of plant and machinery – percentage utilization; amount of downtime.
7 Health and safety – accident frequency/severity rates; health and safety audit reports
8 Employee relations – incidence of disputes and grievances; results of employee attitude surveys

9   Employment – absenteeism and timekeeping figures; disciplinary actions and appeals.
10 Employee development – achievement of multi-skilling development programme.

FURTHER READING

Williams S, 'Objectives' in Neale F (ed) (1992) *Performance Management*, Institute of Personnel and Development, London.

22

CONDUCTING PERFORMANCE AND DEVELOPMENT REVIEWS

REVIEW MEETINGS

As has been mentioned several times earlier, effective management of performance is a continuing process – managing performance throughout the year. But periodical reviews are necessary for managers and individuals to jointly consider how things are going and to agree on reward objectives and plans in the light of the review or changing circumstances. In a sense, this is a stocktaking exercise.

The important thing to remember, and this point cannot be emphasized enough, is that this should not be a formal annual event in which you parade your subordinates in front of you in turn, tell them what you think of them, define or re-define their objectives, rate them and fill in the form. It is ludicrous to believe that in situations where change is the only thing remaining constant that it is possible to tie performance management down to a single annual event. Performance reviews should be held as and when necessary. And they can be almost completely informal. If you ask people 'How are things going?' and they tell you, that is a performance review. If you drop by someone's office and say: 'Thank you, that was a good job well done' you have conducted a performance review. When you have to call someone into your office and say: 'We don't seem to be making enough progress – what's the problem and what can we do about it?' you are reviewing, and therefore managing, performance.

However, these are examples of on-the-spot reviews, and although they are how performance is managed on a day-to-day basis, both parties – you and the members of your team – will benefit if an overview of progress and a general discussion of objectives and plans for the future takes place on a somewhat more formal and regular basis. It can be once a quarter, twice a year or even once a month in a fast-moving situation. But a year's gap between reviews is too long.

In this chapter reviewing and discussing performance and development needs (the two go together) are discussed under the following headings:

☐ Who is involved?

☐ General guidelines on conducting a performance and development review or discussion with an individual.

☐ Preparing for the discussion.

■ How to analyse individual performance and development needs.

☐ How to provide feedback to individuals.

☐ Other performance and development review skills.

☐ Completing the discussion with individuals.

☐ Typical individual review problems and how to solve them.

■ Conducting team review meetings.

WHO IS INVOLVED?

The one-to-one meeting

The most typical situation is a meeting between the manager or team leader and the individual. This is a joint affair. You are acting in partnership with the member of your team to promote both your interests. Your aim should be to ensure that the meeting is run as a dialogue to which you both contribute, without either party dominating it.

In a one-to-one review meeting the individuals will analyse their own performance and development needs and you will provide feedback. You then, together, agree on a development action plan.

Upward assessment or feedback

The individual review meeting can, and indeed should, include an opportunity for individuals to comment on how they perceive they are being managed by you. This feedback should aim to identify things which you can do which will improve their performance.

This is, of course, a delicate process, which depends on the creation of mutual trust and a willingness on your part to accept constructive criticism, and on their part to be constructive, and to base their views on actual experiences rather than emotional reactions. Upward assessment or appraisal does not work when managers are autocratic and their subordinates are cowed. But then, if this is the situation, the relationship is so flawed that performance improvement will only be achieved by grudging submission rather than willing agreement.

In some organizations, upward assessments are made by getting team members to complete a questionnaire and feeding the results back to their manager anonymously. A typical statement in a questionnaire to which responses will be invited could be worded like this:

> 'My manager makes it absolutely clear to me what I am expected to do.'

The people completing the questionnaire could be asked to tick what they believe to be the most appropriate one of the following comments: fully agree, partly agree, partly disagree, fully disagree.

The argument for upward assessment is that bosses will learn more about how they manage by comments from the receiving end rather than from above. In some organizations, upward assessments are made by getting team members to complete a questionnaire, the results of which are fed back anonymously to the manager.

Upward assessment or 180-degree feedback is perhaps most effective when all the parties concerned agree that it is worth doing voluntarily.

Peer assessment

Peer assessment takes place when fellow team members or colleagues assess one another for their contribution to team effort and their performance as team workers – collaborating well with others, communicating well and working flexibly. Again, the argument in favour of peer assessment is that team members know more about how they work together than their manager or team leader. Peer assessment can also be carried out by internal customers for service providers. But, like upward assessment, it works best when it is a voluntarily agreed process.

360-degree feedback

360-degree feed back or assessment combines assessments from individuals' managers, direct and indirect reports, peers (fellow team members) and, often, internal and external customers. Individuals may also be asked to assess themselves. The emphasis is on interpersonal skills and behaviour. The feedback should be directed at describing behaviour rather than judging it.

The usual approach is to use structured questionnaires, which are completed anonymously and are confidential to the individual. However, organizations which have introduced 360-degree assessment usually provide some form of counseling which enables people to interpret the feedback and prepare action plans for self-development.

OVERALL GUIDELINES ON CONDUCTING PERFORMANCE AND DEVELOPMENT DISCUSSIONS

Performance and development discussions or review meetings enable a perspective to be obtained by both parties on past performance as a basis for agreeing development plans for the future. The discussion should enable individuals to reflect on what they have done and how they have done it. They are then in a better position, in conjunction with their managers, to look ahead. Using the joint analysis of performance as a means of obtaining historical perspective is a necessary part of a performance and development discussion, but reaching agreement about what should be done next is what the discussion is really all about.

The basis of the performance and development discussion

This discussion provides the means through which the five key elements of performance and development reviews can take effect. These are:

1   Measurement – assessing results and progress against agreed targets, standards and development plans.
2   Feedback – providing individuals with information on how they have been doing (this can work two ways, ie upwards as well as downwards).
3   Positive reinforcement – emphasizing what has been done well so it can be done equally well if not better in the future; only making constructive criticisms, ie those that point the way to improvement.
4   Exchange of views – ensuring that the discussion involves a full, free and frank exchange of views about what has been achieved, what needs to be done to achieve more and what individuals think about the work, the way they are managed and their future.
5   Agreement – jointly coming to an understanding about what must be done by both parties to improve performance, develop knowledge,

skills and capabilities and overcome any work problems raised during the discussion.

Key aspects of the discussion

When you get together with someone to conduct a performance and development review your aim should be to engage in a dialogue about that person's work and development. The discussion should take the form of a free-flowing conversation in which both parties are fully involved. But, like a selection interview, this is a conversation with a purpose, that purpose being to reach firm and agreed conclusions about the future – revised objectives, any areas for improvement, development needs and how improvements will be achieved and development needs satisfied.

Remember that when you are conducting a review you are not acting as prosecutor, jury and judge combined. You are not just weighing the evidence and passing sentence – 'You're in box 3, not box 2'. You are there to help individuals understand what they are expected to do, improve their performance and develop their skills. A review meeting is an exercise in leadership. Your principal aim should be to use the discussion as a means of motivating people. You should be more of a coach and a counsellor than a boss.

There is no one right way of conducting a performance and development discussion. And there is no disguising the fact that it is difficult to do well. Managers are often reluctant to do it, either believing wrongly that they have better things to do or simply being nervous about giving feedback. Even if they do not mind doing it they do not always do it well.

To carry out a good performance and development review requires high levels of inter-personal skills. But do not despair. These skills can be practiced and developed and, if this process is supported by the organization, training, coaching and continued guidance should be made available. You will get off to a good start if you are aware of what skills are needed and how to use them. Then it is a matter of putting your skills to the test. If you are conducting a review meeting for the first time it is a good idea to involve someone with whom you get on well and who will be able to give you frank but positive feedback on how you did. A few pilot tests will enable you to approach any more difficult meetings with confidence.

Guidelines for conducting performance and development discussions

The following are the basic guidelines which are developed more fully in later sections of this chapter:

Preparing for and conducting the meeting:

prepare carefully

work to a clear but flexible structure

create a supportive atmosphere

let the individual do most of the talking

encourage self-assessment

keep the whole period under review

- no surprises – do not suddenly launch criticisms about past behaviour which should have been raised at the time

- be positive – give praise where praise is due and criticize constructively.

Use interpersonal skills:

- seek information by asking the right questions

- listen

be sensitive to the other person's concerns

- observe and respond to non-verbal signals

be open to criticism

test understanding

reach agreement.

Complete the discussion:

check understanding

summarize and confirm plans

make a record of the agreement on future objectives and the personal development plan.

PREPARATION

Setting up meetings

You should set up meetings a few days in advance to give both you and the individual concerned time to prepare along the lines described below. Brief individuals on why the meeting is going to take place, emphasizing its positive nature – it will not be a fault-finding exercise. You should do as much as you can to reduce any fears about the forthcoming discussion.

Preparation by the manager

You should consider the points you want to bring out in the discussion in advance. You will need to illustrate these points with actual examples. Your role is to bring out the facts not to indulge in value judgements and unsupported opinions.

The basis for the discussion should be any performance agreement and development plan which emerged from an earlier meeting. This should set out objectives and a personal development plan.

If this is the first time you have held a review meeting with someone your aim should be to concentrate on the future (there may, of course, be no past to consider). The future will be defined in terms of objectives at this stage and you need to think about these by reference to the person's role definition, which should set out the key result areas. If no such definition exists the first thing you will have to do at the meeting will be to agree what these areas are, and then discuss objectives for each area. The development plan can then be considered by reference to what people have to be able to do and your joint understanding of what they need to learn to do it well.

The following is a checklist of the points you should consider at a performance review:

Performance and development analysis

- How well do you think the individual has done in achieving the agreed objectives over the period? – provide examples.

- How well have any improvement, development or training plans as agreed at the last review meeting, been put into effect? – provide supporting evidence.

■ Are there any aspects of performance which deserve particular praise and should be mentioned during the meeting? – be specific, provide examples.

■ Are there any aspects of performance which have not been up to standard and should be pointed out to the individual? – be specific, provide examples.

■ What approach are you going to adopt to ensure that any criticisms you make are constructive (ie they lead to plans to overcome the problem) and will be accepted by the individual?

■ What are the factors which you think may have affected the performance of the individual? – consider factors which were both within and beyond the individual's control. Try to think of any particular events or observed behaviour which may have influenced the results achieved.

Support for the individual

■ Are you satisfied that you have given the individual sufficient guidance and support? Is there any additional guidance or help which you could provide?

■ Are you satisfied that the individual has the amount of resources and/or authority needed to carry out the work effectively?

Development needs

■ Are there any areas where knowledge, skills or capabilities need to be developed?

■ Is there any additional experience, coaching or training from which the individual would benefit?

The individual's present and future

■ Is the best use being made of the individual's skills and abilities? If not, what should be done?

■ Is the individual ready to take on additional responsibilities in the present job? If so, what and when?

■ Would the individual benefit from getting wider experience?

■ What is the individual's potential in this organization?

Content of performance agreement and development plan

- What changes, if any, are required to the individual's role definition and its key result areas?

- What objectives for each of these key result areas would you like to agree over the next period?

- What sort of work or performance improvement plan would you like to agree with the individual?

- What sort of personal development plan would you like to see adopted by the individual?

- What action do you need to take personally to provide additional guidance or coaching?

Preparation by the individual

It is equally important to get individuals to prepare for the meeting. The following is a checklist as a basis for self-assessment and for noting points to be raised during the discussion.

Individual's preparation checklist

- Taking each of any key result areas in turn, how well have I done?

- To what extent have I achieved any objectives as agreed at the last meeting?

- If I have not managed to achieve these objectives, why?

- How well have I got on with implementing my personal development plan?

- Are there any specific aspects of the work where there may be room for improvement or further learning? If so, what am I going to do about them?

- What objectives do I believe should be set for each of my key result areas over the next period?

- What steps do I think will be necessary to ensure that I achieve these objectives?

- Would I have benefited from better, guidance, help and training from my manager/team leader? If so, what form should it take?

CONDUCTING THE REVIEW MEETING

Essentially, the review meeting is about:

- where individuals have got to
- where they are going
- how they are going to get there
- what they feel able to do
- how they feel about the support and guidance you provide
- what they believe they need to learn and how they are going to learn it.

To conduct an effective review meeting you have to:

- work to a clear but flexible structure
- create and maintain the right atmosphere
- know how to open the discussion
- let the individual do most of the talking
- encourage self-assessment
- keep the whole period under review – no surprises
- base assessments on evidence – events and observed behaviour
- provide feedback – recognizing achievements, reinforcing strengths and, as necessary, criticizing constructively
- adopt a joint problem-solving approach
- use interpersonal skills
- complete the meeting with an agreement on objectives and an action plan.

Structuring the meeting

Every performance and development meeting is a unique occasion. You should plan and conduct it in accordance with the needs and personalities of both parties. You should not try to stick to a rigid agenda and the discussion should proceed flexibly – responding to issues and comments as they arise. But you should retain a reasonable amount of control. It is your job to steer the meeting to a positive conclusion in an hour or so.

Bearing in mind these caveats, a typical framework would look something like this:

- a review of achievements compared with agreed objectives, taking each of the key result areas in turn

- a review of progress in implementing the personal development plan

- a general discussion of any matters of concern about the job

- a discussion of the individual's aspirations

- a discussion and agreement on objectives for the next period

- a discussion and agreement on a personal development plan.

Creating the right atmosphere

You won't get anywhere if, having changed the date several times, you haul individuals into your office, plonk them down in front of a barrier provided by a formidable desk, fire a battery of questions and criticisms at them for 20 minutes or so and then spend a minute or two ticking boxes in a form provided by the personnel department.

This may seem to be an exaggeration but all too often it happens along these lines. And it's a waste of everyone's time. You need to:

- inform individuals in advance of the date and time of the meeting – and stick to it

- put individuals at their ease – don't hit them with criticisms at the outset

- start the discussion with an invitation to individuals to talk to you generally about how they have progressed since the last meeting – say something along the lines of: 'Would you like to tell me about how you feel you have been getting on since our last review meeting?'

Let the individuals do most of the talking

During the meeting you will want individuals to feel free (within certain limits) to talk about their work and objectives. You need to give them plenty of time to talk through the issues and put forward their own ideas.

Encourage self-appraisal

To get positive results from the meeting you have to try to involve people actively in the review process. If you can get them to analyse and assess their own performance as a basis for discussion this is likely to produce more positive attitudes. It will also reduce defensive reactions which can happen when the criticisms come from above.

You can initiate a discussion by asking such open questions as:

- How do you feel you have done?
- What are you best at doing?
- What do you think have been your major achievements recently?
- Are there any parts of your job you find difficult?
- Are there any parts of your work in which you feel you would benefit from further training?

Keep the whole period under review

You should not just refer to recent events, although because they are fresh in your mind you may be tempted to do so. You should review performance over the whole period and encourage the individual to do the same.

No surprises

Do not deliver unexpected criticisms – there should be no surprises. The focus of the discussion should reflect day-to-day events and contacts. It should be concerned only with events or behaviours which have been noted and discussed at the time they took place. Feedback on performance should be immediate and continuous, it should not wait until the review meeting. If you say to an individual 'What about that mistake you made last January in preparing the schedule?' and this is the first time he or she has been made aware of it, the only reaction you will get is a hostile one.

Base assessments on evidence

Any comments you make on the performance of individuals should be based on evidence – actual events and observed behaviour. You are not there to criticize the person. You are there to provide helpful feedback on your observation about what people have done and how they have been carrying out their work. Any comments you make should be supported by evidence and your aim should be to get agreement on how that evidence should be interpreted and what the implications are for the future development and behaviour of the individual. Your interpretation of the event may not be the same as the individual's but you have to attempt to reconcile any differences.

So you need to say something like this: 'Do you remember that situation last September when you presented me with your sales budget? Can you recall what happened?' If the recall is correct you could say next, 'Well, what did you learn from that?' If the recall is incorrect you might have to say: 'Well, I remember it somewhat differently; would you agree that it went like this? I made a note of it at the time to that effect'. You may reach an impasse sometimes but it is worth trying hard to get agreement. You could then comment on what has been said about the lessons learned. If you agree you could simply say: 'Good, so what have you been doing about it?' If you are not satisfied on actions taken you might have to comment 'Yes, but what about...?' or, 'Yes, but have you thought of...?' At this stage you might have to become more directive but always by putting questions for the person to consider. Incidentally, the phrase 'Yes, but...' is useful on some occasions. It conveys that you accept in general what has been said, however there is, in your view, more to it which ought to be discussed.

Giving feedback

Giving feedback based on fact not subjective judgement is an important part of a performance and development discussion. In this respect at least performance meetings have some of the characteristics of a system in that they provide for information to be presented (feedback) to people on their performance, which helps them to understand how well they have been doing and how effective that behaviour has been. The aim is for feedback to promote this understanding so that appropriate action can be taken. This can be corrective action where the feedback has indicated that something has gone wrong or, more positively, action can be taken to make the best use of the opportunities the feedback has revealed. In the latter case, feedback acts as a reinforcement and positive feedback can be a powerful motivator because it is a recognition of achievement.

Guidelines on giving feedback

■ *Build feedback into the job*. To be effective, feedback should be built into the job. Individuals or teams should be able to find out easily how they have done from the control information readily available to them. If it cannot be built into the job it should be provided as quickly as possible after the activity has taken place, ideally within a day or two.

- *Provide feedback on actual events.* As mentioned above, feedback should be provided on actual results or observed behaviour. You should, for example, say: 'We have received a complaint from a customer that you have been rude. Would you like to comment on this?' You should not say: 'You tend to be aggressive.'

- *Describe, don't judge.* The feedback should be presented as a description of what has happened. It should not be accompanied by a judgement. If you say: 'I have been informed that you have been rude to one of our customers: we can't tolerate this sort of behaviour' you will instantly create resistance and prejudice an opportunity to encourage improvement.

- *Refer to specific behaviours.* Relate all your feedback to specific items of behaviour. Do not transmit general feelings or impressions.

- *Ask questions.* Ask questions rather than make statements: 'Why do you think this happened?' On reflection, is there any other way in which you think you could have handled the situation?', 'What are the factors that influenced you to make that decision?'

- *Get people to work things out for themselves.* Encourage people to come to their own conclusions about what they should do or how they should behave. Ask questions such as: 'How do you think you should tackle this sort of problem in the future?', 'How do you feel you could avoid getting into this situation again?'

- *Select key issues.* Select key issues and restrict yourself to them. There is a limit to how much criticism anyone can take. If you overdo it, the shutters will go up and you will get nowhere.

- *Focus.* Focus on aspects of performance the individual can improve. It is a waste of time to concentrate on areas which the individual can do little or nothing about.

- *Show understanding.* If something has gone wrong show that you understand that there may have been circumstances beyond the individual's control which affected the result.

Adopt a joint problem-solving approach

In this approach you abandon the role of a judge and become a helper. You are not telling people what to do, you help them to work it out for themselves. You don't hand an appraisal down to an appraisee. Instead, a discussion takes place on any work problem individuals have met. They are encouraged to think through their own solutions to the problems, including any changes in their behaviour to achieve improvement. You must ensure that people make suggestions which are both realistic and practical and that they accept the responsibility for taking the actions required with your help as necessary.

You can encourage people by asking questions such as:

■ 'How do you propose to do that?'

■ 'What are the specific steps you think you need to take?'

■ 'Do you think you will meet any problems in getting this done?'

■ 'What would you do if you found you were not getting the information on time?'

The 'what if?' approach is often fruitful as a means of generating ideas as well as for exploring the practicality of a proposed course of action. It can be used to prompt individuals who are slow in coming up with ideas themselves. Ask questions such as:

■ '*What if* we had a look at the filing system to see if we could simplify it? What would that mean doing?'

■ '*What if* we called a meeting of your most important clients to get their ideas on what sort of service they want from you? How would you approach such a meeting?'

Interpersonal skills

Interpersonal skills are the ones you use when you are relating to other people: building and maintaining relationships, getting them to do something, telling them something, asking them something, seeking their help or co-operation and so on. Interpersonal skills involve both verbal behaviour (asking or replying to questions, making statements, persuading, negotiating etc.) and non-verbal behaviour (facing people, looking at them, reacting physically to what they say or do by nodding or smiling).

Interpersonal skills are used in all forms of interviewing (selection, disciplinary etc.) as well as in performance and development discussions. Basically, the same skills are used but they may be applied differently to meet the demands of the situation. The main skills used are questioning, listening, influencing and non-verbal behaviour (body language).

Questioning

As in the case of selection interviewing, open questions to create an atmosphere of calm and friendly enquiry should be used extensively. They can be expressed quite informally, for example:

'How do you think things are going?'

'What do you feel about that?'

'How can we build on that for the future?'

'What can we learn from that?'

Open questions can be put in a 'tell me' form, such as:

'Tell me, how did you handle that situation?'

- 'Tell me, how is this project going?'

- 'Tell me, what do you think your key objectives are going to be next year?'

The important type of question is the probe question which seeks specific information on what has happened and why. Probe questions can:

- show interest and encouragement by making supportive statements followed by questions: 'I see, and then what?'

- seek further information by asking 'Why?' or 'Why not?' or 'What do you mean?'

- explore attitudes: 'To what extent do you believe that…?'

- reflect views: 'Have I got the right impression, do you feel that…?'

Listening

You must listen carefully, bearing in mind the old saying that hearing is with the ears, listening is with the mind. Good listeners:

concentrate on the speaker

are alert at all times to the nuances of what is being said

- respond quickly when appropriate but do not interrupt unnecessarily

ask questions to clarify meaning

comment as necessary on the points made to demonstrate understanding but not at length.

Influencing

Although you want people to think things through for themselves you may need to influence them to go in the right direction. The influencing skills you can use are:

- *Asserting* – making your views clear.

- *Persuading* – using facts, logic and reason to make your case.

- *Bridging* – drawing out the other person's point of view; demonstrating that you understand their concerns and appreciate what they are getting; giving credit to their good ideas, joining your views with theirs.

- *Attracting* – conveying your enthusiasm, getting people to feel that they are part of an attractive project.

Body language

Words are not the only means of communication. Body language can convey important messages. The most important things to do if you want to achieve good rapport are to:

- face people squarely and maintain good eye contact

- show that you are interested by leaning slightly forward rather than lolling back

- smile encouragement from time to time and nod in agreement – but don't overdo it, a constant grin while nodding like a china doll will be counter-productive.

COMPLETING THE MEETING

Main steps

The main steps to take when you complete the meeting are to:

- *Check understanding* – ensure that individuals comprehend what has been said and agreed. There should be no doubts or misapprehensions.

- *Agree objectives* – obtain agreement to new or revised targets, projects, standards or personal development objectives, or re-affirm existing objectives.

■ *Plan ahead* – agree the means by which objectives are going to be achieved in the form of a performance agreement (performance improvement plan) and a personal development plan.

■ *Agree on further reviews* – when the next review is to take place, how performance and the implementation of the personal development plan will be monitored in the meantime.

■ *Complete documentation* – you may have to complete a more or less elaborate form issued by the personnel department. This will record the data systematically and can be checked by your boss to ensure that you have carried out the review thoroughly and fairly (this 'grandparent' assessment is one way of helping people to believe that they will be assessed properly). But you may simply record your joint agreement to objectives and plans on a piece of paper, copies of which both parties keep for future reference. This can become a working document and there is always the danger that forms will be locked away in a filing cabinet. Some organizations require a rating of performance at this stage and this process is discussed below.

Rating

Organizations often ask managers to summarize their judgements on people's performance by rating them on some sort of scale, for example: excellent (A), highly acceptable (B), acceptable (C), not entirely acceptable (D) and unacceptable (E). It is often argued that ratings are a convenient way of summing up judgements (note the word) which might otherwise by submerged in verbiage. And if there is a performance-related pay scheme (PRP), there has to be some sort of process of ticking in boxes to determine what size a pay increase should be (PRP schemes – their advantages and their notable disadvantages, are discussed in chapter 31).

But there are powerful arguments against ratings, namely that:

■ to sum up the total performance of a person with a single rating is a gross over-simplification of what may be a complex set of factors affecting performance

■ it is difficult to attach any real meaning to words such as 'acceptable' or 'average'

■ they are subjective and it is hard to achieve consistency between different raters

■ to label people as 'average' or below average', or whatever equivalent terms are used is both demeaning and demotivating.

A number of organizations are accepting the force of these counter-arguments and do not require rating.

FURTHER READING

Edwards, L (1997) *Interviewing*, The Industrial Society, London.
Fisher, M (1995) *Performance Appraisals*, Kogan Page, London.
France, S (1997) *360-degree Appraisal*, The Industrial Society, London.

23

PERSONAL DEVELOPMENT PLANS

Personal development plans are perhaps the most important output of performance management processes. They are agreed during performance and development review meetings and progress in implementing them is reviewed at consequent meetings, although progress should also be monitored continuously. Personal development plans include development activities such as:

- self-managed learning – the process by which individuals take responsibility for their own learning needs

- coaching (see Chapter 26)

- development through monitoring (see Chapter 28)

- action learning (see Chapter 28)

- distance learning – correspondence courses

- project working – getting involved in projects which extend their skills

- job enlargement – being given additional, wider responsibilities

- secondment

- developmental career moves, often lateral (ie in new roles at a broadly similar level, which will extend the individual's experience, knowledge and skills

- formal training, but only when a training need has been identified which is best met by a training programme

PURPOSE OF PERSONAL DEVELOPMENT PLANS

A personal development plan may concentrate on the development required to improve performance in the current job. It may extend to the development required for future career moves and is thus part of a career development programme. Career moves could be by promotion or by lateral development to gain expertise in new areas of work. The latter is particularly important in smaller organizations when there are limited opportunities for promotion but more scope for lateral development.

PREPARING A PERSONAL DEVELOPMENT PLAN

Personal development plans are prepared on the basis of the outcome of performance and development reviews. These, as described in Chapter 22, consist of a joint examination of progress and achievements – comparing what people have done and how they were expected to do it. In other words, the objectives they have attained and the capabilities they have demonstrated.

The personal development plan, as its name implies, is very much the property of individuals. They have to set the direction in which they want to develop and decide on the actions required to get there. Your role as a manager is to provide guidance as necessary in preparing the plan and to support them when it comes to implementation. Of course, you should also monitor progress and stimulate action or provide further support as required. The steps required to prepare a personal development plan are:

1 *Identify development needs*
   These can be defined in terms of knowledge skills and capabilities (competencies). These needs should be specified as precisely as possible in terms of what people have to know and be able to do when the plan has been implemented.
2 *Set goals for meeting these needs* (personal development objectives). These can be defined under headings such as:
   ■ the extension of relevant knowledge

   ■ the improvement or acquisition of skills, especially transferable skills, which will enable them to extend their role and take on new responsibilities

   ■ the development of specified areas of capability or competence

- enlarging the current role

- working towards future developments in the current role

- extending a career laterally across the organization to roles at broadly the same level but which will enrich the individuals expertise and capabilities

- increasing potential for provision in general or, possibly, in a specified direction.

3 *Prepare action plans for meeting the development needs*
Action plans specify both the means by which needs will be satisfied and how individuals and their managers will check that they have been met. The areas could include any of the following:

- learning new skills or improving existing skills during the normal course of work, with coaching as appropriate from managers, teams leaders, mentors or specialized trainers (learning on the job)

- taking on additional responsibilities or moving to a different role in the team (job rotation) and acquiring additional skills (multiskilling) through coaching and with the help of co-workers

- being appointed a member of a project team to develop something new, to achieve a task or to solve a problem, extending knowledge and skills through their experience (learning on the project) with guidance and coaching as required

- spare-time study to learn new skills, acquire extra knowledge or obtain a qualification (distance learning, guided reading, attending courses provided by local educational institutions)

- attending in-company or external training courses designed to help people learn new skills and/or increase knowledge

- action learning programmes as described in chapter 28.

4 *Implement the plans*
Individuals should be encouraged, or indeed, expected to monitor their own progress but their managers should review how things are going from time to time.

5 *Evaluate*
Evaluate the outcome of the personal development plan and decide if anything more needs to be done in any existing or new area.

THE ICL APPROACH TO PERSONAL DEVELOPMENT PLANNING

The ICL Learning Guide states that the aim of the booklet is to:

> ... help you to increase your personal value through learning by stimulating ideas for developing your own personal capability: skills, knowledge, attitudes and experience. It will help you to achieve better performance in the Company and better employability for you... We learn most of what we know and what we can do from experience, both at work and outside of work. Learning is not just about attending training courses. By systematically exploiting our experience in a disciplined way we and the Company will benefit from achieving your full potential. The more we understand about learning, the more we are likely to achieve our ambitions.

The guide specifies how people can increase their personal value by identifying their learning needs in appraisals and review of achievement and performance, assessment, benchmarking, using ICL's assessment and career guidance/development centres and consulting a career counselor. Guidance is given on learning styles and details are given of 31 learning options The method of completing a personal development plan is summarized as follows:

■ identify your learning needs

■ identify your learning style profile

■ review options available

■ note down your earning needs under the headings; knowledge, skill, attitudes and experience (the advice is given –'Think about what, specifically, you will need to know and do differently'

■ against each need, note down the specific action chosen, who is responsible for effecting the action and by what date

■ ensure that your personal learning plan is implemented, reviewed and updated as necessary

■ ensure that a formal review with your manager takes place at least once a year, preferably twice, to establish that all is going according to plan, or to adapt the plan to meet new needs.

FURTHER READING

Gannon, M 'Personal development planning' in M Waters (ed) (1995) *The Performance Management Handbook*, Institute of Personnel and Development, London.

Honey, P and Mumford, A (1986) *The Manual of Learning Styles*, Peter Honey.

Institute of Employment Studies (1995) *Personnel Development Plans*, Brighton.

24

MANAGING UNDER-PERFORMERS

Managing performance is always a positive process. It is about improvement and development. Its aim is to help the good to be even better. When people are not achieving the results expected of them – when performing less well than they could, then steps can and should be taken to identify the causes and help people to do something about it, in their own interests as well as yours.

Managing performance, as has been said a number of times earlier (but is worth repeating) is always a continuous process. If people are not performing up to their potential, if they are not using or developing their skills efficiently, then action should be taken at the time. You don't wait for several months until a formal performance review. Essentially, as Valerie and Andrew Stewart say, managing poor performance is about spotting that there is a problem, understanding the causes of the problem and attempting a remedy. These basic approaches are described in more detail in this chapter.

STEPS REQUIRED TO MANAGE UNDER-PERFORMERS

The first steps required to manage under-performers are:

Identify and agree the problem

Analyse what happened and what the shortfall from the target or standard has been. This is part of the feedback process and the aim should be to come to an agreement on what the problem is.

Establish why the shortfall happened

Your aim should be to establish jointly with the individual why performance was not up to expectations. This means agreeing on the facts and the context in which the problem occurred. The causes of the problem can be analysed under the following headings:

The problem is caused by something or somebody else:

☐ unforeseeable changes in job requirements arising from external or internal pressures or unexpected alternatives in what the organization, department or team has to do, including shortened deadlines

☐ expected resources – people, money, time – are not available

☐ lack of co-operation with others

■ interference by others.

But these possible causes have to be real – no insubstantial excuses. And at managerial and possibly other levels, it is not unreasonable to expect that people should foresee problems and avoid them.

The problem is caused by the manager:

■ failure to clarify requirements and expectations – aims, standards and priorities

■ failure to provide adequate training, guidance, information, support and encouragement

■ failure to provide the resources required

■ expecting too much – setting unreasonable or unattainable targets or standards

☐ arbitrarily changing objectives, tasks and priorities.

As a manager, these are possible causes of failure which are down to you. It is necessary to be honest with yourself and decide what action you need to take.

The problem is down to the individual:

☐ lack of application and effort

☐ lack of interest

☐ negative or uncooperative action

- failure to get priorities right
- lack of knowledge
- lack of skill
- failure to understand tasks or objectives
- lack of confidence.

But you have to consider the extent to which you may have contributed to problems. Did you, for example, give someone a task which the person did not have the skill, experience or capacity to do? Did you fail adequately to monitor progress so that you could step in before things went too far? Did you fail to provide leadership or adequate motivation? Performing below par is not necessarily the entire fault of the individual. You may not have done enough to prevent it happening. Again, you have to be honest with yourself and be prepared to discuss with the individual how together you can ensure that the problem does not recur.

These causes will probably overlap. It is most unlikely that there is any single cause to a problem of under-performance. For example, the individual may lack of ability, but this may have been compounded by new and unforeseen demands and a failure to ensure that the individual has the necessary knowledge and skills.

In identifying causes, both parties should try to avoid getting into an over-defensive position. Respect is gained through admitting mistakes, not defending them against all-comers.

Decide and agree on the action required

Action may be taken by the individual, by you or, often, by both of you working together. This could include:

The individual:

- changing behaviour – with guidance from the manager
- changing attitudes – this is up to the individual, managers can help to change behaviour, but attitudes are more personal and deeply embedded, although individuals can change over time if they accept that this is necessary
- improving or extending knowledge or skills or learning new skills.

The manager:

- providing more support
- coaching and counselling
- providing learning opportunities.

Joint:

- clarifying expectations
- developing abilities and skills – joint, in that individuals should be expected to take steps to improve themselves but managers should provide help as required by coaching or the provision of additional experience or training
- preparing and implementing action plans involving both parties.

Whenever action is agreed, it is necessary for both you and the individual to understand how you will know that it has succeeded. You can provide feedback but individuals should be encouraged to monitor their own performance.

Resource the action

This means ensuring that the coaching, training, guidance, experience or facilities are provided or made available. This is your responsibility as a manager.

Monitor and provide feedback

Both you and the individual should monitor performance, ensure that feedback is provided or shared, and agree any further actions required.

FURTHER READING

Stewart, V and Stewart, A (1982) *Managing the Poor Performer*, Wildwood House.

25

MANAGING TEAM PERFORMANCE

It is just as important for you to be able to manage the performance of your team effectively as for you to manage individual performance well. Managing team performance is a matter of agreeing team objectives and plans and getting the team as a whole to review its performance and decide what action it needs to take. Managing team performance can be carried out best by developing self managing teams which decide on methods of work and the planning, scheduling and control of their work.

TEAM OBJECTIVES

Work objectives

Team objectives, like individual objectives are concerned with targets, standards of performance, the projects teams are expected to complete, and programmes for developing team effectiveness.

Team objectives should be completely integrated with organizational and function/departmental objectives. Thus if at organizational level a drive to improve levels of customer service has been launched this may be translated into expected levels of service and standards at departmental level. Teams can then get together to decide on their specific targets for such aspects of their work as speed of response or turnaround, and customer satisfaction levels. These may often be expressed as improvement targets: 'As a team we agree to improve speed of response from an average of two days each enquiry to one day within the next six months'.

So far as possible, teams should be given scope to consider and propose their own targets and standards. Clearly these have to be acceptable to you as supporting the achievement of your own targets. But the more the team as a body of people think for themselves and agree targets, the more likely it is that they will work well together to achieve their aims.

Team process objectives

Teams shall be asked not only to agree and propose work objectives but also to consider objections for the ways in which the team functions – the process of working together, operating flexibly, reaching agreement, resolving problems, making plans and monitoring progress. Teams should be encouraged and helped to analyse these processes, assess areas for improvement and agree on what needs to be done.

TEAM PERFORMANCE REVIEWS

Team performance review meetings analyse and assess feedback and control information on the team's achievements against its targets, standards, work plans and team process objectives.

The points covered by such a meeting could be as follows:

General feedback review:

- progress of the team as a whole
- general problems encountered by the team which have caused difficulties or delayed progress
- overall helps and hindrances to the effective operation of the team.

Work and process review:

- specific aspects of the work which went well or not so well
- how well the team has functioned (a check list for analysing team process is given below)
- identification of any new problems encountered by team members
- identification of any ways in which team performance in such areas as output, quality, speed of response or customer service could be improved.

Group problem solving:

- analysis of reasons for any problems
- agreement of steps to be taken to solve them or to avoid their re-occurrence in the future.

Update or develop new objectives and work plans:

- review of new requirements, scope for improvement and innovation opportunities
- agreement of new or revised targets or standards
- agreement of process objectives to improve team effectiveness
- agreement of plans to achieve objectives and standards.

If you are a departmental manager you should encourage team leaders to get their teams to carry out team reviews along these lines. As a team leader you should guide and facilitate team reviews, but the more you can leave the team alone to get on with it the better.

CHECKLIST FOR ANALYSING TEAM PROCESSES

- How well have we worked together?
- Does everyone contribute?
- How effectively is the team led?
- How good are we at analysing problems?
- How decisive are we?
- How good are we at initiating action?
- Do we concentrate sufficiently on priority issues?
- Do we waste time on irrelevancies?
- To what extent can people speak their minds?
- If there is any conflict, is it openly expressed and is it about issues rather than personalities?

Part 5

Developing people

26

THE LINE MANAGER'S RESPONSIBILITY FOR DEVELOPING PEOPLE

As a line manager you have to deliver results. You are there to ensure that your department or team makes an effective contribution to achieving the purpose of the organization and that performance continuously improves. You cannot achieve these aims unless you give special consideration to developing the people in your department or team. And this is your responsibility, you cannot pass it over to the personnel or training departments. They can help, but ultimately it's up to you.

Your aim should be to ensure that you have the skilled and capable workforce you need. To do this it helps if you understand:

- what learning involves (dealt with in this chapter)
- how people learn (this chapter)
- the principles of planned learning (this chapter)
- the concept of a learning organization (this chapter)
- how to identify learning needs (Chapter 27)
- how to manage learning and development (Chapter 28)
- how to act as a coach or mentor (Chapter 29).

WHAT LEARNING INVOLVES

Learning takes place when new or changed knowledge or skills have been acquired or developed which can then be put to use permanently or at least over extended periods of time. Learning is achieved through:

- education – the increase of knowledge through systematic instruction or self development, drawing out latent abilities and developing mental powers

- training – the systematic modification of behaviour and development of skills through instruction, working and planned experience

- experience – the development of skills and capabilities through action, reflection and personal observation

- practice – putting something we have learned into effect until it has been fully absorbed and is part of our regular behaviour and performance.

HOW PEOPLE LEARN

Learning is a continuous and natural process. And the best learning is achieved through practical experience – by doing things. People learn best when:

- they are motivated to learn – when they see that the learning will benefit them

- the learning is seen as relevant by the learner

- they learn by doing – 'I hear and forget, I see and remember, I do and understand'

- they are helped to learn from their mistakes

- they are provided with feedback on how they are doing, preferably by monitoring their own progress (self-checking)

- they are given scope as far as possible to learn at their own pace.

CONDITIONS FOR EFFECTIVE LEARNING

The main conditions for learning to be effective are:

■ Individuals must want to learn or at least should be encouraged to believe that it will satisfy their needs. Learning should be seen as useful and the learner should gain satisfaction from learning.

■ Learning should be an active process. Learners should be actively involved in the learning programme and with whoever provides the training.

■ Learners should have well defined targets and standards which they find acceptable and can use to judge their own progress.

■ Learners need guidance. They require a sense of direction and feedback on how they are doing. Self-motivated individuals may provide much of this for themselves but help and encouragement should be available when necessary.

■ Learners need feedback and reinforcement. They should know how well they are doing and in a prolonged learning programme intermediate steps are required in which learning can be reinforced.

■ Learning methods should be varied to suit whatever has to be learned and the needs of the learner. There are many techniques available, such as learning on the job with suitable guidance (experiential learning), mentoring, and formal training.

Time must be allowed to absorb the learning. All learners are on some form of 'learning curve' as they progressively acquire the knowledge and skills they need. Different people have different learning curves and the pace of learning should be varied to accommodate them. Sufficient time should be allowed for practice and familiarization and learning may be planned to take place progressively. This means allowing pauses at the end of each stage of a learning programme to consolidate through practice what has been learned at the previous stage before moving on.

PLANNED LEARNING

Planned learning is the process of systematically deciding what learning is required and then putting it into effect. It consists of the following steps:

■ identify and define learning needs
■ define the learning required

- define learning objectives

- plan learning programmes or events

- decide who provides for the learning to take place

- implement the learning programme or event

- evaluate how much learning has taken place

- amend and extend arrangements for learning as necessary.

THE LEARNING ORGANIZATION

The concept of the learning organization has become popular in recent years. Basically a learning organization is seen as one in which learning is treated as a continuous process that is fundamental to business success. The learning organization is one which continually improves by defining and developing the capabilities it needs to achieve its purpose, now and in the future.

The notion of a learning organization is somewhat abstract. It is often expressed as an aspiration rather than a reality. It is a philosophy of learning which tends to ignore or skate over the practicalities of implementing it.

But the concept has its uses. It focuses attention on the fact that organizations should be concerned with learning from their past and present successes and failures in order to achieve future success. This can be a deliberate and systematic process. At Book Club Associates, for example, an annual two-day conference for managers was held during which task forces analysed trends and events over the previous year to establish what could be learned from them which should influence next year's business plans. In the same firm, systematic efforts were made to analyse the core competences as they developed over time. This was followed by decisions on what needed to be done to ensure that people made the best use of the learning that had taken place and expanded that learning in the future. A constant and familiar cry of the Chief Executive at Board and management meeting was 'What have we learned from this?' 'What are we going to do about it?'

The learning organization concept also emphasizes that learning should be a continuous process which is the responsibility of line managers, not the personnel or training department. Line managers must learn from their own experiences (success and failures) and must encourage their teams to do the same.

FURTHER READING

Garratt, R. (1990) *Creating a Learning Organization*, Institute of Directors, London.

Reay, DG (1994) *Understanding How People Learn*, Kogan Page, London.

27

IDENTIFYING LEARNING NEEDS

AIMS

Learning needs analysis aims to define the gap between what people know and can do and what they should know and be able to do. It is concerned with assessing the difference between what is and what should be. The 'what should be' is whatever people need to learn to be better in their present jobs. It is also about they need to learn to develop – to take on extra responsibilities, move to higher level or more responsible jobs, acquire a wider range of skills (multiskilling) and increase all round capability or competence.

METHODS OF ANALYSING LEARNING NEEDS

The three main methods of analysing learning needs for individuals at departmental or team level are job and learning analysis, the preparation of learning or training specifications, performance and development reviews, and surveys.

Job and learning analysis

The techniques of job and skills analysis as described in Chapter 13 provide the basic data for the analysis of learning needs. This analysis should specify what job holders need to know and to be able to do and additionally identify:

- any problems faced by job holders in learning basic skills and applying them successfully

- any weakness in the performance of existing job holders attributable to deficiencies in knowledge or skill which can be rectified

- any areas where levels of capability or competence are clearly not up to standard

- any areas where future changes in work processes, methods or job responsibilities indicate a learning need

- how effectively learning takes place at present.

The output of the job analysis should be a learning specification as described below. But the analysis will provide some information on its effectiveness of existing learning methods which will help when it comes to making plans to meet learning needs (see chapter 28).

Learning specification

A learning specification spells out the characteristics or attributes people in particular jobs or roles should have to perform them effectively. The learning specification provides both the means to identify what needs to be done (the gap between what is and what should be) and the basis for the design and evaluation of learning or training programmes.

The characteristics or attributes which need to be analysed and recorded as the basis for a learning specification are:

- *Knowledge* – what individuals need to know to carry out their work well. It could be professional, scientific, technical or business/commercial knowledge. Or it could be about how to operate or use machines, equipment, systems, software or materials. It might be about the customers or clients dealt with, the products or services sold or its problems or faults that frequently occur and how to solve or correct them.

- *Skills* – what individuals need to be able to do if expected results are to be achieved and knowledge used effectively. Skills may be manual, intellectual, mental, perceptual or social.

- *Capabilities* – the work-based competences and behavioural competencies needed to achieve the required levels of performance.

- *Attitudes* – the disposition to behave or to perform in a way which is in accordance with the requirements of the work.

■ *Performance standards* – what fully capable people have to be able to achieve.

Detailed learning specifications may be set out under all these headings but a basic specification for induction training could concentrate on only two things: what the role holder needs to know and what the role holder needs to be able to do. The other information on behavioural competencies and performance standards could be contained in the role profile. This is the most usual approach if role profiles are available. The learning specification then concentrates on the particular aspects of knowledge and skills required by fully competent role holders. An example of such a specification for a product manager at Book Club Associates is given below.

Performance reviews

Performance reviews as described in Chapters 20 to 25 are a prime, and possibly the most important, source of information on learning needs. The analysis of performance compared with objectives and of capability or competence compared with a role profile is the basis for the agreement of personal development plans. These are an expression of learning needs and how they can be satisfied.

Learning surveys

Additionally, and possibly with the help of training specialists, you can assemble all the information obtained from the other methods of analysis in order to provide a comprehensive basis for the development of a learning strategy for your department or team. It may be necessary to supplement this information by carrying out a special survey in which individuals are asked to say what they feel this need to learn.

Learning surveys pay particular attention to which existing arrangements are meeting learning needs. Further information on the effectiveness of learning or training programmes can be derived from training evaluations as described in Chapter 28.

When you have done whatever you can to identify learning needs you will be in a position to define learning objectives and develop learning programmes for individuals or groups of people as discussed in Chapter 28.

LEARNING SPECIFICATION	
Role title: Product Manager	Department: Marketing
What the role holder must understand	
Learning outcomes	Learning methods
■ The book club market	Coaching: Marketing Manager and Advertising Manager
■ Market research availability	Coaching: Market Research Manager
■ Interpretation of marketing data	Coaching: Operations Research Manager
■ Book club fulfilment operations	Coaching: Fulfilment Manager
■ Creative department operations	Coaching: Creative Group Leader
■ Book ordering and stock control	Coaching: Book Production Manager
■ Principles of direct mailing and data based marketing	Institute of Direct Marketing courses
What the role holder must be able to do	
Learning outcome	Learning method
■ Prepare club budget	Coaching: Budget Accountant
■ Prepare marketing plans	Coaching: Mentor
■ Conduct tests	Coaching: Operations Research Department
■ Prepare member recruitment campaigns	Read: Product Manager's Manual
■ Select advertisement lead lists and one shots	Read: Product Manager's Manual Coaching: Club Editor and Inventory Manager
■ Specify requirements for advertisements and leaflets	Coaching: Mentor Coaching: Creative Group Leader
■ Analyse results of recruitment campaigns	Coaching: Mentor Read: previous analyses
■ Prepare marketing reports	Coaching: Mentor Read: previous reports Observe: marketing review meetings
Notes on learning methods	
■ Mentoring provided by Marketing Manager and designated Senior Product Manager.	
■ Induction programme prepared by Development and Training Manager.	
■ Additional training courses to be planned as appropiate in project management, report writing, presentation skills and assertiveness.	
■ Review of progress to be made by Marketing Manager and Development and Training Manager.	
■ Product Manager to manage own learning in accordance with programme.	

Table 27.1   An example of a learning specification

28

MANAGING LEARNING AND DEVELOPMENT

In one sense, your role as a line manager or team leader involves you continuously in the management of learning and development. New starters have to receive induction training to enable them to carry out their work. They will then need to learn new skills or increase and extend existing skills as they develop and are given new tasks. Every time you give an instruction or set a task and later check that the work has been done presents a coaching opportunity to you and therefore a learning opportunity for the individual. This chapter contains a summary of the different aspects of learning and development setting learning objectives:

■ setting learning objectives

■ helping people to learn new skills or improve existing skills

■ managing continuous development

■ evaluating the effectiveness of learning.

THE DIFFERENT ASPECTS OF LEARNING AND DEVELOPMENT

Learning and development takes place at the following stages and in the various ways as set out below:

■ induction training

- learning on the job
- learning off the job.

Induction training

People need to be provided with the information and help they need to settle down in their new job and to learn how to develop or apply their skills to the work they will be expected to do. Induction courses may be provided by the company and these will give general information about the organization, the policies that affect employees, procedures such as performance reviews, health and safety matters and opportunities for learning. But the line manager or team leader has the most important role to play in ensuring that new starters quickly settle down and reach the expected standards of performance. This can be achieved by coaching and nominating guides from the team in which the individual is working to help him or her to understand what is required and to learn about the work. The role of managers as coaches and the use of guides are described later in this chapter. Additionally, an organization may develop mentoring processes as also described below.

Learning on the job

It is often said that experience is the best teacher – people learn by doing. This implies, correctly, that they mainly learn on the job. But they need guidance and help so that they learn to do the right things in the right way. They should not be thrown in at the deep end to struggle for survival. They should not be allowed to pick up bad habits because they have not been given the opportunity to learn about how best to carry out their work. It is your job as a manager or team leader to ensure that this does not happen by coaching and by providing guidance or arranging for it to be available.

Learning off the job

'Off the job' training in the form of courses can be useful in helping people to learn new skills and to complement learning on the job. But such training can only supplement on the job learning, it cannot replace it. The use of formal training is discussed later in this chapter.

HELPING PEOPLE TO LEARN

Your approach to helping people to learn should be based on your understanding of their learning needs (see Chapter 27 on techniques of identifying them). There are a number of approaches available and you should select the most appropriate technique or combination of techniques depending on the person who is involved and the type and level of skill that has to be learned.

Different approaches will, for example, be necessary for:

■ new starters who may need instruction in basic skills or help in adapting their existing skills to their new work

■ more experienced people who need to become multiskilled or to learn new skills on taking up extra responsibilities

■ experienced people who lack skills or whose skills are inadequate.

People can be helped to learn in a number of ways as described below.

Coaching

Coaching is a person-to-person technique designed to develop individual knowledge, skills and attitudes. As defined by the Industrial Society, coaching is 'a skill of facilitating the learning, development and performance of another person is most effective if it takes place informally as part of the normal process of management or team leadership.

Your aims as a coach

In your role as a coach you should aim to:

■ provide guidance on how to carry out specific tasks as necessary, but always on the basis of helping people to learn rather than spoon-feeding them with instructions on what to do and how to do it

■ help people to become aware of how well they are doing and what they need to learn

■ use whatever situations arise as learning opportunities.

This could be described as a 'directive' approach, except that the emphasis is more on helping people to learn than on 'telling' them how to do it.

The coaching sequence

Coaching can be carried out in the following stages:

1   Identify the areas of knowledge, skills or capabilities where learning needs to take place to qualify people to carry out the task, provide for continuous development or improve performance.
2   Ensure that the person accepts the need to learn.
3   Discuss with the person what needs to be learned and the best way to undertake the learning.
4   Get the person to work out how they can manage their own learning while identifying where they will need help from you or someone else.
5   Provide encouragement and advice to the person in pursuing the self learning programme.
6   Provide specific guidance as required where the person needs your help.
7   Agree how progress should be monitored and reviewed.

One of the fundamental skills of coaching is to raise awareness and generate responsibility *in the other person*. When the emphasis is on this type of skill, coaching becomes an important way to achieve empowerment in the sense of giving people more scope or 'power' to exercise control over and take responsibility for their work. The GROW model adopted by the Industrial Society provides a useful framework on which to base a coaching session. This emphasizes the importance of:

■   Goals – getting agreement on what the coaching aims to achieve.

■   Reality – ensuring that the coaching addresses the real issues which concern both parties.

■   Options – identifying and evaluating the different approaches that are available.

■   Will – helping the person to work out how the learning will be applied.

Learning through the performance management process

Performance management processes are based on an agreed performance and personal development objectives and plans. The personal development plan should initiate what people need to learn and how that learning should be accomplished. Reviews should establish what has been learned and any more learning that may be required. Learning can be reinforced during review discussions by obtaining an answer to the question: 'What did you learn from that?'. Thus development reviews can encourage people to learn from their experience by analysing and reflecting on what they have been doing and drawing conclusions on what they have learned and still need to learn.

Performance review discussions provide opportunities for coaching or at least identifying where coaching might be helpful (and this process of identification should be carried out mainly by the individual – the manager's role is to facilitate self awareness, not to tell people what they need to learn).

Counselling in the full sense of the word is not part of this discussion. As defined by the British Association of Counselling, counselling is '... an activity which gives the client the opportunity to explore, discover and clarify ways of living more resourcefully and towards greater well being'. This is something which is best carried out by skilled and professionally trained people. Managers can act as coaches in the ways described above but they should not attempt to take on the role of therapists.

Controlled delegation

Controlled delegation means that you do not simply tell people what they have to do. Instead you:

1 Generate agreement and mutual understanding on what needs to be done and why.
2 Agree with them what they are expected to achieve – always delegate by the results you expect and ensure that these expectations are defined and agreed.
3 As necessary, encourage them to tell you how they propose to do the work, providing guidance if necessary.
4 Discuss with them the knowledge and skills this will need.
5 If there are any gaps, agree any learning required and how it is to happen.
6 Monitor progress and review results and discuss what has been accomplished (the more individuals are encouraged to monitor their own performance and are able to get the information to do so, the better.
7 Evaluate with the person concerned the effectiveness of any learning processes that have taken place and, where necessary, agree on any further learning required (again, self-evaluation should be encouraged).

Demonstration

Demonstration is the process of telling or showing people how to carry out a task and then allowing them to get on with it. It is the most commonly used – and abused – training method. It is direct and the learner is actively engaged. But in its crudest form – 'here's what to do, now get on with it' – does not provide a structured learning system where people can understand the sequence of training they are following and can proceed by deliberate steps along the learning curve. If you do it yourself, taking account of the techniques of job instruction discussed below it can work well. But relying on another member of your team to carry out the training by saying in effect: 'This is what to do, this is how I do it' and leaving it at that is dangerous. The methods used by the person's colleague may be wrong and he or she probably has no idea about how best to help people to learn effectively. The person undergoing the training therefore picks up bad habits and only partially learns how to do the task. They are often confused by someone who is so used to doing it that they cannot put themselves into the place of the learner. This sort of empathy is an essential characteristic of a good trainer, which not everyone has. People not only need to have this natural ability they also need to be trained to train.

Job or skill instruction

The techniques of job or skill instruction are based on the principles of how people learn as described in Chapter 26. The learning programme and objectives should be determined by skills and training needs analysis. The sequence of instruction should be as follows:

Preparation

- define what has to be learned
- define the standard of performance a fully trained person should achieve in terms of quality, speed and attention to safety
- break down the total task into its elements to determine the learning stages and set performance targets for each stage
- plan the instructional techniques to be used, overall and in each stage
- prepare learners for the instruction, ensuring that they accept that the training will be relevant and useful to them personally – they should want to learn.

Explanation (telling)

explain in simple and straightforward language what is to be covered and what to look for

explain first things first and proceed from the known to the unknown, the simple to the complex, the concrete to the abstract, the general to the particular, and the whole to the parts and back to the whole again

make the maximum use of notes, charts, diagrams and other visual aids.

Demonstration (showing)

■ show the complete operation at normal speed to show the learner how the task should be carried out eventually

demonstrate the operation slowly and in correct sequence, element by element, to indicate clearly what is done at each stage and the order in which each task is carried out

■ demonstrate each element of the operation again slowly, at least two or three times, to stress the how, when and why of successive actions or movements

demonstrate the whole operation again so that the learner understands how the parts combine to make up the whole.

Practice

■ start with the first element and get the learner to observe you and then repeat the operation under your guidance until the target level of performance has been reached for that element

continue to get the learner to practise each of the successive elements in turn so that in each case the target level of performance is reached

get the learner to combine all the elements and practise the whole task until the learning programme target performance level is attained – the aim is to ensure that the smooth combination of the separate elements is achieved to provide for co-ordinated and integrated performance.

Follow-up

provide additional help with particularly difficult tasks or to overcome temporary set-backs

■ repeat the instruction as necessary and encourage the learner to practise until he or she reaches the target level of performance (experienced worker standard).

Job rotation/planned experience

Job rotation aims to help people learn additional skills by moving them from job to job. It can be an inefficient method of training.

It is better to use the term 'planned sequence of experience' rather than 'job rotation' to emphasize that the experience should be planned and programmed to satisfy a learning specification for acquiring additional knowledge and experience in carrying out different tasks (multiskilling) and in different but related jobs.

The planned experience programme should set out what people are expected to learn in each new activity and job. Someone should be briefed to ensure that the planned learning does take place.

Action learning

Action learning is a method of helping managers to develop their talents by exposing them to real problems. They are required to analyse them, formulate recommendations and then take action. This approach is based on the belief that managers learn best by doing rather than being taught.

Action learning programmes are usually facilitated by an internal or external consultant or 'set advisor' who helps the group or 'set' of four or five managers involved to learn from each other and from their experiences in conducting the project. They are thus learning about the management processes of planning, organizing, co-ordinating, working in a team, monitoring and controlling as they happen.

Providing 'guides'

You can help people to learn, especially in induction periods or when they need to acquire new skills, by nominating fellow team members to act as guides (or, as the Industrial Society terms them, 'buddies'. These are colleagues who can provide on-the-spot help and advice on how to do things and on where information, equipment and other facilities can be obtained. If at a loss, individuals can turn to their guide to get immediate advice. Guides need to be carefully selected and trained in their duties.

Mentoring

Mentoring is the process of using specifically selected and trained people to provide guidance and advice which will help to develop the individuals for whom they have been made responsible. You could be asked to be a mentor, in which case you would be briefed on your responsibilities and how to carry them out. Alternatively, a member of your team could be given a mentor so that he or she could benefit from the individual guidance provided by an experienced individual.

A mentor is a person who enters into an informal 'contract' with a learner and supplies an independent perspective on the context of the learner's work. (If and when they discuss the content of the work, the mentor then takes on the role of a coach.)

The mentor is usually, but not inevitably, senior in age and experience to the learner. Although their meetings will be intermittent, their contract would be relatively long term – months rather than weeks. Their discussions are totally confidential, so care needs to be taken not to disturb the learner's relationship with their line manager.

Aims

As defined in the Industrial Society's guide to their own mentoring scheme, mentoring is essentially about helping people to develop more effectively. The objectives of this scheme are defined by the Industrial Society as follows:

- To assist individuals with their personal development and career progression

- To improve individuals' performance and productivity

- To improve the effectiveness of induction for those members of staff who move to new jobs within the Society

- To improve internal communication.

Mentoring roles

As defined by the Industrial Society the overall role of mentors is to assist learners to reach their full potential through development and personal growth. Their responsibilities include:

- respecting the confidentiality of the relationship and actively building trust

- giving encouragement to the learner to progress and being enthusiastic about the relationship

■ supporting learners' personal development and their learning

■ building the confidence of learners.

More specifically, mentoring roles can include the following (not in order of priority):

1 Sounding board for ideas – someone to test preliminary thoughts on in a safe environment.
2 Supporter – who will give encouragement and develop the learner's confidence.
3 Expert – a source of technical/professional knowledge.
4 Source of organizational knowledge; someone who knows how things work in the organization.
5 Listener/questioner – someone to ask challenging questions.
6 Facilitator – who will help the learner to achieve their goals.
7 Role model – someone who exemplifies good practice.
8 Resource person, able to point to opportunities/possibilities/develop connections in and outside the organization.
9 Coach – who will give encouragement and feedback, in order to help the learner acquire new skills and abilities.
10 Translator – of ideas/jargon, to help the learner make sense of information, organization terminology etc.
11 Challenger – to help the learner to see themselves more clearly, and is not afraid to tell 'uncomfortable' truths.
12 Helper – career/development, who will assist the learner to identify and explore new learning situations and will take an interest in their career development.
13 Counselor – listen sympathetically and help the learner to work out solutions to their own problems.
14 Helper – self-reliance, helping people to take responsibility for their own development.

The roles of the mentor as guide, coach or buddy are shown in Table 28.1 overleaf.

	Mentor or guide	Coach	Buddy
Relationship to learner	Private, individual	Private or public; individual or group	Partly private but some aspects can be public, eg where to find things, how to complete paperwork
Relationship to learner's manager	The line manager can not be the mentor.	The line manager can be the coach.	The line manager normally appoints the buddy/guide from amongst his/her own team
Contact with learner.	Intermittent, medium to long term.	Can be very short term as wells as medium to long term.	Short term and frequent during induction period. May take up considerable time
Main agenda	Context within which learner's work is done, ie help person plan and decide their future.	Content of work; to improve job performance.	Build confidence of learner, eg know their way around, who does what
Proximity	Need not always involve face to face contact.	Difficult to achieve without face to face contact, eg can be done through correspondence or telephone call.	Must be face to face; the two people should ideally work in close proximity
Outcomes	Person better prepared to progress their own development and career	Improved job performance.	Person has completed induction successfully

Table 28.1 The roles of a mentor, a coach and a buddy or guide (as defined by the Industrial Society)

CONTINUOUS DEVELOPMENT

It is not enough for you to arrange for people to learn something about their work when they start in their jobs and then to interject occasional learning experiences in the shape of randomly selected courses during their career. Learning should be treated as a continuous process. Less emphasis should be placed on formal instruction and people should be encouraged and helped to be responsible for their own learning, but you still have to provide them with opportunities to reflect on what they are doing and to plan their learning needs through performance and development processes. You can also help with their development through controlled delegation and planned experience.

As far as possible learning and work should be integrated. This means that you should encourage people to learn from the successes, challenges and problems inherent in their day to day activities.

Your job is to provide conditions favourable to growth. You can do this by the way in which you manage people. This includes how you delegate, how you empower them, and how you guide and encourage promising individuals to fulfill their potential and achieve a successful career in line with their talents and aspirations. You can also ensure that people of promise can be provided with a sequence of experience and learning opportunities which will fit them for whatever level of responsibility they have the ability to reach. But always remember the wise words of Peter Drucker:

> Development is always self-development. Nothing is more absurd than for the enterprise to assure responsibility for the development of a person. The responsibility rests with the individuals, their abilities, their effects.

But he went on to say:

> Every manager in a business has the opportunity to encourage individual self-development, to stifle it, to direct it or to misdirect it – they should be specifically assigned the responsibility for helping all people working with them to focus, direct and apply their self-development activities productively.

More and more organizations are now fostering policies of continuous development, often as part of a programme for gaining Investors in People (IIP) accreditation. They are holding their line managers accountable for implementing the policies and rightly, one of the key competences they require managers to possess is the ability and willingness continually to develop the members of their departments or teams.

EVALUATING TRAINING

The Industrial Society believes that the evaluation of training and development must begin at the planning stage – well before any programme has started. It is crucial to identify a measurable outcome right from the start. It is also important to measure the financial benefits as this helps to gain the support of directors and senior managers. However, it is impossible to evaluate all improvements in terms of money so other measurements must be found. For example, success could be measured in terms of attitude and improved staff morale.

The carousel of development model developed by the Industrial Society as illustrated in Figure 28.1 comprises six stages:

1   Identify business needs. This links with stage 6 (judge benefit to the organization) and is the link which is of most interest to senior managers because it deals with the pay-off from their investment.
2   Define development objectives. This links with stage 5 (use and reinforce learning). Line managers defines the destination at stage 2 and makes sure that learning is applied at stage 5.
3   Design learning process. This links with stage 4 (experience learning process). These stages heavily involve the trainer, and the connection between them produces validation – a necessary but narrow judgement, less far-reaching than the overall process of evaluation which requires all six stages.
4   Experience learning process.
5   Use and reinforce learning.
6   Judge benefit to the individual and the organization.

As Andrew Forrest, Director of Human Resources at The Industrial Society points out, it is essential that line managers and trainers talk to each other in the first three stages – before the learning process begins – and that line managers are totally committed to the outcomes. He also explains that:

> The carousel provides a framework for managers, helping them to clarify objectives and to identify the roles of the various parties involve – usually the learner, the line manager, the senior manager and the trainer. It works best if the senior manager sets the objectives in the first place, but all four must be involved if the evaluation is to work.

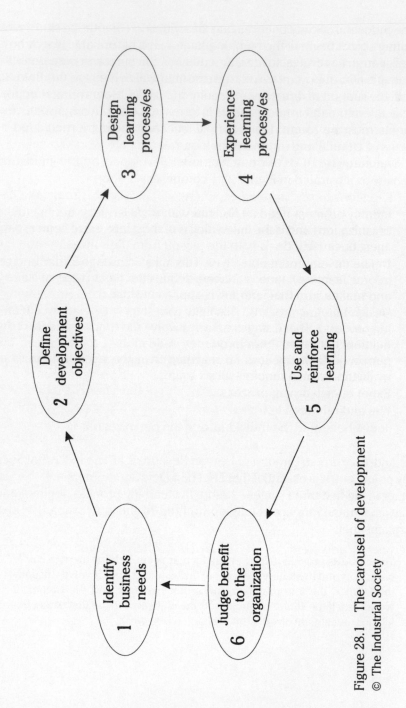

Figure 28.1   The carousel of development
© The Industrial Society

EVALUATING LEARNING

The process of planned learning as described in Chapter 26 starts with setting objectives and ends with evaluation. It is essential to check how well learning activities have succeeded in achieving their objectives so that decisions can be made on the extent to which they are worthwhile and on what improvement are required to make them more effective. Evaluation is mainly concerned with formal training but it is also necessary to review all learning processes, including the implementation of personal development plans, to ensure that they are working well.

Evaluation can take place at four levels:

1   Reactions to the learning experience. Typically, this may take the form of a 'happy sheet' at the end of a course.
2   Learning evaluation – measuring what people have learned by questions or tests.
3   Job behaviour evaluation – assessing what impact the learning has had on the behaviour of people and what effect that changed behaviour has had on their performance. This is the most immediately valid form of evaluation which you can carry out yourself. But you have to be certain that there is a clear link between the cause (the training) and the effect (the performance).
4   Impact on departmental and team performance – from your point of view, this is the ultimate level of evaluation. If you can assess this, then you will be in a strong position to determine what should be done in the future to continue with successful learning activities or to improve or extend them.

FURTHER READING

Harrison, R (1997) *Employee Development*, Institute of Personnel and Development, London.
Kenney, J and Reid, M (1994) *Training Interventions*, 4th edition, Institute of Personnel and Development, London.

Part 6

Managing reward

29

MANAGING PAY SYSTEMS AND STRUCTURES

If you are running an organization, you have to decide what and how employees will be paid. This means fixing rates of pay, creating pay structures and operating pay-for-performance (or competence or skills) schemes. If you are a line manager you will have to work within your organization's pay systems and structures. But this is an area of people management where organizations are increasingly devolving more responsibility to line managers for making pay decisions within the framework of pay policies.

This and the succeeding chapters in the book therefore aim to describe the characteristic features of the pay systems and structures which you may have to develop or work with. They also aim to examine the particular responsibilities you, as a line manager, may have to assume when making pay decisions. This chapter contains an overview of how pay systems and structures are designed and function. The next chapters deal with how jobs are evaluated and priced, how decisions in rates of pay and pay increases are made and what arrangements can be made for what is sometimes called contingent pay – ie pay additional to the base rate which is contingent or dependent on individual performance, competence or skill, or team or organizational performance.

PAY SYSTEMS

A pay system consists of all the arrangements made in organizations for what and how people should be paid for the jobs they do. The system will also provide rewards for how well they, their team or the organization does, and for what they contribute because of the levels of capability (competence) or skills they have achieved.

Objectives of a pay system

The objectives of a pay system are to help the organization and its managers to:

- compete in the job market – attract and retain high quality people
- motivate people – encourage them to achieve superior levels of quality performance
- achieve value for money – ensure that expenditure on pay is cost-effective in that it encourages value-added performance without undue expense.

Pay policies

The pay policies of an organization will be concerned with:

- the achievement of equity – paying people in accordance with their relative contribution
- consistency – paying people consistently according to the level of their job and their performance
- fairness – ensuring that pay decisions are fair in the sense that they do not discriminate against people, are based on objective and unbiased judgements and properly reflect the contribution of the person concerned
- transparency – the pay system is disclosed to people so they know the basis upon which they are rewarded.
- relationships to market rates – the extent to which the organization intends to match market rates or to pay above the average.

FACTORS AFFECTING LEVELS OF PAY

Pay systems and decisions in pay have to take account of the following factors affecting pay levels:

- *Supply and demand* – if people are in plentiful supply pay levels will be lower, if they are much in demand and therefore scarce, pay levels will be higher. This means that the principle of internal equity may have to be sacrificed sometimes to the need to be externally competitive, ie to attract and retain people with a higher scarcity value.

- *The value of the job to the organization* – pay levels are related to the 'size' of the job - the relative contribution to the achievement of the organization's objectives that jobs make. The bigger the job, the more people are paid.

- *The value of the person to the organization* – individuals are paid in line with their contribution - their performance, competence and skill.

- *Affordability* – what the organization can afford to pay.

- *Collective bargaining* – negotiations with trade unions can lead to agreements on rates of pay and other terms and conditions of employment.

PAY STRUCTURES

Pay structures define the different levels of pay for jobs or groups of jobs by reference to internal relativities as established by some form of job evaluation, to external relativities (market rates) and, where appropriate, to negotiated rates for jobs. There are a number of different types of structures, but the main ones as described below are spot rates, graded, broad-banded and job family structures and pay spines.

Spot rates

A spot or individual job rate structure allocates a specific rate for jobs. There is no scope for that rate to progress through a defined pay range or scale. Individuals can, however, earn more pay through incentive schemes or bonuses.

Spot rate schemes are typically used for manual workers where, in its simplest form, there are rates for skilled, semi-skilled and unskilled jobs. Payment-by-result schemes may provide for additional earnings over the base rate for the job.

Some organizations, however, use spot rates for all levels of staff, although they may not use this term. The levels of pay for jobs will be driven by market rates and the decision of the management on the value of the individual to the organization. There is frequently no formal job evaluation scheme and systematic reviews of market rates are not made. Decisions on pay are made in accordance with the judgement of managers on how much a person should be paid in relation to others, what the person is worth in the market place and the contribution they think the person is making. Such judgements are largely subjective and a spot rate system maintained on this basis can function inequitably, inconsistently and unfairly. Typically, rates of pay and the basis of making pay decisions are not revealed. In other words, the system is not transparent.

This approach (it can hardly be called a system or structure) is often used by small to medium sized enterprises in which close control of pay can be maintained and where management cannot be bothered with formal systems because it wants to operate flexibly – reacting and adapting quickly to changing demands.

Organizations which are concerned with being equitable, consistent, fair and transparent are more likely to adopt a graded, broad-banded or pay spine structure which is managed through job evaluation, market rate survey and performance management processes.

Graded structures

A graded pay structure consists of a sequence of job grades into which jobs of broadly equivalent value are slotted. A pay range is attached to each grade which provides for pay to progress through the range in accordance with an individual's performance, competence or skill.

Main features of a graded structure

The main features of a typical graded pay structure are:

- There may be between around six to sixteen grades, depending on the range of jobs to be covered (the highest and lowest rates of pay) the width of the grades, the differentials between grades, and the overlap between adjacent grades (a function of width and differential).

- Grades may be defined by job evaluation in points terms, by grade definitions, or simply by the jobs that have been slotted into the grades.

- The pay range for each grade may be between 20 per cent and 50 per cent above the minimum – thus a '40 per cent' range could span from £20,000 to £28,000. Pay ranges are sometimes described as, for example, 80–120 per cent, so that, if the midpoint (100 per cent) of the range were £20,000 the lower limit would be £16,000 and the upper limit £24,000.

■ Differentials between pay ranges are often about 20 per cent, eg the midpoint of one range could be £20,000 and the midpoint of the next higher range could be £24,000.

■ There is usually an overlap between ranges which can be as much as 50 per cent. For example, the range above a range of £16,000 to £24,000 may be £20,000 to £30,000, an overlap of £4,000 or 50 per cent of the lower range. An overlap provides for flexibility by recognizing that someone with a lot of experience in a job in one grade may be worth more to the organization than someone with little experience in the job placed in the next higher grade.

Advantages of graded structures

The advantages are that they:

■ clearly indicate pay relativities

■ provide a framework for managing those relativities and for ensuring that jobs of equal value are paid equally (a legal requirement, see chapter 35)

■ allow better control over the fixing of rates of pay and pay progression.

■ are easy to explain to employees.

Disadvantages of graded structures

The disadvantages are:

■ defining grade boundaries is a matter of judgement which may not always be easy to defend

■ if there are too many grades, there will be constant pressure for upgrading leading to what is termed 'grade drift' (unjustified progression to higher grades)

■ pay ranges create the expectation that everyone is entitled to reach the top of the scale

■ graded structures can create or maintain rigidity which is at odds with the requirement for flexibility in the new team and process-based organizations.

Broad-banded structures

'Broad-banding', so called, has become more popular in recent years as organizations have delayered and operated more flexibly with increased emphasis on continuous development laterally rather than on promotion upwards through an extended hierarchy.

Main features of a broad-banded structure

The main features of a broad-banded structure are:

- there may be only four or five bands in the structure
- the band width will allow for much more scope for lateral progression – it could be 100 per cent or more
- band boundaries are often, but not always, defined by job evaluation
- bands are not defined hierarchically, A, B, C. etc., instead they may be described in terms of the roles allocated to the band eg senior managers, managers, team leaders and professional/technical staff, support staff
- pay progression is aligned to lateral career progression – expanding roles and taking on new roles at broadly the same level but making a bigger contribution and requiring higher levels of competence
- target rates of pay are determined for the key 'benchmark' roles in a band which are governed by market rates
- there may be pay 'zones' round the target rates which indicate normal progression within a role
- the pay of people can be progressed beyond the pay zone as they develop their competencies and expand their role or move into new roles
- job evaluation is used only to support decisions on allocating roles to bands, it does not determine the positioning of a role in the band which is strongly influenced by market rate relativities
- much more responsibility is usually devolved to line managers to manage pay within the broad-banded structure (how their authority can be exercised is discussed in Chapter 32).

Advantages of broad-banding

The advantages of broad-banding are that it:

- enhances flexibility by reducing the number of vertical break points
- allows for and rewards lateral career development
- offers pay increases for mastering new competences thus promoting continuous development and directing the attention of employees to the opportunities for lateral career growth
- enhances the ability of the organization to reward people for what they bring to the business beyond their job description
- provides for greater flexibility for rewarding people as they grow in their roles and grow their roles
- reduces the time spent on job evaluation because there are fewer levels between which distinctions need to be drawn and job evaluation is not normally used to place jobs within the band.

These advantages are considerable and are particularly relevant in organizations which:

- are seeking a pay structure to fit a new flatter organizational structure where promotional opportunities are few but lateral growth is important
- wish to focus on paying people for what they contribute rather than on paying for the jobs into which people are placed
- need to develop a more broadly skilled and flexible workforce which can take on new challenges, tasks and projects and adapt rapidly to change
- prefer a flexible pay system, not one which is constrained by narrow grades and the bureaucracy surrounding traditional approaches to job evaluation.

But there are considerable disadvantages and broad-banding may not be appropriate for organizations with a strong culture that value a traditional hierarchy where status is recognized and opportunities for upgrading are regarded as very important.

Disadvantages of broad-banding

The disadvantages of broad-banding are that:

- it appears to restrict the number of promotional opportunities

- employees formerly in higher grade may feel that broad-banding has devalued their jobs by placing them in the same band as employees previously in a lower grade

- employees may be concerned at its apparent lack of structure

- managing a broad-banded structure requires considerable effort and skill from personnel specialists and line managers alike

- it may be hard to control pay drift through bands unless very strict budgetary control and monitoring procedures are used

- it may be more difficult to ensure that equal pay is paid for work of equal value, especially if much less use is made of analytical job evaluation.

Job family structures

A job family structure consists of separate pay structures for job families. A job family consists of jobs in a function such as research and development, marketing, finance, computing or personnel which are related through the basic activities carried out and skills used but will be differentiated by the amount or degree of responsibility, competence or skills which are used at different levels.

Each level in a job family may have its own pay range as in a conventional graded structure. Alternatively, pay progression may be managed more flexibly to follow the continuous development of competence and contribution as in a broad-banded structure (job families are often slotted into broad-bands). Job family structures may only be created for certain occupations. Other jobs may be fitted into a more conventional graded structure.

Advantages

The advantages of job family structures are that:

- they enable special treatment to be given to selected key occupations from the point of view of rates of pay and pay progression

- career progression can be planned on the basis of increases in competence or skill

- individuals can easily be made aware of the development opportunities available for them in the job family – this could involve progressing through its levels defined in terms of competence or skill

- a job family can constitute a separate 'market group' where the occupations are subject to particular market pressures – rates of pay could be higher to attract and retain people than elsewhere in the organization, even if internal relativities established by job evaluation indicate that they should be placed in the same pay range.

Disadvantages

Job family structures can:

- be divisive, especially if jobs in families are paid more to match their own market rates
- inhibit career flexibility – moving between different job families
- make it more difficult to achieve equity between rates of pay, for example, between men and women carrying out work at a similar level in different job families or outside the job family structure.

Pay spines

Pay spines consist of a series of incremental pay points (annual pay increases) extending from the lowest to the highest-paid jobs in a structure. Pay ranges of so many increments are then superimposed on the pay scale. A typical increment is 3 per cent and a grade may be covered by 5 such increments. Thus someone who starts at the bottom of a grade will gain a pay increment of 3 per cent for each year of service until the top of the grade is reached after five years. This system may be called a service related fixed incremental pay structure. It is based on the assumption that the value of people to the organization is related directly to their length of service.

Pay spines are found in the public sector and some agencies and voluntary organizations. They are perceived to be fair in that there is only one factor which influences pay increases – time in the job. There is no room for possibly prejudiced decisions about the rate of increase from managers. Everyone knows what is going on. But pay spines or fixed incremental systems can be perceived as being inequitable. High contributors at the lower end of a scale may be paid much less than poor contributors at the upper end who have received more pay for simply being there rather than for performing more effectively. Pay spines can be costly. In times of low staff turnover and where there are few opportunities for promotion – conditions which are typical nowadays in many organizations. People tend to progress inevitably to the top of their scale and may be paid much more than they are worth to the organization or in the marketplace.

FURTHER READING

Armstrong M (1996) *Employee Reward,* Institute of Personnel and Development.

Armstrong M and Murlis H (1998) *Reward Management*, 4th edition, Kogan Page.

Fisher M (1995) *How to Reward Your Staff*, Kogan Page.

30

EVALUATING AND PRICING JOBS

Decisions on how the relative value of jobs should be determined and levels of pay may be made centrally in an organization but you might contribute to them. If there is no formal job evaluation scheme or systematic process of establishing market rates you may be involved in deciding where jobs should be placed in a pay structure and taking pay decisions based on your understanding of market relativities.

In either case you need to understand about job evaluation and market rate surveys as discussed in this chapter. You need to know what to do if you have to take into account the results of formal job evaluation or market rate surveys, and you need to know how to make logical and defensible decisions yourself without the benefit of supporting systems or data.

JOB EVALUATION

Definition

Job evaluation is a systematic process for establishing the relative worth or size of jobs within an organization.

Purposes

The purposes of job evaluation are to:

■ provide a rational basis for the design and maintenance of a pay structure

■ enable consistent decisions to be made on grading and therefore rates of pay

■ establish the extent to which there is comparable worth between jobs so that equal pay can be provided for work of equal value.

Approaches to job evaluation

Job evaluation is essentially a comparative process in which the values of jobs (not people) are related to one another. It is a process which requires judgement, but this judgement can be made more objective and therefore more fair when it is based, as it is in a formal scheme, on systematic job analysis and a framework which helps evaluators make consistent and equitable decisions.

The two basic approaches are non-analytical and analytical.

Non-analytical schemes

In non-analytical schemes whole jobs are compared with one another to be placed in rank order, or jobs are slotted as a whole into a grade in a pay structure by comparing them with a grade definition or with other established 'benchmark' jobs already placed in the grade.

Analytical schemes

In analytical schemes jobs are analysed in terms of a number of factors or characteristics, eg skill, responsibility and effort. These factors are common to all jobs but apply at different levels. Each factor has a maximum points score which may be weighed in accordance with what is believed to be the relative significance of the factor. The levels or degrees at which the factor can operate are defined and a points score or range of points is assigned to it. These factors, their levels and the points scores constitute the 'factor plan' which is used by job evaluation. This involves:

■ scoring jobs factor by factor according to the level assigned to that factor in the job and by reference to the factor plan

■ adding up the factor level scores to produce a total score

■ slotting the jobs on the basis of their scores into job grades which have been defined in points terms.

Use of non-analytical schemes

These are simpler to use but they do not provide a framework within which judgements can be made and they are not much use if you have to defend an equal pay claim.

An attempt may be made to increase the objectivity of a non-analytical scheme by setting out the factors that should be considered, even if points are not allocated to them. If jobs are compared systematically with grade definitions or other benchmark jobs on the basis of a proper analysis of the job being evaluated, then more accurate and defensible decisions will be made.

Some organizations have formalized their non-analytical schemes along these lines and the manager's role in these cases is simply to ensure that jobs are properly analysed in terms of the factors and then to achieve a more objective judgement by systematically comparing one job with another. It is easier to operate within a defined framework.

But recent research has shown that 40 to 50 per cent of organizations do not have any type of formal job evaluation, non-analytical or analytical. This does not mean that they do not evaluate jobs in the sense that they decide on some basis or other that one job is worth more than the same as or less than the other. These sort of organizations are doing this all the time. Whether or not the outcomes of these largely subjective judgements are equitable, consistent or fair is another matter. The chances are that they will not meet any of these criteria. There is too much scope for prejudice, bias, discrimination and half-baked decisions.

This is dangerous. A number of research projects have established that a major reason for dissatisfaction with the job or the organization is the perception amongst employees that decisions on relative job values are unfair, inconsistent, inequitable and unjustified. A major cause of demotivation and a common reason for good people leaving an organization is that they do not consider that they are being paid what they are worth compared with other people. This belief may not be justified but it will be held unless they feel that your decisions are fair and are logically based on objective data.

What line managers can do

If you have to make job evaluation decisions in the absence of a formal scheme these are the things you should do to make appropriate and defensible decisions which will not demotivate people:

1   Ensure that before making a decision the job has been analysed in such terms as:

- *level of responsibility* – what the job holder is accountable for, including contribution (impact on end-results), freedom to act (extent to which decisions have to be made independently) and resources controlled (people, money and assets)

- *characteristics of the work* – mental or physical effort required, complexity, problem-solving, dealing with people

- *knowledge and skills* – technical or professional knowledge, manual and mental skills, interpersonal and leadership skills.

2 Ensure that a job analysis using the same terms is available for any jobs with which you are comparing the job you are evaluating.

3 Compare the two (or more jobs) by reference to each of these criteria.

4 Reach a conclusion on the relative worth of the job by reference to the comparisons.

5 Explain to the job holder the procedure you followed and the reason for your decision (if this is an existing rather than a new job).

Use of analytical schemes

Organizations that have analytical job evaluation schemes either adopt one of the management consultants' 'proprietary brands' for example the Guide Chart method of Hay Management Consultants. Or they develop a tailor-made scheme themselves or with the help of consultants.

In either case, your role as a line manager will be to take part in the process of job analysis for members of your department. This could arise because a new job has been created, an existing job has changed or the job holder has lodged an appeal to the effect that their job is wrongly graded. You could also be a member of a job evaluation panel for the organization, in which case you should have been trained in your duties.

When you are involved in job analysis your responsibility is to ensure that an accurate and comprehensive picture of the job emerges. The job analysis techniques with which you will be concerned are basically those described in Chapter 13 but you may take part in a special analysis of the job in terms of the job evaluation scheme factors.

Some managers are tempted to exaggerate the level of the job in order to curry favour with job holders, or generally to enhance the status of their own departments, or even to demonstrate that if the job of a subordinate is upgraded their own job will also have to be placed in a higher grade. Such behaviour is, of course, indefensible. If it is practised too widely the whole job evaluation process and the pay system will fall into disrepute and this makes the life of the managers who have been responsible for this happening as difficult as any of the innocent parties.

ESTABLISHING MARKET RATES

To maintain competitive pay levels in order to attract and retain good people it is necessary to know what is being paid in the market place for the jobs with which you are concerned.

You may be tempted to base your conclusions on the pay information provided in advertisements. This temptation should be resisted. Advertisements can be notoriously misleading. You cannot be certain that you are comparing like with like – job titles can mean many different things in different organizations – and the pay figures companies quote in advertisements are often exaggerated.

You need more accurate information and this can be obtained from published surveys or from other organizations. If you have a personnel department, it will obtain and analyse the data for you – but before examining these surveys it is necessary to discuss briefly the concept of a market rate and ways of presenting market rate data.

The concept of a market rate

People commonly talk about the market rate for a job as if there were such a thing as the market rate. There is not. No market rate survey will ever produce a result which states, unequivocally, the correct rate of pay for a job. There is always a wide range of market rates for any occupation as the different surveys indicate when covering the same type of job. The determination of the going rate for a job or a person in a job is as much art as science. This is because:

■ different firms have different policies on what they need to pay

■ individuals have in effect their own market rate – their 'market worth' – which varies widely according to their expertise, experience and the degree to which their talents are unique

■ larger firms tend to pay more, and rates of pay are higher in some labour markets than others.

The accuracy of market rate information may also vary because of the following the factors:

- *Job matching* – the accuracy depends on comparing like with like. But published surveys tend to make comparisons on the basis of very flimsy descriptions of what constitutes the responsibilities of the job. The same can apply to special surveys unless a lot of time and trouble is taken to compare job analyses and even use the same job evaluation scheme to check on comparative levels of responsibility in different organizations.

- *Timing* – surveys may contain out-of-date information because they have been conducted some time before publication.

Presenting information on market rates

Information on market rates is presented as an indication of the average or median and of the spread between the pay figures collected in the survey.

Average or median

The arithmetic average or mean is the form in what 'central tendencies' are usually referred to. It is often used in pay surveys but it can be distorted if there are any extremely high or low values in the distribution of the data.

The median gets over this problems and is therefore more frequently used in pay surveys. This is the value falling in the middle of a distribution of figures. Half the reported rates of pay will be equal to or above the median and half will be equal to or below the median

Measures of spread or dispersion

These are:

- the range which covers the lowest and highest figures in a distribution of pay values for jobs

- the upper quartile is the value in a distribution which a quarter of the values exceed and three quarters of the values are lower than

- the lower quartile is the value in a distribution which three quarters of the values exceed and a quarter of the values are lower than

- the interquartile range is a measure of spread between the upper and lower quartile – it covers the middle 50 per cent of values and is a useful way of expressing dispersion which eliminates extreme figures at either end (and there are usually some of these).

Sources of data – published surveys and other data sources

Published surveys can be obtained, at a price, but some of the larger ones can be consulted in libraries such as the Institute of Personnel and Development or the Institute of Directors.

The surveys available are:

■ general national and regional surveys such as those published by Reward, Monks Publications and PE International

■ local surveys conducted by agencies or consultants

■ sector surveys (eg the voluntary sector) such as those conducted by Charity Recruitment

■ occupational surveys covering professional jobs, specific categories of occupation such as computer specialists or sales staff and office staff – these are published by professional institutions and various specialist publishers or agencies

■ industrial surveys conduced by employees and trade unions

■ management consultants' data bases – the large consultancy firms such as Hay Management Consultants maintain a data base of rates which can be accessed by clients, or on payment of a fee, by non-clients.

■ published data in journals – Incomes Data Services and the IRS Employment Review monitor pay settlements and publish information on trends.

Because the information varies between different surveys the ideal approach is to get hold of several of them, if you can, and come to a judgement on the market rates with which you should compare your rates. This is a somewhat subjective process and produces what is sometimes referred to as a 'derived market rate'.

Sources of data – special surveys

You or your personnel department can conduct your own survey by getting pay information from comparable companies for similar jobs. This may be a local survey for manual workers, sales or clerical jobs but it may extend to the regional or national labour markets if you are recruiting from them.

The advantages of conducting your own survey are that you get immediate and, if replies to your enquiries are truthful, valid data. To encourage people to respond you should promise to let them have an anonymous summary of the survey data.

The steps to take in conducting a pay survey are:

- draw up a list of suitable organizations

- invite the organizations to participate

- prepare information on your jobs (brief description) and distribute them to participating organizations

- analyse the data and distribute a summary (preferably presented if you have had sufficient replies – say 12 or more – in the form if the median, upper and lower quartile figures).

If you regularly contact a number of employees you can encourage them to form a pay 'club' for the collection and analysis of data. Or, if such a club already exists, you can join it (if they will have you, some restrict membership).

Using the data

Market rate data can be used for the following purposes:

- to ensure that your pay levels remain competitive in accordance with your pay policy or 'market stance' – this represents the point where you want to fix your rates, say at the median or between the median and the upper quartile

- to help with decisions on the rates of pay for recruits, possibly to be quoted in advertisements

- to provide guidance at individual pay review times when you look at the rates of pay of existing employees – you can compare them with market rates and then decide on any adjustments required to ensure that the pay of the people you want to retain remains competitive

- to provide guidance on general 'across the board' pay reviews when overall uplifts to pay may be made to ensure that pay levels match the going rates (many organizations are basing reviews on market rate trends rather than rates of inflation although, of course market trends reflect trends in the cost of living)

- to provide guidance on the design of pay structures or the 'pricing' (attaching rates of pay) of jobs in the structure – pay ranges may be designed broadly to cover the interquartile market range for jobs allocated into the grade.

FURTHER READING

Armstrong M and Baron A (1995) The Job Evaluation Handbook, Institute of Personnel and Development.

31

PAYING FOR PERFORMANCE, COMPETENCE OR SKILL

When you pay individuals for their performance you are hoping that they will be motivated by the prospect of extra money as a result of their efforts. You are providing an incentive. But you will also be providing a reward when you recognize their achievement with money. It is useful to remember the distinction between incentives, which look forward, and rewards, which look backwards. Incentives are intended to provide direct motivation, rewards can only motivate indirectly by providing financial recognition, if that is worth having.

People can also be paid for the efforts of their team (team pay) or the results achieved by the organization (gainsharing, profit sharing and profit-related pay). Such payments will not provide direct motivation; they do not 'incentivize'. But they can increase commitment.

Paying for individual performance in the shape of payment-by-result schemes for manual/workers and performance-related pay (mainly for non-manual workers) has a long history. More recently, organizations have developed schemes for rewarding competence or skill.

This chapter starts with a general review of the considerations affecting performance, competence or skills pay. It then deals separately with:

- payment-by-results schemes for manual workers

- performance-related pay

- skill-based pay

- team pay

- paying for organizational performance.

GENERAL CONSIDERATIONS

Criteria

The eight golden rules for paying individuals or teams for their performance as quoted by Armstrong and Murlis are:

1   Individuals and teams should be clear about the targets and standards of performance required, whatever they may be.
2   They should be able to track performance against those targets and standards throughout the period over which the performance is being assessed. They must be able to measure their performance because if you can't measure performance you can't pay for performance.
3   They must be in a position to influence the performance by changing their behaviour or decisions.
4   They should understand what rewards they will receive for achieving the end results – there should be a clear link between effort and reward.
5   The reward should follow as closely as possible the accomplishment which generated it.
6   The reward should be worthwhile.
7   The results required to generate the reward should be attainable, although not too easily.
8   The basis upon which rewards are made should be communicated positively and should be easy to understand.

These rules are in line with the precepts derived from expectancy and goal theory as described in Chapter 4. They also apply in general to competence-related and skill-based pay schemes.

Methods of payment

Rewards can be paid as 'variable pay' which is not consolidated, ie it does not become a permanent part of back pay. This takes the forms of the incentive payments made in payment-by-results scheme, the commission paid to sales representatives, or the cash bonuses paid to people, eg executives, for special achievements or sustained high levels of performance.

Alternatively, payments can be consolidated into base pay. This applies to service related payments and most performance-related pay schemes. In the latter case, however, some companies are moving into variable pay on the grounds that payments for performance need to be re-earned, they should not be perpetuated. Why, it is said, should someone who did well three years ago but badly ever since continue to benefit three years after the event?

PAYMENT BY RESULTS

Payment by results schemes for manual workers relate extra payment to effort and/or output. They are less common now because managements have become increasingly disenchanted with incentive schemes which degenerate because of loose rates or poor control resulting in the phenomenon called 'wage drift' – earnings going up without commensurate increases in effort or output. It is felt by many people that shop floor incentive schemes are more trouble than they are worth and are not cost-effective. Such schemes are no longer appropriate in high technology environments where workers do not control output, where flexibility is important and where results are achieved by collective efforts, as in just-in-time, cellular and group technology systems. In these situations, direct incentives are being replaced by high day rates. A high day rate is a fixed rate which is set at a level significantly higher than the base rate that would be paid if there were a payment-by-results scheme in operation. The high day rate may be broadly equivalent to what workers on average earnings (base rate plus incentive pay) would get, say 30 per cent above the base rate.

A bonus may be paid in addition to the high day rate related to team or organizational performance. When incentive schemes are retained there are two main types, as described below: piecework and work measured schemes.

Piecework

Piecework is the oldest and simplest form of incentive scheme. Operators are paid at a specific rate according to their output – the number of 'pieces' they produce. It is, however, rare except for part time agricultural workers and, often unpleasantly, in the garment industry.

Work measured schemes

Work measured schemes are the most popular form of incentive plan for manual workers. They use work measurement techniques to determine output levels over a period and standard times for tasks. The incentive pay is linked to the output achieved relative to the standard or to the time saved in performing the task.

Work-measured schemes may be appropriate when the following

conditions apply:

- short-cycle repetitive work predominates
- changes to the work mix, tasks or methods are infrequent
- hold-ups and down time are rare
- management and supervision helped by work study engineers can manage the scheme and prevent degeneration
- productivity is so low that the stimulus of an incentive scheme is desirable.

But such schemes are hard to keep under control and can easily degenerate because of loose rates or the erosion of standards. Workers do not always like them because ratings seem to be too subjective and earnings can fluctuate through no fault of theirs.

Choice of approach

You should always be cautious about introducing payment by results scheme. They can be more trouble than they are worth, especially of the stringent criteria mentioned earlier cannot be met and the conditions are not appropriate.

You should also review the operation of a current scheme. If you cannot confidently answer yes to all the following questions you should consider improvements and think again about whether you want it at all.

- Are you convinced that the scheme produces measurable increases in productivity?
- Are you certain that the cost of the scheme is justified by its impact on output?
- Are you sure that the scheme does not affect quality?
- Is the scheme easy to manage and control?
- Have you managed to eliminate loose rates and wage drift?
- Are your managers and supervisors happy with the scheme?
- Are the workers happy with the scheme?

PERFORMANCE-RELATED PAY

Performance-related pay (PRP) offers individuals financial rewards in the form of increase in basic pay (most commonly) and/or cash bonuses which are linked to an assessment of performance.

Reasons for introducing PRP

PRP is introduced and returned because it is usually believed that:

- it is an effective motivator
- it conveys a clear message to employees that high levels of performance are expected and will be rewarded
- it is right and proper to relate pay to performance – high performers should get more than low performers.

The effectiveness of many PRP schemes as motivators has been questioned by many commentators who point out that they usually fail to meet the criteria for a good incentive scheme. A number of research projects have failed to detect a measurable link between PRP and higher levels of performance.

The argument that PRP delivers the right sort of message is more convincing, but this depends on people believing that schemes are working fairly, and often they do not.

Perhaps the most convincing argument for PRP is that it is fair to reward people according to their contribution. If there were no PRP you would have to pay everyone in the same job the same amount of money irrespective of their performance, which does not really make any sense. Alternatively you would have to relate pay entirely to time in the job on the somewhat dubious assumption that the longer anyone does a job the better they will become at it. This recalls the old tag: 'It is all very well saying that someone has had five years' experience, but couldn't that have been one year's experience repeated five times?'

Advantages of PRP

The advantages claimed for PRP can be summarized as follows:

- It motivates.
- It delivers the right message.
- It is fair to reward people according to their performance.

■   It provides a tangible means of rewarding and recognising achievements.

Disadvantages of PRP

The disadvantages of PRP, as pointed out by its many critics, are that:

■   It is not a guaranteed motivator, the performance pay criteria mentioned earlier in this chapter are often difficult if not impossible to meet.

■   It has to be based on some form of performance assessment, usually a rating. But it may be difficult to produce realistic performance measures. As a result, ratings may be – will be, according to some trade unions – unfair, subjective and inconsistent. A further problem with basing pay decisions on performance or merit ratings will occur if they are made during the performance management review process. If it is known that the output of a review meeting will be a rating used to determine the amount of a pay increase there is a real danger that the people at the receiving end of the review will focus all their attention on this outcome. This could seriously prejudice the developmental purposes of the review by diverting attention away from the formulation of personal development plans. Individuals will only be concerned with making the best case possible for themselves and going on to the defensive when they think they are being criticized. It is because they do not want this to take place that many organizations have abandoned the use of ratings and hold their pay reviews at a separate time.

■   If there is undue emphasis on individual performance, teamwork will suffer.

■   PRP can lead to pay rising faster than performance (pay drift). In other words, it is not cost-effective.

■   PRP schemes are difficult to manage well. They rely upon effective performance management processes which many organizations will not have.

Criteria for installing and monitoring PRP

If you have any influence on the introduction of PRP or the continuation of a scheme these are the criteria you should consider before launching it or deciding whether or not it should be retained.

■   Will the proposed scheme or does the existing scheme motivate people?

■ Is it possible to devise or maintain fair and consistent methods of measuring performance?

■ Is there an effective performance management process in place which is based on measuring and assessing performance against agreed targets and standards?

■ Can managers be trained (or are managers properly trained) to rate performance fairly and consistently?

■ Will there be, is there, enough money available to provide worthwhile rewards?

■ Will the proposed scheme or does the existing scheme satisfy the other criteria for an effective performance pay system, namely, clear targets and standards, ability to track performance, ability to influence performance, clarity on the relationship between effort and reward, the reward follows the accomplishment fairly closely?

■ Will the scheme be, or is the scheme, cost effective?

If you are not confident that you can answer all these questions positively in favour of PRP, you need to be very careful about introducing it.

One alternative is to abandon PRP as a means of adding performance-related increases to the base rate and replace it with a system which only awards cash bonuses as and when they are earned for notable and measurable achievements. In addition, you could consider a cash bonus for someone who has achieved sustained levels of high performance as demonstrated by exceeding targets and standards over an extended period.

Another alternative which a number of organizations are turning to is competence-related pay.

COMPETENCE-RELATED PAY

How it works

Competence-related pay provides for pay progression to be linked to assessments of the levels of competence people have achieved. Typically, the headings in a competence profile or framework are used as the basis for assessment. The level of competence expected from a fully effective individual in a role is defined and the actual levels achieved are compared with requirements.

In some schemes people are assessed against each competence heading and an overall assessment is then made which may be expressed on a scale such as: exceeds to level of competence required, fully competent, not yet competent but developing at the expected rate, not yet competent but developing at less than the expected rate. These assessments are then translated into a pay increase.

Measuring competence

The problem with competence-related pay is that of measuring levels of competence. This is easiest when hard, work-based competences are used rather than softer, behaviourally-based competencies. If competence or capabilities are used they will have been defined in output terms ie 'in this aspect of the role the person should be capable of.' The capability will be described in terms of doing something which will produce a result. The measurement of competence therefore starts by reviewing results in each area of capability and thus assessing how effectively the competence has been used.

If this approach is adopted, competence-related pay begins to look suspiciously like performance related pay. But if competence is not about performance, what is it about?

Differences between performance-related and competence-related pay

But there are differences between performance and competence-related pay. These are:

- Competence-related pay is based on an agreed framework of competences or capabilities, some of which are generic (applicable to a number of roles), some of which are specific to particular roles.

- Competence-related pay is not based on the achievement of specific results expressed in the form of targets or projects to be completed, but it can be said to be concerned with the attainment on a continuing basis of agreed standards of performance.

- Competence-related pay looks forward in the sense that it implies that when people have reached a certain level of competence they will be able to go on using it effectively into the future; conversely, performance-related looks backwards – this is what you have just achieved, this is your reward for achieving it.

- Competence-related pay is based on agreed definition of competence requirements expressed in the language of role holders and on agreements about the evidence that can be used to assess levels of competence; in contrast performance-related pay is often, although not always, based on managerial judgements which the individuals concerned may find difficult to accept.

Advantages and disadvantages of competence-related pay

The list of differences between competence and performance-related pay given above summarize a number of the advantages of the former. If the organization really believes that successful performance depends on raising levels of competence then some form of competence-related pay makes sense.

But there are problems of measuring competence, and translating any measurements into an overall assessment can seem to be an arbitrary process. Competence-related pay also seems to ignore the fact that performance is about delivering results. That is why some organizations have introduced hybrid schemes in which base pay is related to competence but out-of-the-ordinary achievements are rewarded with cash bonuses. Many people think that this is the best way forward.

Conditions necessary to introduce competence-related pay

You or your organization should not contemplate the introduction of competence-related pay lightly. The following demanding criteria need to be met if it is to work:

■ well researched and analysed competence frameworks must be in place

■ reliable, fair and consistent methods of assessing competence must be available

■ managers, team leaders and employees generally should be trained in how the process operates and must be convinced that it is workable and fair.

Competence-related pay is generally more likely to be appropriate for 'knowledge workers' in organizations where the values and processes focus on flexibility, adaptability and continuous development.

SKILL-BASED PAY

Skill-based pay provides employees with a direct link between their pay progression and the skills they have acquired and can use effectively. It works as follows:

- skill blocks or modules are defined incorporating individual skills or clusters of skills which workers will use

- the skills blocks are arranged in a hierarchy

- the additional pay which will be awarded for the successful acquisition of the skills required in each skill block is determined – this shows how the pay of individuals will progress as they gain extra skills (typically, payments per module average about £300 in UK firms with skill-based pay)

- methods of verifying that workers have acquired the skills and can use them effectively are established

- arrangements for 'cross-training' are made which consist of learning modules for each skill block.

Advantages and disadvantages of skill-based pay

Skill-based pay is a means of encouraging the development or acquisition of skills, especially in circumstances when flexibility and consequently multiskilling is required. But it is expensive to introduce and maintain because of the training and accreditation requirements, and companies which have introduced it have too often found themselves paying for skills which are used infrequently, if at all.

TEAM-BASED PAY

Team-based pay provides rewards to teams or groups of employees carrying out similar and related work which is linked to the performance of the team. Performance may be measured in terms of outputs and/or the achievement of service delivery standards. The quality of the output and the opinion of customers about service levels are also often taken into account.

Team pay is usually paid in the form of a bonus which is shared amongst team members in proportion to their base rate of pay (much less frequently, it is shared equally). Individual team members may be eligible for competence-related or skill-based pay but not for performance-related pay.

Advantages of team pay

Team pay can:

- encourage effective team working and co-operative behaviour
- clarify team goals and priorities
- enhance flexible working within teams
- encourage multiskilling
- provide an incentive for the team collectively to improve performance
- encourage less effective team members to improve to meet team standards.

Disadvantages of team pay

The disadvantages of team pay are that:

- it only works in cohesive and mature teams
- individuals may resent the fact that their own efforts are not rewarded specifically
- peer pressure which compels individuals to conform to group norms could be undesirable.

Conditions suitable for team pay

Team pay is more likely to be appropriate when:

- teams can be readily identified and defined
- teams are well-established
- the work carried out by team members is inter-related – team performance depends on the collective efforts of team members
- targets and standards of performance can be determined and agreed readily with team members
- acceptable measurements of team performance compared with targets and standards are available
- generally, the formula for team pay meets the criteria for performance pay set out in the first section of this chapter.

PAYMENTS RELATED TO ORGANIZATIONAL PERFORMANCE

Payments related to organizational performance aim to:

- enable employees to share in the success of the business

- increase the identification of employees with the organizations, ie their commitment

- focus the attention of employees on what they can contribute to the success of the business.

They do not provide direct motivation. The main ways of relating pay to organizational performance are profit-sharing, gainsharing and profit-related pay.

Profit-sharing

Profit-sharing schemes provide eligible employees from a pool, the size of which is influenced by profit performance. Cash payments are distributed in accordance with a formula. They are usually expressed as a percentage of base pay.

Gainsharing

Gainsharing schemes provide for employees to share in the financial gains made by a company. Typically, the performance indicator used to calculate the money available is added value (the difference between the value of sales and the amount spent on materials and other purchased goods and services). Added value is the preferred indicator because it is in effect the wealth created by the people in the business.

Gainsharing differs from profit-sharing and, in this respect, is preferable, because it is based on factors which are within the control of employees. The calculation of profits depends on many considerations which have nothing to do with productivity. A key aspect of gainsharing schemes is that it can be used to involve employees in analysing the reasons for results as measured in added value terms. Discussions can take place on how they can contribute to improve those results and increase their shares accordingly. Gainsharing can be called participation with teeth.

Profit-related pay

Profit-related pay is a government sponsored scheme which arranges for a proportion of pay to go up and down with profits. The major attraction of the scheme was the tax advantages it provided (up to certain limits, profit-related pay was free of income tax). But these advantages have now been removed and it is not such an attractive proposition.

Examples

The following are three examples of approaches to pay progression and performance pay.

New grading structure at Kimberley Clark

The grading structure established by Kimberley Clark, the paper product manufacturer, consists of established systematic benchmarks for skills acquisition and long-term career development. It is supported by regular individual performance reviews. It was introduced because managers had identified a serious problem with the system of individual salary progression via the attainment of skills credits. Like a number of other manufacturers who have experimented with such approaches, the company found that people ended up 'chasing skills', rather than developing them in a way that met business needs. They could get additional payment for being qualified to operate a particular piece of equipment in addition to their usual machine, regardless of whether they would ever be required to use it.

By contrast, the new grading structure, covering all manufacturing employees, from trainee operator right up to team leader, is based on five salary bands, with progression within bands, and promotion between them, linked to the acquisition and use of a very broad range of both 'hard' technical and softer behavioural skills.

Progression through the grading structure at GKN Westland helicopters

The introduction of the new production pay structure in 1994 allowed cell team members to develop skills on an individual basis. Each grade within the structure has job specifications attached. If individuals are paid as grade 'C', they can be required to do any job which is classed as a grade 'C' task, provided it is within safety and training limitations. The job evaluation process is conducted by the grading committee which is made up of four managers and four union representatives, chaired by the employee relations manager. When the new structure was introduced certain existing jobs were evaluated in order to establish appropriate job relativities and hence the pay scales.

When new skills are needed in the production process, agreement is reached between the manager and job-holder. A job description is generated against the appropriate criteria, such as length of experience, training, accountability and responsibility. The grading committee evaluates the criteria and places the job in the grading structure. If extra skills are added to the job it will move up to the next skill grade within the structure.

Heatherwood and Wexam Park Hospitals Trust

The performance-related pay scheme in this Trust rewards five levels of performance: excellent, superior, good, average, and poor. For those on Trust contracts, each level of performance attracts a given percentage increase in base salary.

At the heart of the scheme is the individual performance and development review. A 'contribution profile' has been established for every non-medical job in the Trust. This sets out the skills and contribution required in a particular job and acts as the blueprint against which the job holder's performance can be assessed. The profile establishes the standard or level of contribution required in the following six categories: occupational skills, interpersonal skills, leadership skills, and planning and administration skills. For each of these competency areas, jobs are categorised into one of six levels, ranging from the lowest level A, up to level F.

The review process has three stages. At the beginning of the year employees discuss with their line manager their objectives, their job contribution profile and their training and development needs. Through the year there are informal progress reviews. At the end of the year, the formal assessment takes place, where the manager employee and manager evaluate performance against both objectives and the job contribution profile. Finally, the manager decides he overall rating which determines the level of pay award. There are guidelines on deciding the rating and various safeguards are built into the system to ensure consistency across the Trust. An important control is the 'grandparent' system whereby a second level manager oversees the whole process. Employees who disagree with their rating can appeal to their 'grandparent manager', but there is no further appeal procedure.

Each department and the Trust as a whole has a target range of distribution ratings to control the payroll increase. On the basis of a normal distribution, the target is for 60 per cent of employees to be assessed in the middle range of 'good' with 20 per cent as 'superior' or 'excellent' and 20 per cent as 'average' or 'poor'.

FURTHER READING

Armstrong M and Murlis H (1998) *Reward Management*, 4th edition, Kogan Page.

32

REVIEWING PAY AND MAKING PAY DECISIONS

Increasingly, line managers are getting more involved in decisions concerning general, 'across-the-board' pay reviews and are taking on more responsibility for reviewing the pay of individual employees and for making pay decisions when recruiting people. This chapter covers:

■ general pay reviews

■ reviewing individual rates of pay

■ deciding on rates of pay for recruits.

GENERAL PAY REVIEWS

Considerations affecting reviews

General, across-the-board, pay reviews may follow a pay settlement with trade unions or a staff association. More commonly, they are based on the decisions of management. These decisions are influenced by four considerations:

1   Inflation – increases in the cost of living. But few if any managements can afford to commit themselves automatically to compensate people for the impact of inflation to protect their standard of living by maintaining the real value of their pay. Such a policy would be a hostage to fortune. Inflation rates may be reasonably low at one point in time but there is no certainty that they may not go up in the

future to levels which companies cannot afford to match with pay increases. Some companies take the hard view that there is no obligation on their part to protect the real value of their employee's earnings. There may be occasions, they say, when poor performers should receive no increase at all or an increase which is less than inflation, thus effectively reducing their real earnings. Many companies are now taking the line that their main concern is to maintain competitive pay levels, in which case they take account of 'going rates' or market rate trends.

2   The going rate – this is the rate of increase other similar organizations are applying generally. If everyone else in the same industry or area is awarding, say, 3 per cent, a company may well decide to do the same.

3   Market rate trends – more companies are now saying that the main criterion for pay reviews should be trends in market rates, generally, or differentially for distinct occupations. They argue that increases in market rates, like going rate trends, are influenced by inflation, so why bother about the latter? What is most important, they say, is to ensure that their rates of pay remain competitive.

4   Affordability – whatever the rate of inflation, the going rate or market rate trends, the ultimate factor governing pay increases (general or individual) is how much the business can afford.

Timing

The most common practice is to have an annual pay review on a fixed date. But there is no reason why it should be held annually. There could be interim reviews during the year. Reviews could be held as and when required, with periods longer than a year between them if there is no reason for holding them, or if the company believes that it cannot afford a general increase.

Delaying reviews will, of course, upset employees, especially if an annual review has been the norm, and the reasons for delay would have to be explained to them. If there are trade unions, this would be a matter of negotiation.

Consolidating general and individual reviews

Some companies are now consolidating general and individual reviews. This means that the amount available for individual increases covers both market rate trends and rewards related to the individual's performance or competence. Companies such as ICL go further than this and have a policy which states that they are concerned with paying whatever a person is worth (both to the company and in the market place). This means that they start from a decision on what an individual should be paid in total and do not talk in terms of a percentage increase above the present rate.

Control in some companies such as Book Club Associates is exercised over total payroll costs in departments. This covers all expenditure on people and allows for pay increases arising from promotions as well as individual reviews and, of course, the headcount. This 'total payroll budgeting' approach means that the traditional pay review budget of x per cent is no longer used.

INDIVIDUAL REVIEWS

Your role as a line manager in conducting individual pay reviews will vary considerably according to company policy, although you will almost certainly always be controlled by a payroll or pay review budget.

Budgets

The most common practice is to issue a pay review budget of, say, 3.5 per cent to managers and ensure that pay proposals do not exceed that budget. Alternatively, as referred to above, a total payroll budget is agreed. Within the budget the approaches adopted by organizations vary from total central control, to allowing considerable freedom to line managers, with various forms of intermediate control between these two extremes.

Total central control

If there is an across-the-board increase, total central control means that this is imposed across the organization. If there is some form of performance, competence or skill pay, the centre will impose the increases within an overall budget by reference to the performance ratings of managers.

Forced distribution

In an entirely centralized approach, performance ratings will be governed by a system of forced distribution. This involves managers distributing their ratings amongst their staff in the proportion laid down by the centre, for example:

A	=	Excellent	–	5%
B	=	above average	–	15%
C	=	average	–	60%
D	=	below average	–	15%
E	=	poor	–	5%

A decision is made at the centre that these ratings should be rewarded by percentage increases, say:

A	=	5%
B	=	4%
C	=	3%
D	=	2%
E	=	0%

This would give an overall percentage increase of just under 3 per cent. The forced distribution and/or the percentage increases for different ratings can be flexed to produce different overall percentages.

Pay matrix

A more refined version of this approach is to have a policy which states that pay increases should be governed not only by the performance or merit rating but also by the position of an individual in the pay range for the job. The jargon term for this is 'compa-ratio'. This ratio gives the position of a person's salary in the pay range. For example, a typical range extends 20 per cent on either side of the central point, e.g. 80 per cent (£16,000) – 100 per cent (£20,000) – 120 per cent (£24,000). The compa-ratio would then be 100 per cent for someone paid £20,000, between 100 and 120 per cent for someone paid between £20,000 and £24,000, and between 100 and 80 per cent for someone paid between £20,000 and £16,000.

Companies often have a policy which states that the rate of increase in a range should reduce as progress is made through the range. In the jargon, this is a 'decelerated pay increase model'. The rationale for this approach is that individuals are likely to make more progress in their earlier period in a range and should be rewarded accordingly. The rate at which they progress later may be limited by their own capacities or the scope for improvement in the role.

The rate of increase should therefore be reduced. In any case, it is argued, pay increases in a range are added cumulatively to the base rate and a lower percentage increase in the higher reaches of the range would still mean a greater cash increment. A typical pay matrix is shown in Figure 32.1.

Rating	% increase according to position in pay range			
	80–90%	91–100%	101–110%	111–120%
Exceptional	12	10	8	6
Very effective	10	8	6	4
Effective	6	4	3	0
Developing	4	3	0	0
Ineligible	0	0	0	0

Figure 32.1   A pay matrix

The amount of increase depends entirely on the rating. If forced distribution is used, this means that it is dictated from the centre, as is the increase related to position in the range.

Ranking

Another centralized approach to individual pay reviews is to get managers to rank their staff according to the points they award through merit rating (a largely discredited approach to performance appraisal which allocates points under various characteristics such as judgement and initiative according to the individual's perceived merit in this area).

A central decision is then made on how increases should be distributed according to the rank order, for example, the top ten per cent get a 5 per cent increase, the next 15 per cent get 4 per cent and so on.

Contribution of line managers

The only contribution that line managers make to these processes is to allocate ratings and that is constrained by the forced distribution. They are therefore perceived by many line managers as being arbitrary and as removing from them any scope for exercising their leadership qualities in managing and motivating their staff. Some managers, however, quite like pay decisions to be made on this basis – they do not have to explain to staff the reasons for their increase and can indeed hide behind 'management' decisions. But this could hardly be described as a commendable attitude. It is surely better for line managers to have to make decisions on pay, even within clear guidelines, and then to have to explain or even defend them to their staff.

Intermediate approaches to guiding individual pay reviews

The four intermediate approaches to guiding individual pay reviews are described below in declining order of centralized duration and control. In each case, overall control would be exercised to ensure that payroll increases were kept within the pay review budget.

Issue guidelines and a non-mandatory scale.

A scale is issued showing as guidelines the amount that could be awarded for each level of performance rating. But a forced distribution of the ratings is not required.

Issue guidelines on recommended increases but without a rating scale.

Managers are asked to produce recommendations on the size of increase they would want each member of their staff to receive. The guidelines simply state that the recommendations should set out who should be given:

- an above average increase, say between 4 and 6 per cent
- an average increase, say 3 per cent
- a below average increase, say 2 per cent
- no increase at all.

This approach leaves a fair degree of freedom to managers, but they would be required to justify any unusual distributions, eg large numbers of high and low increases and, a far more common failing, everyone or a very high proportion of staff being recommended an average increase. The latter approach is adopted by managers who do not have the courage to single out people to be paid more or less than others and want an easy life by giving everyone the same.

Organizations may adopt this method when they are against including ratings in their performance management process because they are invidious and arbitrary. They also want to separate pay review recommendations from the performance and development review. This is because, if the review were perceived as mainly existing to inform pay decisions (as merit rating schemes often did), then the developmental purposes of performance management would suffer.

Of course it is recognized that there is a 'read across' from a performance and development review to a separate performance pay review although this would not be so blatantly linked to performance review ratings. It also allows the pay review to take into account other reasons for awarding above or below average increases, for example the fact that an individual's pay differs significantly from the market rate for the job.

Issue average and min/max guidelines

The average performance pay award, say 3 per cent, is laid down, and restrictions are issued on the maximum and minimum pay increases that can be awarded, say 5 per cent and 2 per cent respectively. This method can be used in the same way as the second approach described above when there are no performance ratings and the pay and performance reviews are separated.

Issue budget for pay increases only

Managers are informed of the budget for their payroll increase as a result of the pay review, say 3 per cent. They are then free to distribute this pool of pay award money amongst their staff. Policy guidelines would be issued to the effect that managers would be expected to make sensible decisions on the distribution of rewards and would have to justify unusual ones.

Complete or at least considerable devolution of pay decisions to line managers

A few organizations devolve almost complete responsibility to line managers to make pay decisions as long as they keep within their budgets. But gross inconsistencies between departments would have to be justified and close attention has to be paid to ensuring that people carrying out work of equal value are paid equally.

Conducting the review

The steps taken by Bass Brewers to conduct a pay review are set out below.

- Budget centre managers propose and obtain agreement to their payroll budget which will allow for any pay increases.

- Budget centre managers are issued with printouts showing the distribution of the rates of pay of their staff. These could be accessed on a PC screen through a password.

- Information on the latest market rates for the different jobs in the managers' department is also issued.

- Managers examine the rate of pay of each of their staff in turn, giving consideration to:

  - how the rate compares with market rates

  - the level of competence and contribution of the role holder

  - how the rate compares with what other people carrying out the role at the same level of competence and contribution are receiving.

Managers take into account the above considerations and decide what the appropriate rate of pay for the individual should be.

Managers consider the increase necessary to bring the individual's rate to the appropriate level and they may decide that the increase should be made in more than one stage.

Using a computer model, managers calculate the effect of their interim decisions on their payroll (this calculation may be done on their behalf by personnel)

If the impact of the first proposals are out of line with the payroll budget limits, managers adjust their recommendations (a process of iteration). The computer model can be used to make a series of 'what if' calculations.

The final proposal, which must not produce an increase in payroll above the budget, is submitted to personnel.

Personnel reviews the proposals and questions any that seem out of line with pay policy.

A peer review takes place in which managers present their pay recommendations to their colleagues who question any unusual proposals or ones that conflict with what they are doing. This peer review process is another way of devolving responsibility to line managers for not only making pay decisions but also for monitoring the overall pay review process to ensure that it is consistent with company policy.

Mangers make amendments to their proposals in the light of the comments of personnel and their peers.

Pay review aims

Your aim in conducting a pay review is to ensure that as far as possible within the framework of your budgets and company policies:

- the rate of pay for your key roles and your fully competent staff in those roles are competitive so that you can attract and retain high quality people

- your pay decisions demonstrate that you value your staff and are prepared to recognize that value in financial terms

- the pay progression of individuals matches increases in their competence and contribution

- significant differences do not exist between the pay of people in similar roles who have reached the same level of competence and are performing equally well

- your decisions are reached on objective grounds by reference to the role carried out by individuals and their level of competence and contribution in that role

- your decisions are not prejudiced on sexual or racial grounds – people carrying out work of equal value and performing at the same level should be paid equally

Pay review considerations

The considerations you should take into account in achieving these aims are:

- your payroll or pay review budget
- the pay policies and guidelines of the organization
- the market rates for the roles in your department
- the present rates of pay of the members of your department
- your judgement of the performance, competence and potential of individuals in comparison with their colleagues
- the need to be fair, consistent and equitable in making pay decisions
- the need to be transparent – to explain to people how you make decisions and why they have been made
- the impact of your decisions on other parts of the organization.

DECIDING RATES OF PAY FOR RECRUITS

You may be constrained by the pay policy of the organization on what you offer a recruit. You may be required to offer the rate for the job or make an offer at the lowest point in the scale or, where appropriate for particularly well-qualified people at a high point within limits. You may be limited to say, only paying 25 per cent above the lower limit or, exceptionally, at the mid-point as long as the person is competent to carry out the work at the same level as would be expected from a fully experienced and capable employee.

What you have to be careful about is offering a rate of pay which is higher than someone already with you who is doing the work perfectly well. This is an issue which managers frequently have to face when they want to attract someone good from elsewhere who is already being paid the market rate or even above and, usually wants an increase in pay to make the move worthwhile. If you do engage someone at a higher rate than existing staff this will inevitably cause dissatisfaction and you won't be able to keep it secret. These things get out.

In these circumstances you simply have to use your judgement. You have to answer the question, 'Is this person so important that I must run the risk of upsetting existing members of staff?' If the answer is yes, you may have to go ahead but be prepared for negative reactions from existing staff. If you find yourself in this situation your aim should be to redress the balance as soon as you can.

FURTHER READING

Armstrong, M (1996) *Employee Reward*, Institute of Personnel and Development.

Part 7

Employee relations

33

MANAGING EMPLOYEE RELATIONS

Employee relations as covered in this chapter involves industrial or trade union relations, dealing with people collectively by processes of involvement and participation, and handling grievances. An important aspect of trade union relations – negotiating – is covered in Chapter 34.

APPROACHES TO EMPLOYEE RELATIONS

Four approaches to employee relations have been identified by Industrial Relations Services (December 1997):

- Adversarial: the organization decides what it wants to do, and employees are expected to fit in. Employees only exercise power by refusing to co-operate.

- Traditional: a good day-to-day working relationship, but management proposes and the workforce reacts through its elected representatives.

- Partnership: the organization involves employees in the drawing up and execution of company policies, but retains the right to manage. This approach is becoming more prominent and is discussed later in this chapter.

- Power sharing: employees are involved in day-to-day and strategic decision-making.

INDUSTRIAL RELATIONS

The old days of powerful industrial relations directors who spent their life confronting aggressive and militant trade unions have largely gone. With a few exceptions, the power of the trade unions in the workplace has diminished considerably over the last twenty years. The popular view is that this is entirely because of the trade union legislation programme of the Conservative government. Clearly this contributed to the decline of union power by such means as outlawing the closed shop and requiring unions to conduct secret ballots agreeing to strike action before taking such action.

But union power nationally has largely decreased for structural reasons – the decline of manufacturing industry, which is the traditional base of union power, and the rise of the fragmented service industry where unions are much less in evidence The 1990 Workshop Industrial Relations Survey established that the proportion of workplaces recognising trade unions has declined from 52 per cent in 1984 to 40 per cent in 1990; only 29 per cent of workplaces established since 1984 have recognized trade unions.

The decline in union power has been one reason for the virtual disappearance of the strong, union-bashing industrial relations director. The other reason is that those trade unions which still have representation in the workplace have on the whole been less militant. This is evidenced by the considerable decline in the number of strikes. The explanation for this decline has primarily been economic pressures leading to high unemployment. Unions have sometimes had to choose between taking strike action leading to closure or survival on the terms dictated by employers.

Managing with trade unions

Although trade union powers have diminished and managements have tended to seize the initiative, many firms are content to live with trade unions, although they may give industrial relations lower priority. They often feel that it is easier to continue with a union because it provides a useful, well-established channel for communications and for the handling of grievance, discipline and safety issues. In the absence of a crisis, managements may not want to waste time and money in developing alternatives.

Managing without trade unions

The workshop survey mentioned above found in 1990 that the

characteristics of union-free employee relations were as follows:

- employee relations were generally seen by managers as better in the non-union sector than in the union sector

- strikes were unheard of

- labour turnover was high but absenteeism was no worse

- pay levels were generally set unilaterally by management

- employee relations were generally conducted much less formally than in unionized firms.

- managers generally felt that they were free to manage work as they felt fit

- there was more flexibility in the use of labour

- employees were two and a half times as likely to be dismissed as those in unionized firms.

Many of these differences could be explained by the generally smaller size of the non-unionized firms and the fact that a number of them were independent rather than being part of a large group.

The role of the line manager in industrial relations

In unionized firms in the situations described above, the importance of the informal relationships between line managers and trade union representatives is considerably increased.

Such relationships take place wherever it is felt that discussion is necessary on issues such as methods of work, allocation of work and overtime, working conditions, employee grievances, health and safety, achieving output and quality standards, discipline or pay (especially when a payment-by-results scheme is in operation). Such contacts happen on a day-to-day basis, although more formal arrangements can be made for participation, involvement and communications as described later in this chapter.

Aims

Your aim should be to control and maintain harmonious working relationships, not because you want peace at any price but because it will get the work done better. You should constantly strive to create a climate of trust in which inevitably there will be disagreements but where such disagreements can be resolved because both sides believe in each other's good intentions, are honest and open with one another, and trust each other. If there is conflict, your objective should be to end it by achieving an agreement which integrates the various views. There may have to be some compromises, but the objective should be to achieve a win-win solution.

Achieving the aims

To build a climate of mutual trust you should:

- keep your word – don't make promises you can't fulfil

- rely more on deeds than words – it is inconsistency between what is said and what is done which undermines trust

- establish and maintain informal relationships with trade union representatives – explosive situations can be defused by quiet, off-the record words; it is much harder when you are confronting a union committee in a meeting (remember that they will want to report success back to their members)

- be friendly but not easy-going

- be firm when you have to be firm – you will only earn the respect of shop stewards and their members if you are prepared to stick to your guns and where necessary press home your point of view

- adopt a problem-solving approach to dealing with issues; aim to achieve a joint solution to the problem rather than just accommodating different points of view

- try to achieve agreement on what the problem is, what objectives are to be attained by solving it and what is the most acceptable approach for both parties from the alternatives that have been identified

- listen to grievances and suggestions and don't dismiss them out of hand

- tell people 'why' – if you don't feel they have a grievance or if you believe that it won't work, explain why in terms they will understand, but be prepared to listen and explain again

- express your views strongly if you need to, but never lose your temper

- do not delay your response to approaches from trade union representatives, but don't over-react

■ if you cannot let someone have an immediate answer, tell them when they can have it, but keep your promise

■ your motto in dealing with trade unions should be 'think before you act' – if you are meeting full time officials you can be fairly certain that they will have got the facts and put their case together; you must do the same (and this applies equally to approaches from shop stewards)

■ anticipate possible adverse reactions to what you intend to do or to a new company policy

■ explain why the action or policy is necessary, obtain reactions and listen to them, amending your plans or doing your best to persuade management to amend its policy if you are convinced that there is a better way (there will, of course, be occasions when you have to say 'this is the way it has to be' but still explain why).

These approaches to dealing with issues concerning employees are just as relevant in situations where there is no trade union. There may be no official representatives but your aim should still be to create a climate of trust by dealing with people individually and collectively along the lines described above. But in the absence of trade unions, as well as in their presence, the process of involvement and participation, communications and grievance handling as described in the rest of this chapter are the key to success in building and maintaining a productive climate of employee relations.

PARTNERSHIP

The Department of Trade and Industry and Department for Education and Employment report on partnerships at work (Partnerships with People, DTI 1997) concludes that partnership is central to the strategy of successful organizations. A growing understanding that organizations must focus on customer needs has brought with it the desire to engage the attitudes and commitment of all employees in order to effectively meet those needs, says the report.

The report was based on interviews with managers and employees in 67 private and public sector organizations identified as 'innovative and successful'. It reveals how such organizations achieve significantly enhanced business performance through developing a partnership with their employees.

There are five main themes or 'paths' which the companies identified as producing a balanced environment in which employees thrived and sought success for themselves and their organizations:

■ Shared goals – 'understanding the business we are in'. All employ-ees should be involved in developing the company's vision, result-ing in a shared direction and enabling people to see how they fit into the organization and the contribution they are making. Senior man-agers in turn receive ideas from those who really understand the problems – and the opportunities.

■ Shares culture – 'agreed values binding us together'. In the research, 'company after company acknowledged that a culture has to build up over time... it cannot be imposed by senior executives but must rather be developed in an atmosphere of fairness, trust and respect until it permeates everyactivity of the organization'. Once achieved, a shared culture means that employees feel respected and so give of their best.

■ Key business benefits of shared learning include an increasing receptiveness to change, and the benefits of increased company loyalty brought by career and personal development plans.

■ Shared effort – 'one business driven by flexible teams'. Change has become such an important part of our daily lives that companies have learnt that they cannot deal with it in an unstructured way, says the report. The response to change cannot be purely reactive, as business opportunities may be missed. While teamworking 'leads to essential co-operation across the whole organization', care must be taken to ensure that teams do not compete with each other in a counterproductive way. It is essential that the company develops an effective communication system to ensure that the flow of informa-tion from and to teams enhances their effectiveness.

■ Shared information – 'effectiveness communication throughout the enterprise'. While most companies work hard at downward com-munication, the most effective communication of all 'runs up, down and across the business in a mixture of formal systems and informal processes'. Many companies with unions have built successful relationships with them, developing key partnership roles in the effective dissemination of information, communication and facilita-tion of change, while others have found representative works coun-cils useful in consulting employees and providing information.

Moving on

An important point which emerged from the research is that there are three levels, or stages, within each of these five paths – levels 'at which certain elements of good practice must be established before the company moves forward to break new ground'.

Examples

The following are two examples of partnership in practice.

Partnership in practice at Legal & General

Partnership between management and manufacturing, science and finance union MSF at Legal & General is seen by both sides as a way of improving employee relations and increasing the involvement and commitment of staff while addressing the rapidly changing business climate. It provides a workplace philosophy based on employer and union working together to achieve common goals, such as fairness and competitiveness. Both sides recognize that, although they have different constituencies and at times different interests, these can best be served by making common cause wherever possible.

Partnership at Perkins Engines

The launch of an environmental management policy at gas and diesel engine manufacturer Perkins Engines has had a major impact on working practices and employee relations at the company's four UK sites in subsequent years. Our case study focuses on how the company has created an environmentally friendly workforce.

Built on an existing total quality (TQ) programme, the company uses TQ tools, including task based project teams, to identify and carry out environmental improvements in areas such as energy efficiency, waste minimization, waste disposal and recycling.

It has been helped in its drive for environmental improvement by the AEEU engineering union, whose senior shop stewards at the company's Peterborough site initiated an environmental awareness-raising campaign with management support. At the outset of the campaign, a survey found that only 10 per cent of employees knew how to go about making environmental improvements or where to go for information. After one year, this figure had risen to 60 per cent.

WHAT IS INVOLVEMENT AND PARTICIPATION?

Involvement and participation covers processes designed to:

■ convey information to employees on business initiatives, decisions and results

■ enable employees to play a greater part in business decision making in order to increase their commitment.

Aims

The Institute of Personnel and Development has affirmed that the involvement and participation by employees in any organization should aim to:

■ generate commitment of all employees to the success of the organization

■ enable the organization better to meet the needs of its customers and adapt to changing market requirements, and hence to maximize its future prospects and the prospect of those who work on it

■ help the organization to improve performance and productivity and adopt new methods of working to match new technology, drawing on the resources of knowledge and practical skills of all its employees

■ improve the satisfaction employees get out of their work

■ provide all employees with the opportunity to influence and be involved in decisions which are likely to affect their interests.

According to the Confederation of British Industry, involvement promotes business success by:

■ increasing trust and a shared commitment to an organization's objectives

■ demonstrating respect for individual employees and drawing on a full range of their abilities

■ enabling employees to derive the maximum possible job satisfaction.

Forms of employee involvement and participation

Five forms of employee involvement and participation have been identified by Professor Mick Marchington:

1 Downward communications – briefings and meetings to inform and 'educate' employees so that they accept management plans and

initiatives.

2 Upward problem solving – quality circles or improvement groups, total quality teams and suggestion schemes designed to tap into employee knowledge and opinion either in small groups or at an individual level.

3 Task participation – getting individuals or teams to analyze and organize the work they do.

4 Consultative and representative participation – enabling employees to take part through their representations in management decision making. This is seen by management as a means of addressing employee grievances as well as getting their views.

5 Financial involvement through such schemes of profit-sharing, gainsharing and employee ownership.

Project teams

There is a sixth form of participation or involvement which was implied but not specified by Marchington. This is when management forms project teams, working parties, or task forces which consist of managers, employees and, if they exist, employee representatives.

The project team, or whatever it is called, is formed as an ad hoc body by management given a remit to develop a new process or investigate a work problem and come up with a solution. It may be involved in such activities as developing a new job evaluation or performance management scheme. Or it may look into problems in areas such as quality, customer relations, productivity or absenteeism.

The important reason for setting up such teams is that they should come to a joint agreement on what should or needs to be done. They are often involved in consulting employees, surveying employee attitudes, communicating proposals and plans and helping with implementation. The aim is to achieve as much 'ownership' as possible of the proposal or solution.

A good example of such a project team was provided by Triplex Safety Glass which set up a joint management/staff/trade union working party to develop job evaluation. The union convenor was on the working party and played a major part in the scheme's development, even presenting joint recommendations to top management.

Empowerment

When employees are genuinely involved in decision-making through processes of involvement and participation they are in effect being empowered. In other words, they are being given more scope to influence what they do and to take responsibility for it.

Mechanisms for involvement and participation

The main mechanisms for involvement and participation are joint consultation, works councils, team briefing, quality circles or improvement groups, and attitude surveys. These are described below.

Joint consultation

This is the most familiar kind of participation, involving union or elected employee representatives. The aim is to provide a means of jointly discussing problems which concern both management and employees so that mutually acceptable solutions can be sought through the exchange of views and information. Joint consultation committees frequently exist at departmental or plant level.

Works councils

Works councils have broadly the same function as joint consultation committees except that they cover the whole organization. Some works councils have wider membership than typical joint consultation committees, including representatives of managers, professional and technical staff who are not trade union members.

The European Union works council directive requires any UK company with more than 100 employees working elsewhere in the European Community to set up a works council.

Team briefing

The concept of team briefing as developed by the Industrial Society is a method of ensuring consistent two-way communication by involving everyone in an organization, level by level, in face-to-face meetings in which information about the company and its policies which affect employees is presented, reviewed and discussed. Team briefing aims to overcome the gaps and inadequacies of casual briefings by injecting some order into the system.

Line managers and team leaders play a key role in the team briefing process. Once it has been initiated at top level it is they who are responsible for calling meetings, briefing those attending and, importantly, listening to what they say and passing reactions upwards to more senior management.

The essential features of team briefing are that:

■ it covers all levels in the organization but with the maximum number of steps from top to bottom

- it is run by the team leader of the group at each level who must be trusted.

- the subjects cover organizational, developmental and team plans, progress in implementing plans, and information about people and the personnel policies that affect team members

- briefing groups work to a brief prepared at top level which is cascaded down the organization, but relevant information can be added at any level

- the briefing group process should cater for any reactions or comments to be fed back to the top thus providing for two-way communications

- briefing groups should be held at least once a month

- the team briefing system should be led by a senior manager who prepares briefs, trains group leaders and ensures that it functions effectively.

Quality circles

Quality circles, often now called improvement groups, are small groups of volunteers who are engaged in related work and who meet regularly to discuss and propose ways of improving working methods or arrangements under a trained leader. They use systematic analytical techniques in which they have been trained to defuse and solve problems.

Quality circles were popular in the 1980s when it was believed that they were one of the secrets of Japanese success. A full system of quality circles is demanding to set up and maintain and, although they can provide a sound method of involving people in improving work methods, they have often been launched with much enthusiasm only to fade away after a year or two.

Suggestion schemes

Suggestion schemes provide a process for employees to submit ideas and tangible rewards for those whose suggestions have merits. They can be a valuable means for employees to participate in improving organizational effectiveness in such areas as work methods and administrative procedures. Properly managed, they can help to reduce the feelings of frustration common in all organizations where people believe they have good ideas but can get no one to listen to them.

Attitude surveys

Attitude surveys are valuable ways of involving employees by seeking their views on matters that concern them. They are usually run by a personnel department or outside specialists on their behalf. The impact of attitude surveys is much enhanced if the results are fed back to employees and management is seen to act on the information they provide.

Role of line managers in involvement and participation

The approaches described above provide the means for increasing employee commitment and ownership of the processes that affect them at work. But none of these systems will work without the wholehearted involvement and support of line managers and team leaders. They must:

■ be aware of the issues that concern their team members

■ be aware of new developments and plans which will affect team members about which they may well feel they should be informed and would like to contribute from their own perspective and know-how

■ understand that participation and involvement, although it is extra work, can make life easier by ironing out problems and generating worthwhile ideas from people

■ appreciate that there is endless scope for people to misinterpret new ideas or developments and resist change unless they are made aware of what is happening and why, and have the opportunity to comment on it from their own viewpoint and contribute their suggestions

■ not rely on the formal methods of involvement and participation, but instead, should seize any opportunity to involve people on a day-to-day basis in matters that concern them.

HANDLING GRIEVANCES

It is sometimes said that the best way to settle grievances is to get the facts, obtain agreement on the issues involved and then work through to an equitable and amicable solution. Of course it is not as easy as that. The problem, whether it is one presented to you by trade unions as a collective grievance, or one brought up by an individual, is frequently based on matters of opinion. It is essential to penetrate the facade presented by

the problem or grievance and find out what is really concerning whoever raises it. To do this it is necessary to:

■ Encourage people to define the problem for themselves by listening
  to what they have to say and prompting them with brief
  well-directed questions. These questions should be entirely neutral.
  Your aim is to get the facts as perceived by the individual and to
  understand the person's viewpoint. It is often helpful to ask a sum-
  marising or reflecting question: 'Is that what you mean?' 'Is that how
  you feel?' At this stage you should not make any judgmental or dis-
  missive remarks.

■ Allow people to have their say. Sometimes they only want to let off
  steam – get it off their chest – and just listening to them will help.

■ Listen attentively to what people have to say.

■ Ask questions to draw them out and to ensure that you understand
  the point they are making or the reason for their grievance. Your aim
  is to get to the root of the matter.

■ Observe behaviour. While listening take note of gestures, manner,
  tone of voice and how people respond to questions.

■ Don't become heated or argumentative. Listen carefully and
  respond calmly.

■ Don't belittle the grievance or dismiss it out of hand. Even if you are
  reasonably certain that the grievance is groundless or frivolous,
  don't say so. You might get an angry reaction. You don't want the
  meeting to turn into a slanging match. Your approach should be to
  do your best to get individuals to concentrate on the facts.

■ If you think there is something in the complaint, take time and trouble to identify causes rather than dwelling on symptoms. You will
  then be in a position to agree remedial action to be taken by you, the
  individual or jointly.

■ When you feel individuals have had their say and you have got the
  complete picture, get them to summarize the problem and suggest
  a solution. If this response is not forthcoming, help them with a
  crystallising question such as: 'Am I right in thinking that this is your
  problem...?' If you get an answer, you will then be in a position to
  ask: 'Well, what do you think should be done about it?'

■ If you are satisfied that something needs to be done, discuss the
  practicalities of the individual's suggestion with the aim of getting
  agreement on what can and can't be done.

- If agreement is reached, summarize the action that will be taken, spelling out who takes it and when. Get individuals to confirm that they understand what is going to happen and are satisfied with it.

- Take notes throughout the meeting and summarize the outcome in writing.

Grievance procedure

A grievance procedure should be based on a policy statement to the effect that employees should:

- be given a fair hearing by their immediate supervisor or manager covering any grievances they may wish to raise

- have the right to appeal to a more senior manager against a decision made by their supervisor or manager

- have the right to be accompanied by a fellow employee of their own choice when raising a grievance or appealing against a decision.

The procedure should be staged as follows: (1) the initial hearing by the immediate supervisor or manager (2) if a satisfactory conclusion is not reached at that meeting, a hearing with a more senior manager and (3) the right of final appeal to a director or equivalent. Time limits should be laid down for the intervals between meetings.

FURTHER READING

Gennard, J and Judge, G (1997) *Employee Relations*, Institute of Personnel and Development.

34

NEGOTIATING

The tendency is for union negotiations to be handled at local level rather than centrally. This means that line managers are more likely to be involved. This chapter examines approaches to the conduct of such local pay negotiations.

PREPARING FOR PAY NEGOTIATIONS

Your first step is to define three things:

■ the target settlement you would like to achieve

■ the maximum you would be prepared to concede

■ your opening offer.

These decisions will sometimes be made for you by higher authority and you have to do the best you can to achieve the targets set for you.
  Your next step is to prepare for the negotiation session.
  You should:

■ Estimate what you believe will be the union's opening claim and what they might be prepared to settle for. This estimate can be based on settlements in similar firms with the same unions (get the data from publications such as IRS Pay and Benefits Bulletin and by contacting other employers) and your own or others' experience on the normal tactics adopted by the union

■ List the arguments that they are likely to use in supporting their case.

- List your own counter arguments.

- Obtain the data you need to support your case.

- Pick your negotiating team – you should be supported by at least one other person.

- Decide on the roles of team members, for example who takes the lead and when, who deals with particular points etc.

- Brief team members.

- Rehearse team members in their roles during negotiations.

- If you are on good terms with the trade union leader you can sometimes go in for 'corridor negotiation.' This means exchanging informal, off-the-record and unattributable views on what you would each regard as a reasonable settlement. With that in mind, you can proceed to bargain hard round the negotiating table but you know where you are likely to end up. This is a delicate process and can only be entered into if there is complete trust between the two of you. Some people feel strongly that it is unethical, but if both parties truly believe that a peaceful settlement is more likely to be achieved quickly this way, there is much to be said for it.

OPENING

Your opening tactics should be as follows:

- open the negotiation with some fairly general comments about the claim and your initial reactions to it

- challenge the other side's position as it stands, do not destroy their ability to move

- explore attitudes, ask questions and, above all, listen in order to assess the other side's strengths and weaknesses, their tactics and the extent to which they may be bluffing

- make no concessions of any kind at this stage

- be non-committal about proposals and explanations (do not talk too much)

BARGAINING

After the opening, the main bargaining phase takes place in which the gap is narrowed between the initial positions. The following tactics can be employed:

- always make conditional proposals: 'If you will do this, then I will consider doing that' – the words to remember are 'if... then'

- never make one sided concessions, always trade off against a concession from the other party: 'If I concede X, then I expect you to concede Y'

- negotiate on the whole package; don't allow the other side to pick off item by item

- keep the issues open to extract the maximum benefit from potential trade-offs.

Bargaining conventions

There are a number of unwritten bargaining conventions which experienced negotiators follow. You could expect full time union officials and trained shop stewards to abide by these conventions. You should do the same. The main conventions are:

- both parties are using the bargaining process in the hope of working towards a settlement

- while it is preferable to conduct negotiations in a civilized and friendly manner; attacks, hard words, threats and controlled shows of temper can be used to underline a negotiator's determination and to shake the opponent's confidence – but these are treated as legitimate tactics and should not be allowed to alter a basic belief in each other's integrity

- off-the-record discussions are mutually beneficial as a means of testing attitudes and intentions and smoothing the way to a settlement

- each side should be prepared to move from its original position, and the negotiations normally proceed by alternative offers and counter-offers leading towards a settlement

- conditional offers can be withdrawn but firm offers cannot, neither can concessions

- the terms of the final agreement must be implemented without amendment.

CLOSING

When and how you should close is a matter of judgement and depends on your assessment of the strength of the union's case. There are various closing techniques:

- making a minor concession which is traded off against an agreement to settle: 'if you will agree to settle at X, then I will concede Y'

- doing a deal such as splitting the difference

- summarizing your position and saying: 'This is as far as we can go'

- applying pressure through a threat of the dire consequences that will follow if an offer is not accepted

- giving the other party a choice between two courses of action.

The union will try to force you into revealing the extent to which you have reached your final position. But don't allow yourself to be pressurized. Don't make a final offer unless you mean it. However, you can state that: 'This is as far as I am prepared to go' and bargaining conventions accept that further moves may still be made on a quid pro quo basis from this 'final position'.

1

THE LINE MANAGER'S
RESPONSIBILITY FOR PEOPLE

The responsibility of the line managers for people is best understood within the context of what managers have to do.

WHAT MANAGERS DO

Management is often defined as 'getting things done through people'. This is something of a cliché, but no less true for all that. By definition, managers cannot do everything themselves (although some try and fail). They have to rely on other people.

Managers are sometimes said to spend their time planning, organising, motivating and controlling. But this is an over-simplification implying that managers neatly parcel up their days into thirty minutes planning, one hour organizing etc. In practice, the work of managers is quite fragmented. It depends more on the demands of the situation and on the people concerned than on any theoretical division of the task into clearly differentiated elements. It is better to regard management as being about:

- getting things done
- maintaining momentum and making things happen
- finding out what is going on
- reacting to new situations and problems
- responding to demands and requests

Part 8

Managing the employment relationship

■ Help people to work out for themselves where they need to improve and what they need to learn.

■ Give people the opportunity to enhance their skills and abilities, encouraging them to develop themselves.

■ Trust people and treat them as adults.

■ Involve people so that they can contribute their ideas.

■ Let people know about the things that matter to them at work.

■

■ Reward people according to their contribution.

35

THE LEGAL FRAMEWORK

Line managers are the people who have the prime responsibility for managing the employment relationship which is concerned with how employers treat their employees and how employees respond in return. The employment relationship covers specific aspects of employment, such as health and safety (Chapter 36) and downsizing (Chapter 37). It is also concerned with approaches to dealing with individual employee problems, especially discipline (Chapter 38), managing attendance (Chapter 39) and counselling (Chapter 40), as well as all the areas discussed earlier in this book.

This chapter covers the legal framework which provides much of the basis upon which the various aspects of the employment relationship are dealt with, that is:

■ contracts of employment

■ unfair dismissal

■ redundancy

■ maternity rights

■ equal pay

■ sex discrimination

■ sexual harassment

■ race discrimination

■ disability discrimination

■ health and safety.

CONTRACTS OF EMPLOYMENT

Contracts of employment are conveyed in a letter of appointment, a written statement of express terms (pay, hours, holidays, pensions etc.) and documents such as staff handbooks, work rules and collective agreements which are incorporated into the contract by being expressly referred to in the letter of appointment or the written statement.

It makes sense to spell out in your offer letter the key terms: the job, pay, hours of work, holiday arrangements, period of notice, and pension and pay entitlements. It is also a good idea to have the disciplinary rules which apply to employees ('works rules') recorded in writing and given to employees. These rules will set out offences which will result in instant dismissal, eg falsifying time sheets, fighting at work, abusive behaviour.

The law requires you to issue written particulars of the terms of employees within 13 weeks after they start work (employees working less than 16 hours a week are excluded from these provisions).

The written statement

The written statement should set out:

- the name of the employer and the employee
- starting date
- start of continuous service
- rate of pay and how it is calculated
- the intervals at which remuneration is paid (eg weekly, monthly)
- hours of work
- entitlement to holidays and holiday pay, including entitlement to accrued holiday pay on terminating employment
- provision of sick pay, if any
- length of notice – employer and employee
- the job title
- the disciplinary rules and procedures applying to the employee (reference can be made to a document specifying these rules which is accessible to the employee).

Changes in terms of employment

Any change in the terms of employment must be notified not more than one month after the change individually or by a notice placed in an accessible place.

CheckList

- Ensure that the terms and conditions as listed above are clearly defined.

- Prepare standard contract documents – offer letters, written statements and works rules.

- Give employees information on the duties their job entails, orally at the interview, or preferably, in writing in the form of an outline job description. But avoid too precise a description of the job. It is best to avoid problems of the 'it's not in my job description' variety by incorporating at the end of the job description a catch-all phrase such as 'and such other duties as may have to be carried out by the job holder to achieve the overall purpose of the job'.

- To avoid problems arising from likely changes to the location of employment, it is advisable to include a clause in the offer letter to the effect that the employee might be required to move to other places of work eg to a different branch or region.

UNFAIR DISMISSAL

Legally, dismissal takes place when an employer terminates an employee's contract with or without notice. A contract can also be terminated:

- by demotion or transfer

- by 'constructive dismissal' – when employees terminate their employment because of their employer's behaviour to them.

Basic legal tests of unfair dismissal

The two basic questions that industrial tribunals have to ask when hearing an unfair dismissal care are:

■ was there sufficient reason for the dismissal – was it fair or unfair?

■ did the employer act reasonably in the circumstances?

Fair reasons for dismissal

The main situations when dismissal is fair are:

■ incapability – this covers the employee's aptitude, health, and physical or mental qualities

■ misconduct

■ not having the qualifications for the job

■ redundancy – when this has taken place in accordance with an agreed procedure.

Unfair dismissals

Dismissals are unfair when:

■ the employer has not dismissed the employee with good reason for incapability, misconduct, lack of qualifications or redundancy

■ a constructive dismissal has taken place

■ there has been a breach in the agreed redundancy procedure.

Reasonable in the circumstances – rules

In general, the rules on what constitutes reasonable behaviour on the part of employers when dismissing employees are in accordance with the 'principles of natural justice'. These are:

■ employees should be informed of the nature of the complaint against them

■ employees should be given the chance to explain

■ employees should be given the opportunity to improve, except in gross cases of incapability or misconduct

■ employees should be warned of the consequences in the shape of dismissal if specified improvements do not take place

■ the employer's decision to dismiss should be based on sufficient evidence

- the employer should take any mitigating circumstances into account

- the offence or misbehaviour should warrant the penalty of dismissal rather than some lesser penalty.

These rules provide good guidelines for any manager involved in handling cases of incapability or ill discipline. The Advisory, Conciliation and Arbitration Service (ACAS) has produced a Code of Practice on Disciplinary Practice and Procedure which should be studied.

Unfair dismissal checklist

- Draw up and agree a disciplinary procedure which is in accordance with the ACAS Code of Practice. The procedure should consist of three stages: (1) informal oral warnings (2) formal oral warnings which can be made in writing and set out the consequences of further offences or failure to improve and (3) final written warnings which specify the penalty, eg dismissal, for a further offence or failure to improve. The employee should have the right to be accompanied by a representative or colleague at any hearing and should have the right of appeal to a higher authority.

- Ensure that you know, and that your subordinates know, your authority to take disciplinary action and the procedure to be followed.

- If you are dismissing someone, arrange for a colleague to be present at the meeting.

- Make sure you get all the facts and analyse the evidence objectively.

- Remember the principles of natural justice set out above.

- Take notes of the actions you have taken at each step and why. This may refer to any evidence that you have of misconduct or incapability and may be produced if the dismissal is referred to an Industrial Tribunal.

- Draw up rules on what constitutes 'gross industrial misconduct' and therefore makes an employee who commits the offence liable to instant or summary dismissal.

- If you need time to collect the evidence on a gross industrial misconduct case you can suspend the employee before hearing the case.

- Word final warnings carefully. It is usually advisable to indicate a date when conduct will be reviewed rather than committing yourself to a date on which action will or will not be taken, depending on the employee's conduct. A typical position which managers can find themselves in a poor time-keeping situation is when they warn employees that disciplinary action will be taken if their time-keeping does not improve to the standard required over, say, the next week. The employee then improves but relapses promptly. Clearly you cannot allow this to go on, so you must make it clear that the improvement in time keeping has to be maintained and if it relapses at any time seriously, then specified disciplinary action will be taken. You do not name any time period but say that you will review the position regularly.

- If in any doubt about disciplinary action, consult a personnel specialist who knows about employment law. If one is not available and/or in serious cases, consult a solicitor who has employment law expertise.

- Handle disciplinary interviews with care (see Chapter 38).

REDUNDANCY

The law on redundancy requires employers to consult with the representatives of a recognized trade union. Such consultation should begin at the earliest opportunity or within 30 days if 10 or more employees may be made redundant over a period of 30 days or less; or at least 90 days if 100 or more employees may be made redundant at one establishment over a period of 90 days or less. The union has to be informed of its reasons for redundancy, how many employees are to be made redundant (not who is to be made redundant) and how the redundancy will be carried out.

Employers are required to notify the Department of Education and Employment if they intend to make 10 or more employees redundant over a relatively short period.

Whether or not there are trade unions in your establishment, you should be aware of and comply with your company's redundancy procedure (if it has one). If not, the way you should tackle a 'downsizing' requirement is described in Chapter 37.

MATERNITY RIGHTS

The legislation on maternity rights contains a number of highly complex provisions and if in any doubt, get expert advice.

The essential legal provisions are that employees who fulfil the qualifying conditions have rights as summarized below:

- Statutory maternity pay which, at present, is payable for a minimum period of 18 weeks.

- The right to return to work within 29 weeks after having the baby. This applies if the employee has continued to be employed up to the 11th week before the expected week of confinement, has been continuously employed for two years, supplies a medical certificate, and informs you that she will be absent from work because of her expected confinement and intends to return to work.

- Employees have the right not to be unfairly dismissed for pregnancy if they have two years' continuous service and work more than 16 hours a week.

EQUAL PAY

The equal pay legislation specifies that women and men should be paid the same when work is like, equivalent or of equal value.

Like work

Like work is work of the same or of a broadly similar nature where the differences between what the woman and the man does are not of practical importance in relation to the terms and conditions of employment.

Equivalent work

A woman is employed on equivalent work to a man if her job has been given an equal value to a man's job under a job evaluation scheme.

Work of equal value

A woman is employed on work of equal value with a man in the same employment if the work is equal in terms of the demands made on her, for example, under such headings as effort, staff and decisions.

In a famous case (Bromley and others v H&J Quick Ltd. (1988)) it was ruled that employers would not be able to sustain a claim that work was not of equal value unless an analytical (eg point factor) job evaluation scheme had been used to assess the relative value of the jobs concerned. Thus, to make certain that they have a reasonably good chance of defending an equal pay for work of equal value claim at an Industrial Tribunal hearing, employers have to use an analytical job evaluation process. But the scheme itself must not be discriminatory by incorporating factors or weighting its factors in ways which would be biased against women (or men).

Case law has established that men and women can be paid differently even when the work is of equal value if:

☐ there are real (justifiable) differences in the level of performance

☐ market rate pressures require someone to be paid more to attract them to the job – but the market rate factor must be 'objectively justified'.

Equal pay checklist

■ Establish who is entitled to equal pay by means of a non-discriminatory analytical job evaluation scheme

■ Ensure that any differences in pay between men and women carrying out work of equal value can be objectively justified on the grounds of performance or market rate pressures.

■ Take steps to equalise rates which are clearly discriminatory.

SEX DISCRIMINATION

It is unlawful to discriminate by treating anyone less favourably than someone of the opposite sex in relation to:

☐ who is offered employment

☐ the terms under which employment is offered, including pension schemes and other benefits

☐ the provision of opportunities for promotion, training or transfer

☐ dismissal or other detrimental acts (eg short time)

☐ advertising – it is unlawful to use a 'sexist' job description (eg manager) unless the advertisement states that the job is open to both men and women.

Sex discrimination check list

■ Follow your organization's equal opportunity policy, or develop a policy which spells out that the organization or you is determined to provide equal opportunities to all, irrespective of sex, race, creed, mental status or disability.

■ Ensure that internal and external advertisements do not contain discriminatory statements.

■ Ensure that all employees are treated equally favourably when decisions are made on training, promotion or transfer.

■ Take particular care when interviewing external or internal applicants that you make no discriminatory statements or ask discriminatory questions. Consciously refute any inclination to favour one person over another because of their sex or because, being a woman, you feel that the applicant might take more time off or become pregnant, or be less committed. Make notes of why applicants have been rejected on the grounds of their ability to carry out the work and keep those notes for at least six months.

SEXUAL HARASSMENT

Sexual harassment is conduct of a sexual nature which is imposed by the perpetrator on an unwilling victim and which the victim fears. There is no express reference to sexual harassment in the legislation but it is clear from case law that harassment is covered by the law on sexual discrimination and employees can complain to an industrial tribunal that they have suffered sexual harassment.

What your organization should do, or what you should do, if you are in charge, to combat this serious problem is to:

■ issue a statement that sexual harassment will not be tolerated

■ state that it will be regarded as gross industrial misconduct

■ set up a procedure for hearing complaints

■ handle complaints with sensitivity and due respect for the rights of both the complainant and the accused

■ make arrangements for employees subjected to harassment to obtain counselling.

As a line manager you have the direct and immediate duty to crack down on any cases of sexual harassment.

RACIAL DISCRIMINATION

It is unlawful to discriminate in any way on racial grounds (but there is no law on discrimination based on religion). The approach to be adopted to meet legal requirements is broadly the same as that suggested earlier for sex discrimination.

DISABILITY DISCRIMINATION

Again, the law forbids discrimination against the disabled.

HEALTH AND SAFETY

The Health and Safety at Work Act 1974 spells out that the basic duties of an employer in connection with health and safety are:

- install a safe working system
- provide safe premises, a safe working environment and safe equipment
- employ trained and competent personnel
- give the adequate training and supervision required to create and maintain a healthy and safe place of work.

36

MANAGING HEALTH AND SAFETY

Employers are required by law to prepare and issue a health and safety policy setting out how they intend to provide a healthy and safe place of work. Larger organizations may have specialist health and safety officers to ensure that their obligations in this vital aspect of the employment relationship are fulfilled in every respect.

It is the duty of all employees to observe health and safety policies and regulations and generally to avoid any action which might cause an accident or a hazard to health and safety. But the onus on achieving a healthy and safe environment rests mainly on the line managers and team leaders who are in immediate contact and control over what is going on in the work place. Your responsibilities in this area are to:

■ control occupational health and hygiene problems

■ take steps to prevent accidents

■ conduct safety audits and inspections.

CONTROLLING OCCUPATIONAL HEALTH AND HYGIENE PROBLEMS

Your responsibility for health and hygiene requires you to take the following steps:

■ contribute to eliminating the hazard at source through improving the system of work and making representations to those responsible for maintaining the process, selecting the substances used and setting up appropriate work place arrangements and conditions (eg ventilation) *isolate hazardous processes* and substances so that workers do not come into contact with them

ensure that suitable items of protective equipment and clothing are used and worn.

■ *train your workers on how to avoid* risks to health

maintain plant and equipment to eliminate the possibility of harmful emissions and injuries to people at work

ensure that good training practices in your department

keep premises and machinery clean and free from toxic substances

keep an eye open for signs of undue stress and take steps to deal with it by re-examining the workload of individuals, reconsidering your approach to managing them (are you applying too much pressure?), and if necessary, arranging for counselling to take place.

ASSESSING RISKS

The Management of Health and Safety at Work Regulations 1992 require managements to conduct risk assessments. These are concerned with the identification of hazards and the analysis of the risks attached to them.

A hazard is anything that can cause harm (eg working on roofs, lifting heavy objects, chemicals, electricity etc). A risk is the chance, large or small of harm being actually done by the hazard. Risk assessments are concerned with looking for hazards and estimating the level of risk associated with them. The purpose of risk assessments is, of course, to initiate preventive action. They enable control measures to be devised on the basis of an understanding of the relative importance of risks. Risk assessments must be recorded if there are five or more employees.

Looking for hazards

The following, as suggested by the HSE and others, are typical activities where accidents happen or there are high risks:

receipt of raw materials, eg lifting, carrying

stacking and storage, eg falling materials

movement of people and materials, eg falls, collisions

processing of raw materials, eg exposure to toxic substances

- maintenance of buildings, eg roof work, gutter cleaning

- maintenance of plant and machinery, eg lifting tackle, installation of equipment

- using electricity, eg using hand tools, extension leads

- operating machines, eg operating without sufficient clearance, or at an unsafe speed; not using safety devices

- failure to wear protective equipment, eg hats, boots, clothing

- distribution of finished; jobs, eg movement of vehicles

- dealing with emergencies, eg spillages, fires, explosions

- health hazards arising from the use of equipment or methods of working, eg VDUs, repetitive strain injuries from badly designed work stations or working practices.

The HSE suggests that most accidents are caused by a few key activities. It advises that assessors should concentrate initially on those which could cause serious harm. Operations such as roof work, maintenance and transport movement cause far more deaths and injuries each year than many mainstream activities.

When carrying out a risk assessment it is also necessary to consider who might be harmed, eg employees, visitors (including cleaners and contractors and the public when calling in to buy products or enlist services).

Assessing the risk

When the hazards have been identified it is necessary to assess how high the risks are. The HSE suggests that this involves answering three questions:

1 What is the worst result?
2 How likely is it to happen?
3 How many people could be hurt if things go wrong?

Risk assessment should lead to action. The type of action can be ranked in order of potential effectiveness in the form of a 'safety precedence sequence' as proposed by Holt and Andrews:

- Hazard elimination – use of alternatives, design improvements, change of process

- Substitution – for example, replacement of a chemical with one which is less risky

- Use of barriers – removing the hazard from the worker or removing the worker from the hazard

- Use of procedures – limitation of exposure, dilution of exposure, safe systems of work (these depend on human response)

- Use of warning systems – signs, instructions, labels (these also depend on human response)

- Use of personal protective clothing – this depends on human response and is used as a side measure only when all other options have been exhausted.

Monitoring and evaluation

Risk assessment is not completed when action has been initiated. It is essential to monitor the hazard and evaluate the effectiveness of the action in eliminating it or at least reducing it to an acceptable level. It is also still necessary to carry out regular safety inspections as described below.

SAFETY INSPECTIONS

You should carry out safety inspections to locate and define any faults in the system and the operational errors which allow accidents to occur. Inspections follow up risk assessments with regular and systematic surveys of the work place to identify and deal with hazards before they cause harm. They should be carried out by line managers and supervisors. It is also good practice to nominate other people in your department or team to carry out regular surveys.

Safety inspection procedure

Define points to be covered such as those listed under the heading risk assessment in a check list.

- Divide the place of work into areas and list the points to which attention needs to be given

- Use the check lists to carry out safety inspections at defined intervals. Record the results, the recommended action and the action taken.

- Carry out sample or spot checks on a random basis

■ Investigate special problems such as the use of protective clothing through spot checks or comprehensive reviews

■ Set up a system for workers to report to you any safety hazards they think need attention

■ Set up a health and safety committee in the work place to assist in conducting audits and making recommendations on preventative measures.

PREVENTING ACCIDENTS

To summarise, you can prevent accidents by taking the following steps:

■ recommend and implement plans on building safety into the system

■ identify the causes of accidents and the conditions under which they occur

■ carry out regular inspections, audits and checks and take action on the basis of the information these provide to eliminate hazards and risks.

■ take particular care to ensure that safety equipment and clothing are available and used

■ maintain records and statistics in order to identify problem areas and unsatisfactory trends and to record maintenance carried out

■ conduct a continuous programme of education and training on safe working habits and methods of preventing accidents.

FURTHER READING

Health and Safety Executive (1994) *Essentials of Health and Safety at Work*, London, HSE.

Holt, A and Andrews, H (1993) *Principles of Health and Safety at Work*, London, IOSH Publishing.

IDS Study (1997) *Safety at Work*, London, Incomes Data Services, March

Saunders, R (1992) *The Safety Audit*, London, Pitman.

37

DOWNSIZING

'Downsizing' is one of the most demanding areas of people management with which line managers can become involved. Their responsibilities as discussed in this chapter are to:

■ plan ahead to achieve downsizing without involuntary redundancy

■ take any steps possible to reduce compulsory redundancy

■ encourage voluntary redundancies

■ ensure that the company's redundancy procedure is implemented,
or, if there is no such procedure, conduct redundancy programmes
as described later in this chapter

■ provide whatever help you can to redundant employees to find
other work

PLAN AHEAD

Planning ahead means anticipating future reductions in people needs
and allowing natural wastage to take effect. You need to calculate or
forecast as accurately as you can the amount by which your work force
has to be reduced and the likely losses through employee turnover. You
can then freeze recruitment to allow the surplus to be absorbed by
wastage.

USE OTHER METHODS TO AVOID REDUNDANCY

Natural wastage may not be enough and in any case you may have to act swiftly. The other methods you can use to avoid or at least to reduce the incidence of redundancy include, in order of severity:

- calling in outside work
- withdrawing all sub-contracted work
- reducing or preferably eliminating overtime
- developing work sharing, ie two people doing one job on alternate days or splitting the day between them
- reducing the number of part timers
- temporary lay-offs.

VOLUNTARY REDUNDANCY

You can relieve the number of compulsory redundancies by asking for volunteers and offering them a suitable pay-off. One of the disadvantages of voluntary redundancy is that the wrong people might leave, ie good workers who can easily find other work. You might have to go into reverse and offer them a special loyalty bonus to stay on.

HANDLING REDUNDANCIES

Aims

Your aims should be to:

- treat people as fairly as possible
- reduce hardship as much as possible
- protect your ability to run your business or department effectively.

It may be difficult to reconcile the first two aims with the last but you should do your best.

Legally, as mentioned in Chapter 35, your company might be required to inform the trade union, if there is one, in advance. But if a number of people have to be made redundant it may well fall on you to make a general announcement that downsizing will have to take place. You should let everyone know why this step had to be taken (eg a dramatic and unforeseeable slump in orders) and what had been and is still being done to mitigate its impact (eg striving hard to get new orders). You should not inform individuals until the announcement has been made.

You should also indicate:

- how and when individuals will be informed (as soon as possible after the general announcement)

- the payment arrangements (statutory redundancy pay plus any additional payments the company proposes to make – and should whenever possible)

- steps that will be taken to help people find work, eg outplacement consultants or setting up a 'job shop' in the firm.

When it comes to seeing individual employees you will need to inform them as gently as possible why they have been selected for redundancy and how it will affect them (payment, timing etc) Time should be allowed to describe the help the company will give to find another job and to get initial reactions which might provide guidance on future actions eg counselling.

There may be situations where only one or two people have to be made redundant. Even if a general announcement may seem inappropriate in those circumstances it is still desirable to inform other members of the department or team why this has taken place and to tell them, if that is the case, that there are no other immediate plans for redundancy. But you may not be able to make any promises.

38

HANDLING DISCIPLINARY INTERVIEWS

Handling disciplinary interviews is one of the least attractive parts of a manager's job. But it cannot and should not be avoided, and as Dickens' Mr. A Bagnet said (frequently) in *Bleak House*: 'Discipline must be maintained'. But not with a heavy hand. It must be maintained in accordance with a disciplinary procedure (see Chapter 35) and taking into account the principles of natural justice.

THE PRINCIPLES OF NATURAL JUSTICE

The principles of natural justice are:

1   Individuals should know the standards of performance they are expected to achieve and the rules to which they are expected to conform.
2   They should be given a clear indication of where they are at fault or what rules they have broken.
3   They should be given a chance to explain or defend themselves.
4   Except in cases of gross misconduct, they should be given an opportunity to improve before disciplinary action is taken.

Mistakes to avoid

There are four mistakes you should avoid making.

1   Failure to follow a disciplinary procedure of informal or formal

warnings which provides employees with an opportunity to improve but spells out what will happen if they don't. Managers are sometimes tempted to bypass the system because 'it is an open and shut case'. But this contravenes a fundamental principle of natural justice, that employees should be given a chance to hear and respond to complaints against them.

2 Treating interviews just as a means of establishing guilt or innocence and not as a way of helping employees to improve performance or conduct.

3 Failure to distinguish misconduct, which, if proven, is down to employee, from poor performance, which may be at least partly attributable to poor management.

4 Getting into a bad-tempered argument with the employee. You must be calm, cool and collected.

CONDUCTING THE INTERVIEW

Experienced practitioners such as Alan Fowler and organizations such as ACAS, recommend the following approach to conducting a disciplinary interview:

1 Make sure that you have got all the facts in advance and decide how you are going to tackle the interview.

2 Give employees notice that the interview is going to take place so that they can be prepared and can get a representative to accompany them.

3 Arrange for a colleague to be present to help conduct the interview and to take notes.

4 State the complaint to the employee, giving chapter and verse and giving supporting statements from other people involved where appropriate.

5 Allow employees to give their side of the story and call any supporting witnesses.

6 Question employees and their witnesses and allow them to do the same.

7 Allow time for a general discussion on the issues raised and any other relevant issues.

8 Give employees an opportunity to have a final say and mention any mitigating circumstances.

9 Sum up the points emerging from the meeting as you see them, but allow employees to comment on them and be prepared to amend your summary.

10 Adjourn the meeting so that you can consider your decision on the

basis of what came out in the interview. It is best not to announce the decision during the initial meeting. The adjournment may be only half an hour or so in a straightforward case. It could be longer in a more complex case.

11 Reconvene the meeting and announce your decision. Confirm your decision in writing.

GUIDANCE NOTES FOR A STAFF MEMBER FACING A DISCIPLINARY INTERVIEW, HALIFAX BUILDING SOCIETY

Preparing for the interview

- Ensure you know exactly what complaint is being made against you and why.

- If you feel the complaint is unjustified ensure you are able to present your case clearly.

- Collect any information which may support your case.

- If you wish to be accompanied, it is your responsibility to ensure your representative is aware of the date and time of the meeting.

During the interview

- Remain calm.

- Listen carefully.

- Give honest and accurate answers supported by examples or written evidence if possible.

After the interview

- You will receive written confirmation of the outcome of the interview as soon as possible after the interview.

- If you feel the outcome of the interview is unfair, you have the right to appeal within ten calendar days of the date of the decision; you should appeal in writing to the manager who conducted the disciplinary interview.

- The appeal will be heard by a member of management who has authority over the manager who undertook the initial interview. At least one week's notice of appeal interview must be given.

THE SKILLS NEEDED TO CONDUCT A DISCIPLINARY INTERVIEW

To conduct a disciplinary interview properly, you need to exercise the following skills:

■ keeping control over the meeting while still allowing employees to have their say.

■ handling angry reactions from employees – you must remain calm and, as Alan Fowler suggests, say something like 'I hear what you say but I am not going to enter into an argument about it; now let's move on'.

■ questioning – open questions should be used such as: 'Tell me about what happened', but you may also have to ask probing questions to get closer to the facts: 'Yes, but this is what I've been told by — about what happened. What do you say to that?'

■ counselling – helping employees to see where they have gone wrong and what they can do to put things right.

Counselling skills as described in Chapter 40 are important. If you can end an interview on a positive note about improving performance or behaviour rather than negatively with a punishment, so much the better.

FURTHER READING

Edwards, L (1997) *Interviewing*, Industrial Society, London.
Fowler, A (1995) *The Disciplinary Interview*, Institute of Personnel and Development, London.

39

MANAGING ATTENDANCE

Attendance management is about managing absenteeism and lateness. A recent Industrial Society survey found an average absence rate of 3.6 per cent in the UK although there is a wide spread of average absence rates with significant variations by region, sector and size of organization. The Industrial Society calculates that sickness absence results in approximately 177 million working days lost annually and about £11.2 billion is 'lost' to the economy through sickness absence.

A company with 500 employees and an absence rate of 3.6 per cent (say 8 days a year per employee) could lose 4,000 working days a year. If average earnings were £60 a day this would cost £240,000. A reduction in the absence rate to 2 per cent (and 30 per cent if the organizations surveyed by the Industrial Society had a rate of 2 per cent or less) the cost would be reduced by £135,000, a saving worth some effort to achieve.

MANAGING ABSENTEEISM

Overall approach

The overall approach required to manage absenteeism involves:

- Commitment on the part of management to reduce the cost of absenteeism.

- Trust – the control of absenteeism is best carried out on the basis that employees are to be trusted. Companies who do this provide sickness benefit for all workers. They rely upon the commitment and motivation of their employees (which they work hard at achieving) to minimise abuse. But they reserve the right to review sickness benefit if the level of absence is unacceptable.

Information – sadly, a trusting approach may not be the complete answer, so that accurate information on absence is required. This can be provided by computerized systems.

A documented attendance policy which sets out its organization's view on absenteeism and the rules for sick pay.

Communications which inform employees why absence control is important.

Special studies to identify the causes of absenteeism and propose remedies as required.

Return to work interviews to discuss with employees the position as far as their absence is concerned.

Counselling for employees with absence problems – this may take place during a return to work interview or separately.

Training for managers and team leaders on their responsibilities for absence control and the actions they can take.

■ Disciplinary action – as a last resort this has to be operated fairly and consistently.

Causes of absenteeism

Applying the guidelines referred to above and taking action means that it is necessary for you to understand the likely causes of absenteeism. These may need to be established through a special survey or by analysing the outcome of return to work interviews.

The likely causes of absenteeism, other than genuine sickness, are:

Lack of motivation and commitment, which may be because of the work, the quality of management and supervision, or dissatisfaction with company policies and terms and conditions, including pay.

The job – boring, tiring, stressful, disruptive (constant changes to working patterns), travelling away from home.

Hours of work – unsocial hours, eg shift work, nights

Physical work environment – hot, noisy, uncomfortable, dangerous

Quality of supervision – autocratic, demanding too much, unfair, bullying.

- Fellow workers – hostile, unsupportive, bullying.
- Family or personal problems.
- Outside interests given priority.

Actions to reduce absenteeism

The Industrial Society Survey found that the top ten most effective ways of managing attendance adopted by the 486 respondents were:

- accurate monitoring – 57 per cent
- return to work interviews – 55 per cent
- written absence policy – 50 per cent
- training of line managers – 49 per cent
- motivation – 37 per cent
- discipline – 36 per cent
- communicating absence rates – 33 per cent
- senior management commitment – 27 per cent
- performance appraisal – 26 per cent
- team working – 21 per cent.

What line managers can do

As a line manager or team leader you have the main responsibility for controlling absenteeism. A written company policy, a recognized disciplinary procedure for dealing with absenteeism and senior management commitment and support will help; but ultimately it is up to you.
    This is what you can do:

- Monitor absenteeism accurately – study the records made available to you (ideally they should be computerized) and maintain your own records if necessary. Be aware of any long term absentees and find out why from the medical certificates or by causing enquiries to be made (the Personnel Department, if there is one, will help).

- Conduct return to work interviews – welcoming employees back, enquiring about their health, discussing absence problems, reminding them of their obligations, and agreeing future action. (An example of how these are conducted is given later in this chapter).

- Leadership – lack of motivation and commitment is an obvious cause of absenteeism. You can make the difference by how you manage your people and how you ensure that your team leaders manage their team effectively.

- Job design – you can try to reduce the monitoring of work and stressful conditions when they apply.

- Working hours – if unsocial hours are a genuine problem you can try to adjust them to meet individual needs.

- Discipline – when necessary, you should warn people informally at return to work interviews that their absence levels are unsatisfactory and must be improved or disciplinary action will be taken. If you have to, you can then go through the disciplinary procedure of formal and final warnings before taking action. This will involve special disciplinary interviews which you should conduct along the lines described in Chapter 38.

- Deal with long term sickness – you should deal with long term absence along the lines described below in consultation with the personnel department, if there is one.

- Communicate absence rates – keep your department or team informed of absence rates and indicate where necessary that they need to be improved and what steps should be taken to do so.

- Performance reviews – absenteeism can reasonably be discussed at performance reviews, if it is a problem.

- Team involvement – teams can be involved in investigating the causes of absenteeism in general (not for individuals), monitoring overall absence rates and suggesting remedies to do with work, working conditions and hours. But you should not rely on team pressure to control individual absenteeism. That is your job.

Dealing with long-term absence

As recommended by the Industrial Society the following approach should be adopted in dealing with long term absence:

- There should be regular contact between employee and employer.

- Employees should be kept fully informed if employment is at risk.

- Observing the requirements of the Access to Medical Reports Act, employers should ask the employee's GP when a return to work is expected and the expected capability of the employee.

- Consider whether alternative work is available.

- Where an employee refuses to co-operate in providing medical evidence, or to undergo an independent medical examination, the employee should be told in writing that a decision will be taken on the basis of the information available and that it could result in dismissal.

- Employers should consider redeployment where appropriate.

- After full consultation, where the employee's job can no longer be kept open and no suitable alternative work is available, the employee should be given notice of dismissal. The employee should be paid in full during the notice period regardless of whether they are entitled to, or have exhausted, their occupational sick pay.

EXAMPLE OF AN ATTENDANCE POLICY AND PROCE-DURE – BIRMINGHAM INTERNATIONAL AIRPORT MANAGING FOR FULL ATTENDANCE GUIDE

The return to work interview

It is important that interviews are conducted fairly and consistently, following a basic five part structure. The following points should be covered in the order below:

1 Welcome back
2 Enquire about health
3 Consequences and observations
4 Completion of formalities
5 Future action.

1 Welcome back

It is appropriate to welcome the individual back. This gives you the opportunity to tell them that they were missed and that you value their work and their contribution to the team.

Be genuine. It is not suggested that you make a 'big production number' out of the welcome as that would be counter productive and would make the rest of the interview more difficult to conduct.

2 Enquire about health

You need to be sure that staff are fit for work and it is your duty to make an assessment of this. When a staff member returns to work from a period of non attendance, you should gently explore the reason for absence. In most cases you will not be challenging the reason given for the absence, but it is important that you explore the situation. You need to ascertain:

- if the staff member feels fit to resume duties
- whether the absence is work-related
- what steps the staff member has taken to investigate the cause for themselves
- what preventative measure they are taking to ensure that it does not occur again.

It is particularly important to show care and concern during this exploratory stage of the interview. This is best demonstrated by active listening ie listening carefully and fully to what the staff member has to say, and responding appropriately.

3 Consequences and observations

Every member of staff has a responsibility to come to work when required. We can only maintain the appropriate levels of safety, security and service with a workforce that attends fully.

You should remind staff of the necessity for full attendance wherever possible. You should point out actions you or other colleagues have had to take as a result of their non attendance.

Using the attendance records available you should bring to the staff members attention the facts regarding their attendance during the previous six months. This might include observations as to the number of particular shifts or days being taken off. It is appropriate to make observations if non attendance seems to form a pattern or appears to fall during school holidays.

It should also be pointed out that the Company takes non-attendance very seriously and that it could lead to action being taken under disciplinary or capability procedures.

You should use this opportunity to explore ways in which you can help the staff member to attend as required by the company and to discuss what they can do to better manage their own attendance.

4 Completion of formalities

It is only after this discussion has taken place that you are in a position to complete the certification with the staff member and ask them to sign it. You will be signing to confirm completion and also to confirm that a return to work interview has been conducted.

5 Future action

Before terminating the interview you should make it very clear once again to the staff member that the Company expects full attendance. You should also point out what will happen should the staff member fail to attend in the future. Finally you should test understanding. You need to be sure that the staff member clearly understands what is required of them in the future and what action the Company will take next time they fail to attend for work.

TIMEKEEPING

Controlling timekeeping is a matter of:

- building and maintaining motivation and commitment

- keeping good records

- emphasizing that good timekeeping is important and that disciplinary action will be taken if anyone's timekeeping record is unacceptable.

- taking disciplinary action as necessary through a proper disciplinary procedure (see Chapter 38).

Policies in timekeeping can be negotiated with trade unions. The Continental Can Company's policy includes the following:

> The company trusts its employees to act responsibly and to be at work on time. In the event of this trust being abused and the Company being dissatisfied with an employee's timekeeping record, he or she will be liable to be stopped pay and may be required to comply with a more rigorous form of timekeeping. He or she will also be liable to disciplinary action. The company and its union recognize that it is in the interests of all parties to minimise lateness and will work together in whatever way necessary to this end.

FURTHER READING

The Industrial Society, (1995) *Managing Attendance*.

INDEX